RELIVE THESE THRILLING STORIES FEATURING EXCLUSIVE NEW SCENES!

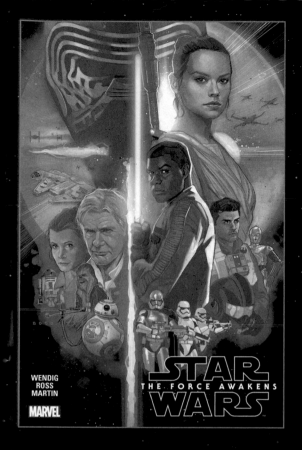
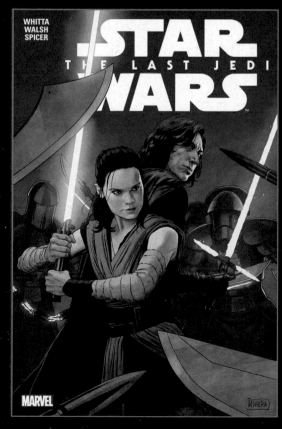

STAR WARS™

JEDI FALLEN ORDER™

DARK TEMPLE

Writer **MATTHEW ROSENBERG**
Artist **PAOLO VILLANELLI** WITH
RUAIRÍ COLEMAN (#5)
Color Artist **ARIF PRIANTO**
Letterer **VC's JOE SABINO**

Cover Art **MARCO CHECCHETTO** (#1),
PAOLO VILLANELLI &
NEERAJ MENON (#2), AND
WILL SLINEY &
DONO SÁNCHEZ-ALMARA (#3-5)

Assistant Editor **TOM GRONEMAN**
Editor **MARK PANICCIA**

Collection Editor **JENNIFER GRÜNWALD**
Assistant Managing Editor **MAIA LOY**
Assistant Managing Editor **LISA MONTALBANO**
Editor, Special Projects **MARK D. BEAZLEY**
VP Production & Special Projects **JEFF YOUNGQUIST**
Book Designer **ADAM DEL RE**
SVP Print, Sales & Marketing **DAVID GABRIEL**
Editor In Chief **C.B. CEBULSKI**

FOR LUCASFILM:

Senior Editor **ROBERT SIMPSON**
Creative Director **MICHAEL SIGLAIN**
Lucasfilm Story Group **STEVE BLANK**
MATT MARTIN
KELSEY SHARPE
EMILY SHKOUKANI
Lucasfilm Art Department **PHIL SZOSTAK**

Special thanks to
LUCASFILM GAMES &
RESPAWN ENTERTAINMENT

STAR WARS: JEDI: FALLEN ORDER — DARK TEMPLE. Contains material originally published in magazine form as STAR WARS: JEDI FALLEN ORDER — DARK TEMPLE (2019) #1-5. First printing 2020. ISBN 978-1-302-91995-5. Published by MARVEL WORLDWIDE, INC., a subsidiary of MARVEL ENTERTAINMENT, LLC. OFFICE OF PUBLICATION: 1290 Avenue of the Americas, New York, NY 10104.

Printed in Canada. KEVIN FEIGE, Chief Creative Officer; DAN BUCKLEY, President, Marvel Entertainment; JOHN NEE, Publisher; JOE QUESADA, EVP & Creative Director; TOM BREVOORT, SVP of Publishing; DAVID BOGART, Associate Publisher & SVP of Talent Affairs; Publishing & Partnership; DAVID GABRIEL, VP of Print & Digital Publishing; JEFF YOUNGQUIST, VP of Production & Special Projects; DAN CARR, Executive Director of Publishing Technology; ALEX MORALES, Director of Publishing Operations; DAN EDINGTON, Managing Editor; SUSAN CRESPI, Production Manager; STAN LEE, Chairman Emeritus. For information regarding advertising in Marvel Comics or on Marvel.com, please contact Vit DeBellis, Custom Solutions & Integrated Advertising Manager, at vdebellis@marvel.com. For Marvel subscription inquiries, please call 888-511-5480. **Manufactured between 3/6/2020 and 4/7/2020 by SOLISCO PRINTERS, SCOTT, QC, CANADA.**

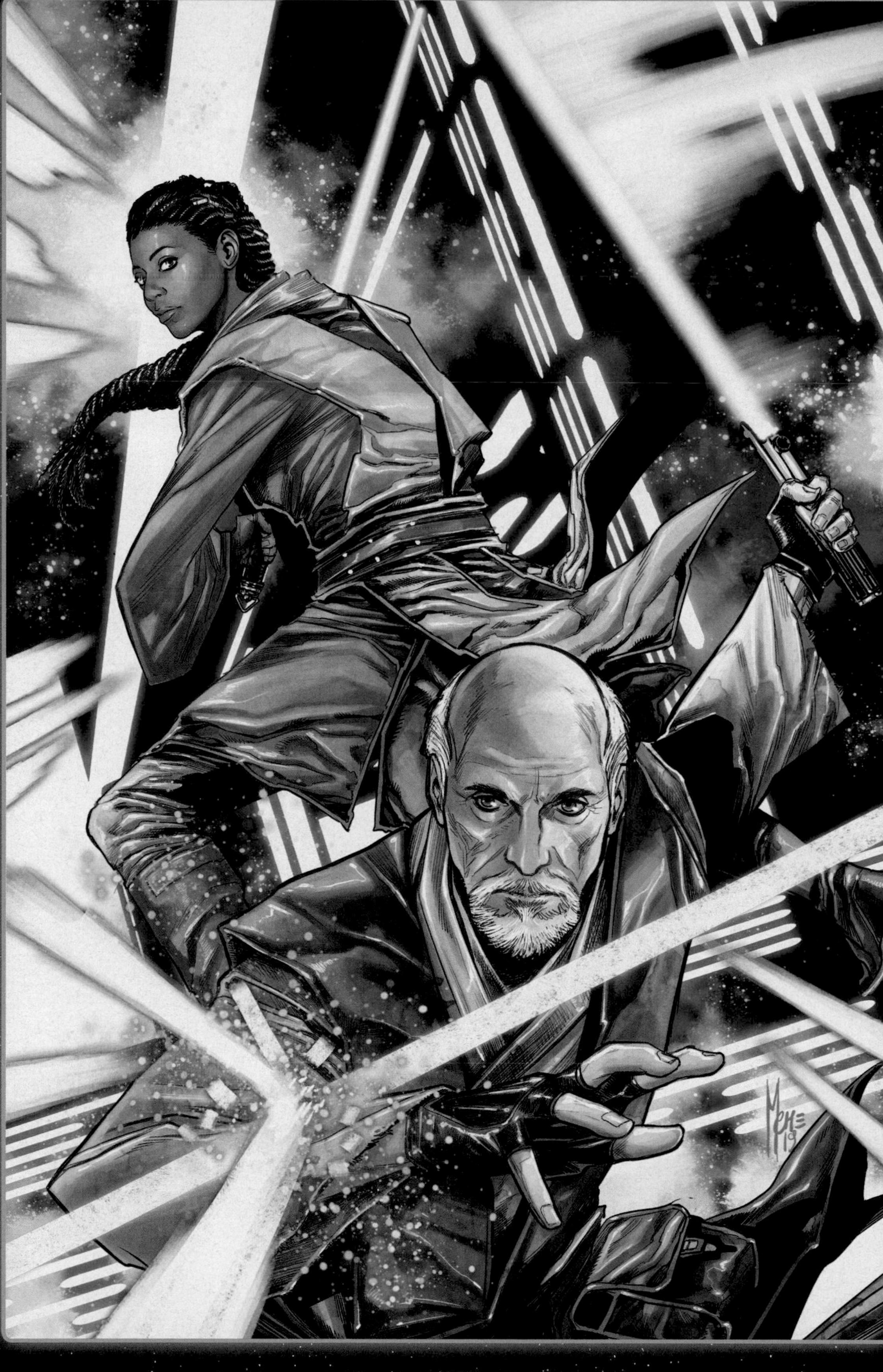

1 – A PLANET DIVIDED

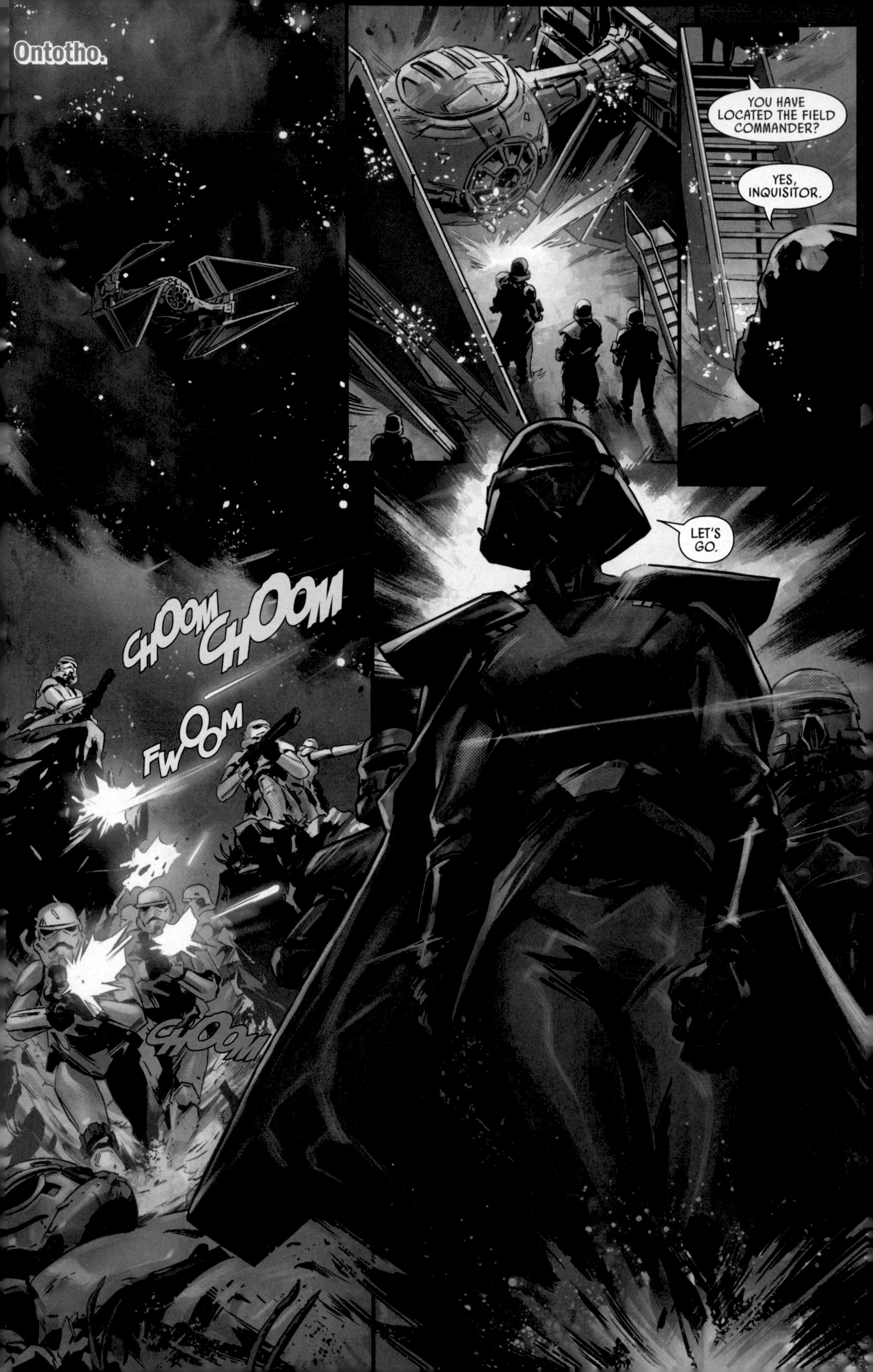
Ontotho.
YOU HAVE LOCATED THE FIELD COMMANDER?
YES, INQUISITOR.
LET'S GO.
CHOOM CHOOM
FWOOM
CHOOM

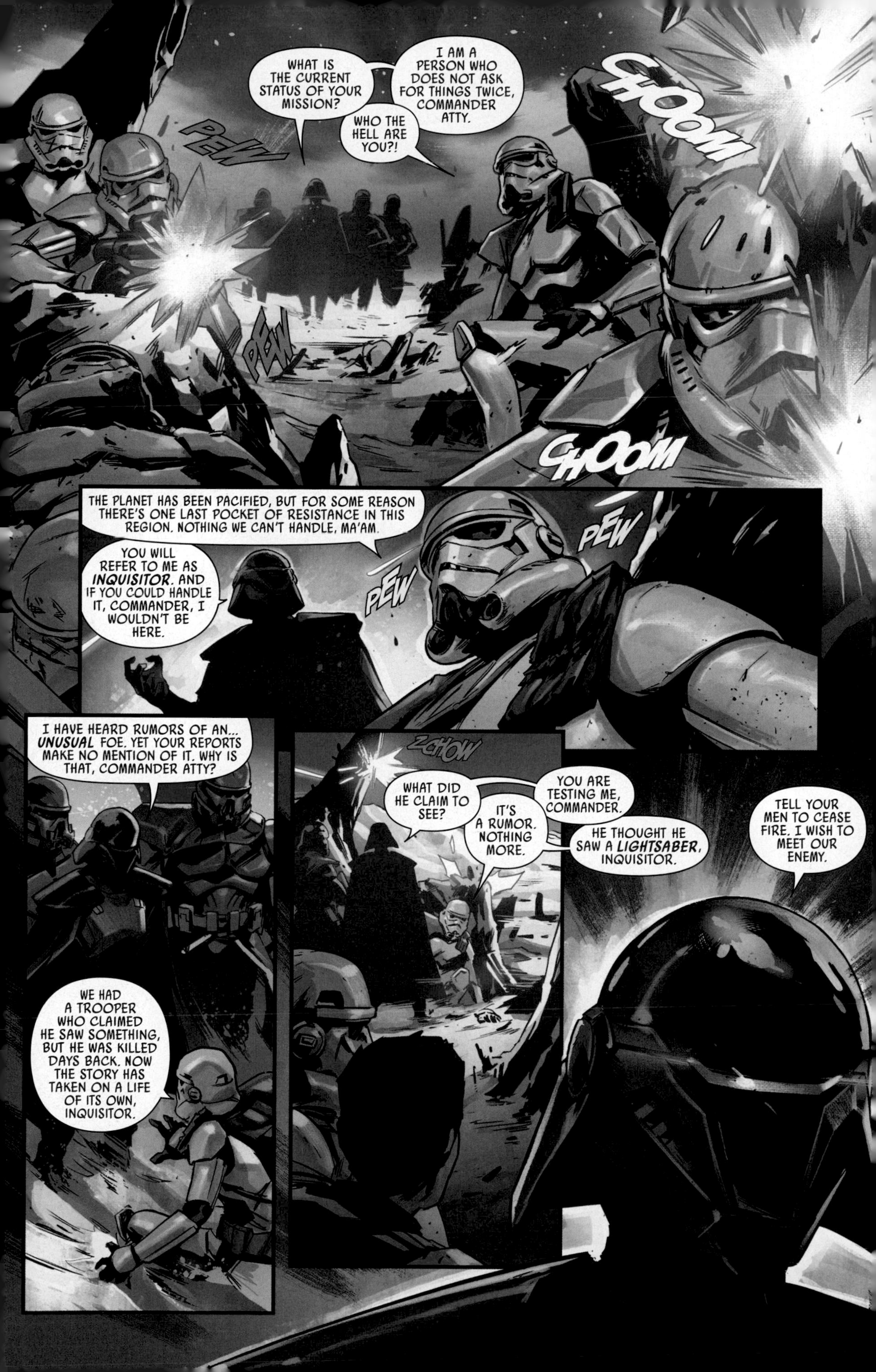
WHAT IS THE CURRENT STATUS OF YOUR MISSION?
WHO THE HELL ARE YOU?!
I AM A PERSON WHO DOES NOT ASK FOR THINGS TWICE, COMMANDER ATTY.
PEW
PEW
CHOOM
CHOOM
THE PLANET HAS BEEN PACIFIED, BUT FOR SOME REASON THERE'S ONE LAST POCKET OF RESISTANCE IN THIS REGION. NOTHING WE CAN'T HANDLE, MA'AM.
YOU WILL REFER TO ME AS *INQUISITOR*. AND IF YOU COULD HANDLE IT, COMMANDER, I WOULDN'T BE HERE.
PEW
PEW
I HAVE HEARD RUMORS OF AN... *UNUSUAL* FOE. YET YOUR REPORTS MAKE NO MENTION OF IT. WHY IS THAT, COMMANDER ATTY?
WE HAD A TROOPER WHO CLAIMED HE SAW SOMETHING, BUT HE WAS KILLED DAYS BACK. NOW THE STORY HAS TAKEN ON A LIFE OF ITS OWN, INQUISITOR.
ZCHOW
WHAT DID HE CLAIM TO SEE?
IT'S A RUMOR. NOTHING MORE.
YOU ARE TESTING ME, COMMANDER.
HE THOUGHT HE SAW A *LIGHTSABER*, INQUISITOR.
TELL YOUR MEN TO CEASE FIRE. I WISH TO MEET OUR ENEMY.

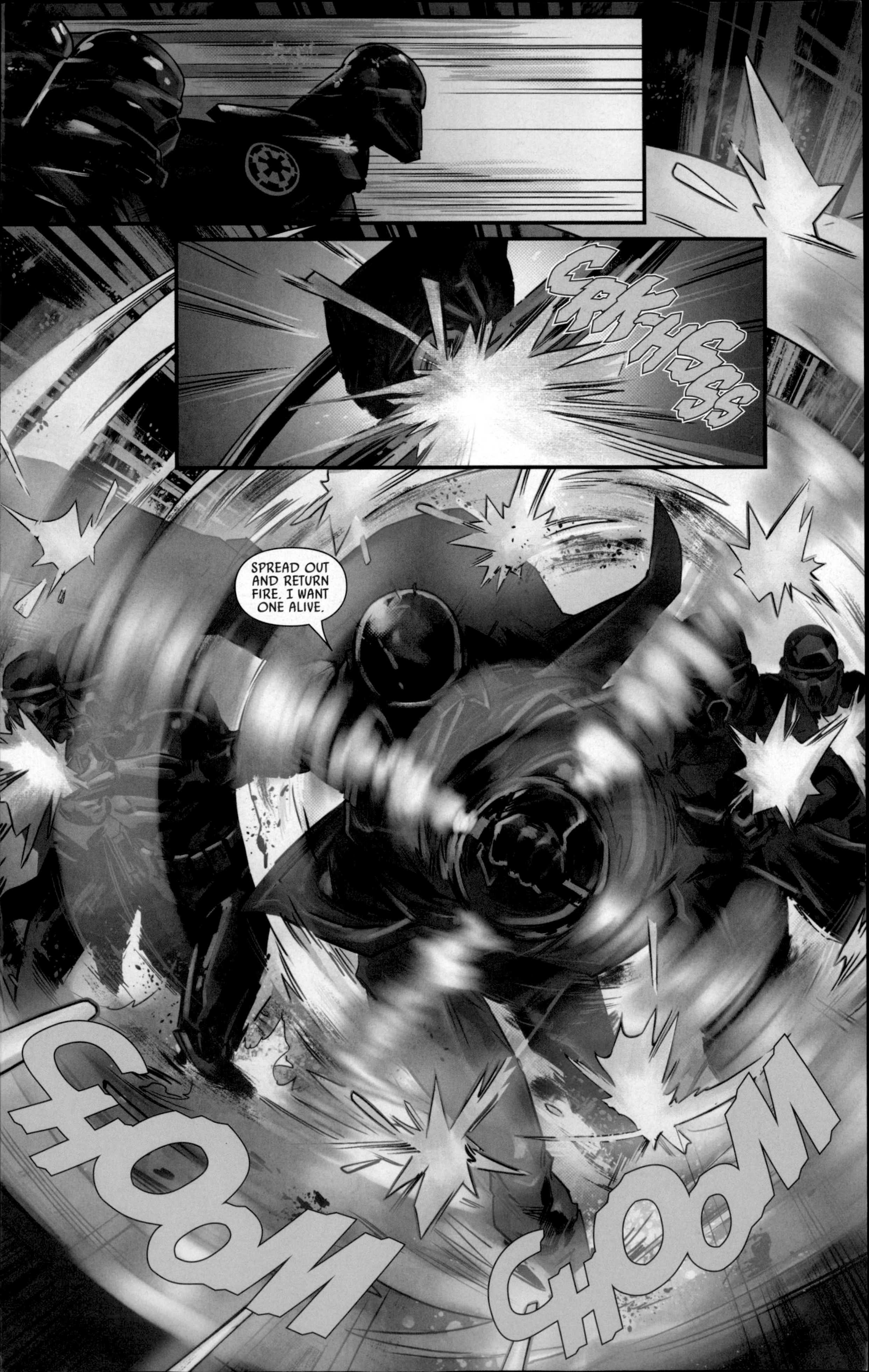
CRKHSSS
SPREAD OUT AND RETURN FIRE. I WANT ONE ALIVE.
CHOOM
CHOOM

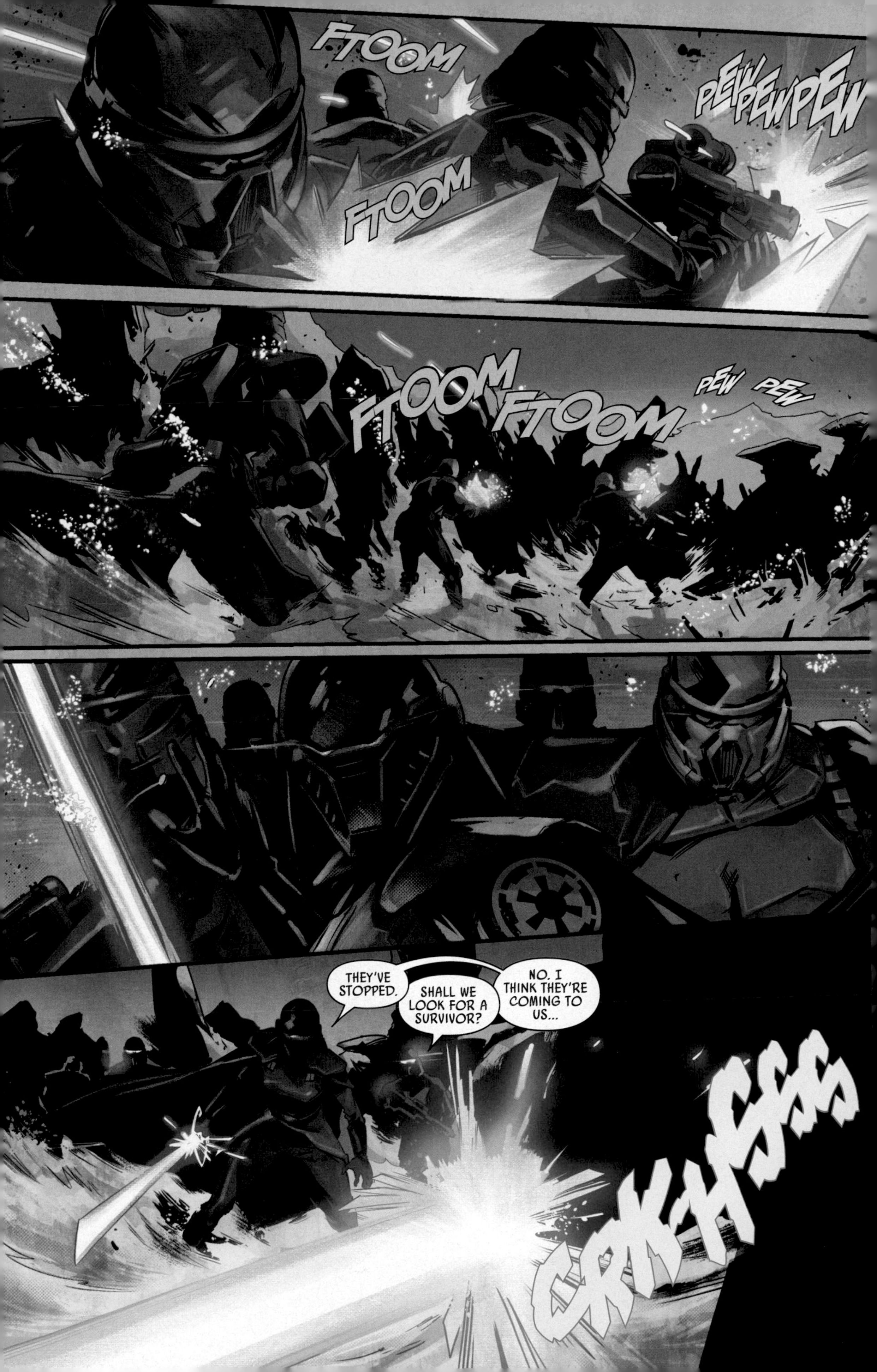
FTOOM
FTOOM
PEW PEW PEW PEW
FTOOM FTOOM
PEW PEW
THEY'VE STOPPED.
SHALL WE LOOK FOR A SURVIVOR?
NO. I THINK THEY'RE COMING TO US...
CRK-HSSS

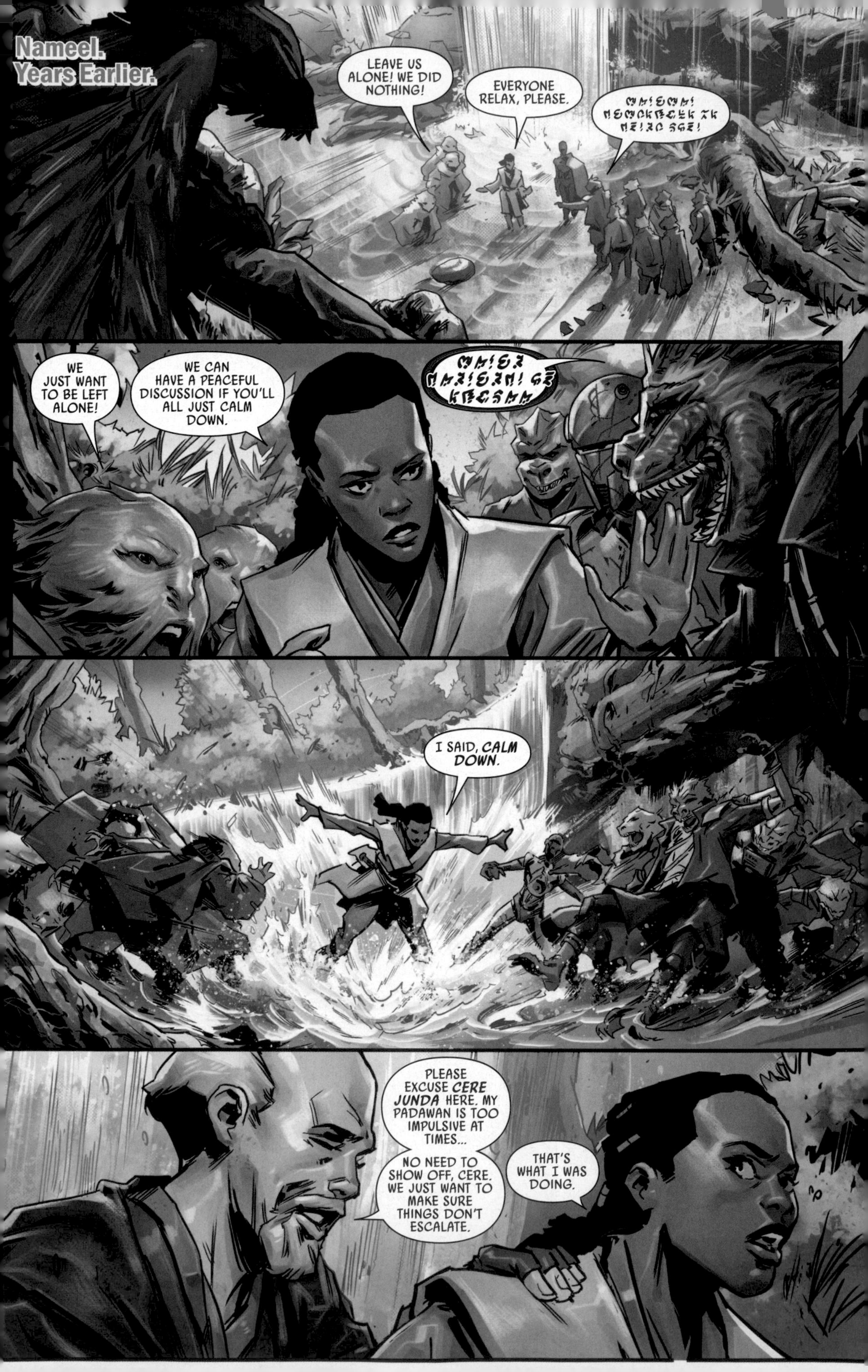
Nameel.
Years Earlier.
LEAVE US ALONE! WE DID NOTHING!
EVERYONE RELAX, PLEASE.
WE JUST WANT TO BE LEFT ALONE!
WE CAN HAVE A PEACEFUL DISCUSSION IF YOU'LL ALL JUST CALM DOWN.
I SAID, CALM DOWN.
PLEASE EXCUSE CERE JUNDA HERE. MY PADAWAN IS TOO IMPULSIVE AT TIMES...
NO NEED TO SHOW OFF, CERE. WE JUST WANT TO MAKE SURE THINGS DON'T ESCALATE.
THAT'S WHAT I WAS DOING.

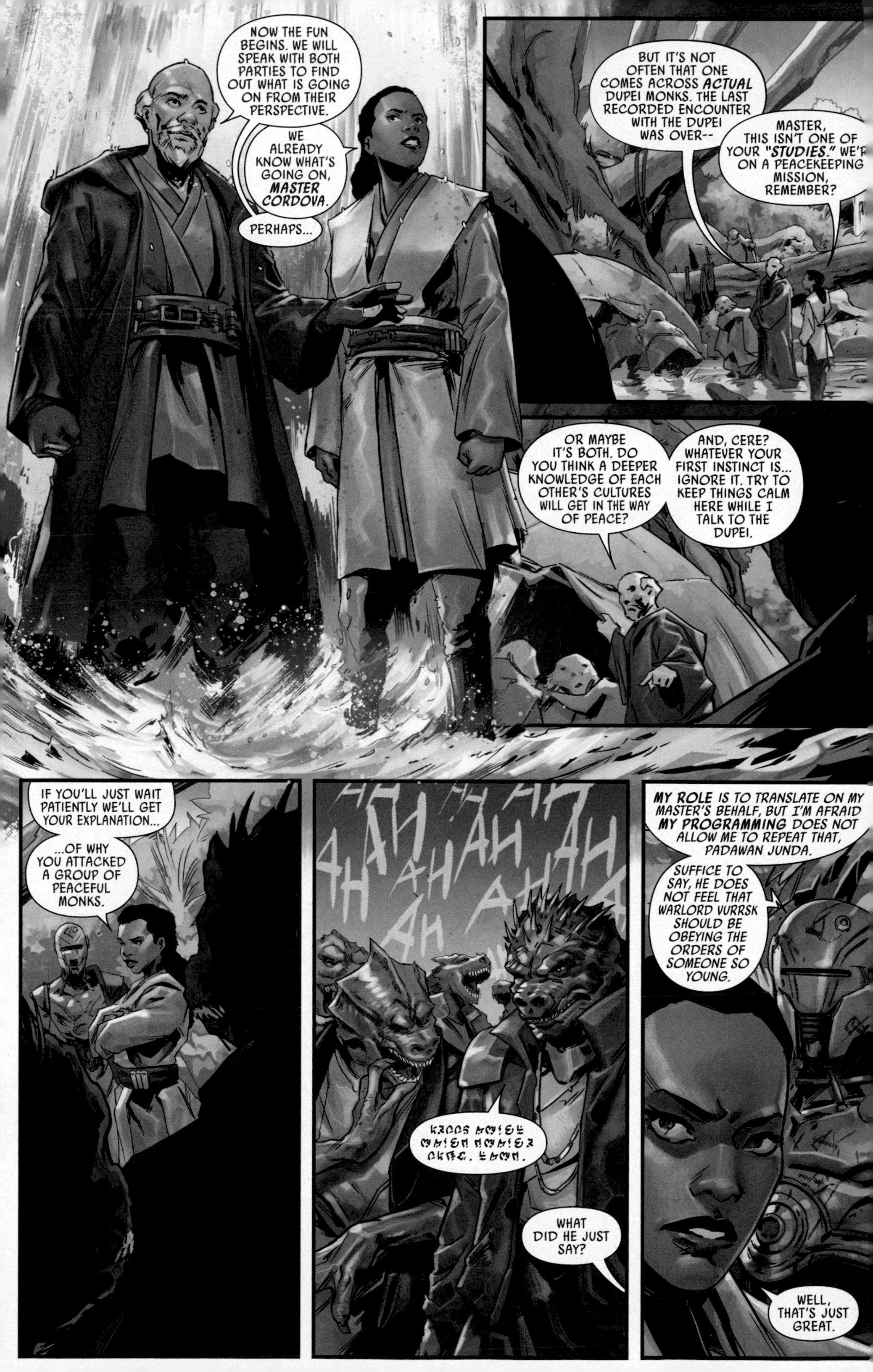
NOW THE FUN BEGINS. WE WILL SPEAK WITH BOTH PARTIES TO FIND OUT WHAT IS GOING ON FROM THEIR PERSPECTIVE.
WE ALREADY KNOW WHAT'S GOING ON, **MASTER CORDOVA**.
PERHAPS...
BUT IT'S NOT OFTEN THAT ONE COMES ACROSS ***ACTUAL*** DUPEI MONKS. THE LAST RECORDED ENCOUNTER WITH THE DUPEI WAS OVER--
MASTER, THIS ISN'T ONE OF YOUR ***"STUDIES."*** WE'RE ON A PEACEKEEPING MISSION, REMEMBER?
OR MAYBE IT'S BOTH. DO YOU THINK A DEEPER KNOWLEDGE OF EACH OTHER'S CULTURES WILL GET IN THE WAY OF PEACE?
AND, CERE? WHATEVER YOUR FIRST INSTINCT IS... IGNORE IT. TRY TO KEEP THINGS CALM HERE WHILE I TALK TO THE DUPEI.
IF YOU'LL JUST WAIT PATIENTLY WE'LL GET YOUR EXPLANATION...
...OF WHY YOU ATTACKED A GROUP OF PEACEFUL MONKS.
AH AH AH AH AH AH AH AH AH AH AH
WHAT DID HE JUST SAY?
MY ROLE IS TO TRANSLATE ON MY MASTER'S BEHALF, BUT I'M AFRAID **MY PROGRAMMING** DOES NOT ALLOW ME TO REPEAT THAT, PADAWAN JUNDA.
SUFFICE TO SAY, HE DOES NOT FEEL THAT WARLORD VURRSK SHOULD BE OBEYING THE ORDERS OF SOMEONE SO YOUNG.
WELL, THAT'S JUST GREAT.

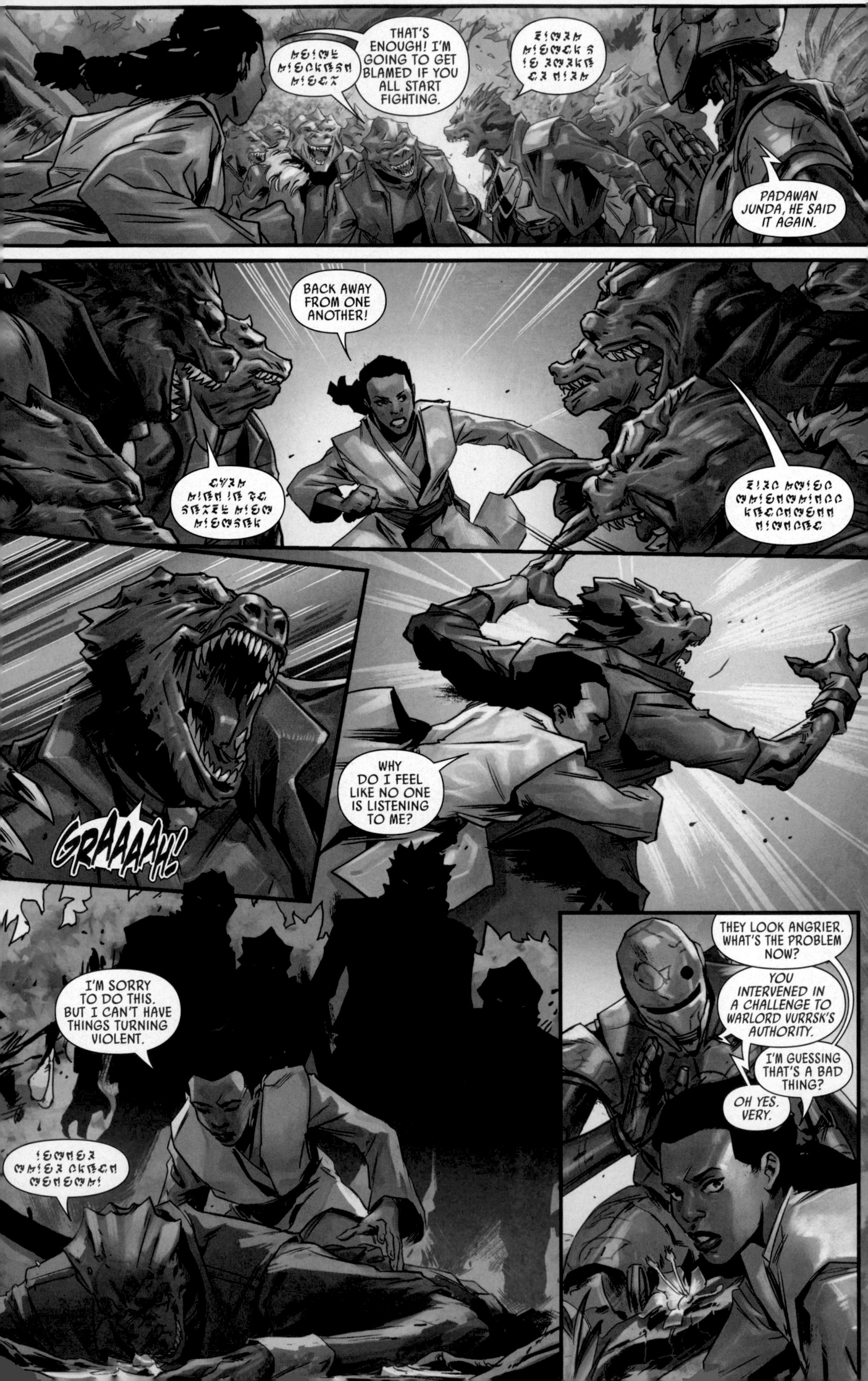
THAT'S ENOUGH! I'M GOING TO GET BLAMED IF YOU ALL START FIGHTING.
PADAWAN JUNDA, HE SAID IT AGAIN.
BACK AWAY FROM ONE ANOTHER!
WHY DO I FEEL LIKE NO ONE IS LISTENING TO ME?
GRAAAAH!
I'M SORRY TO DO THIS. BUT I CAN'T HAVE THINGS TURNING VIOLENT.
THEY LOOK ANGRIER. WHAT'S THE PROBLEM NOW?
YOU INTERVENED IN A CHALLENGE TO WARLORD VURRSK'S AUTHORITY.
I'M GUESSING THAT'S A BAD THING?
OH YES. VERY.

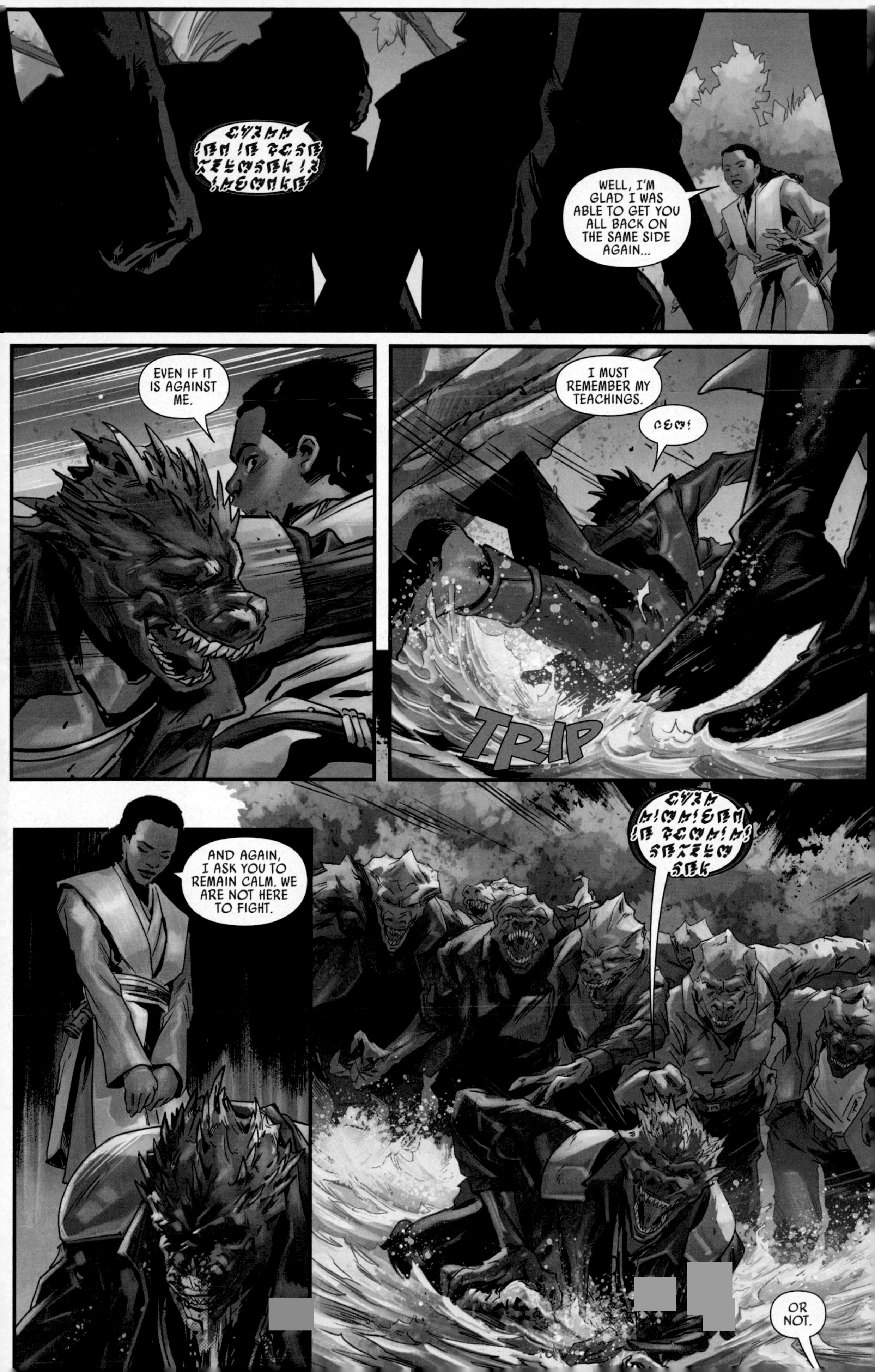

WELL, I'M GLAD I WAS ABLE TO GET YOU ALL BACK ON THE SAME SIDE AGAIN...
EVEN IF IT IS AGAINST ME.
I MUST REMEMBER MY TEACHINGS.
TRIP
AND AGAIN, I ASK YOU TO REMAIN CALM. WE ARE NOT HERE TO FIGHT.
OR NOT.

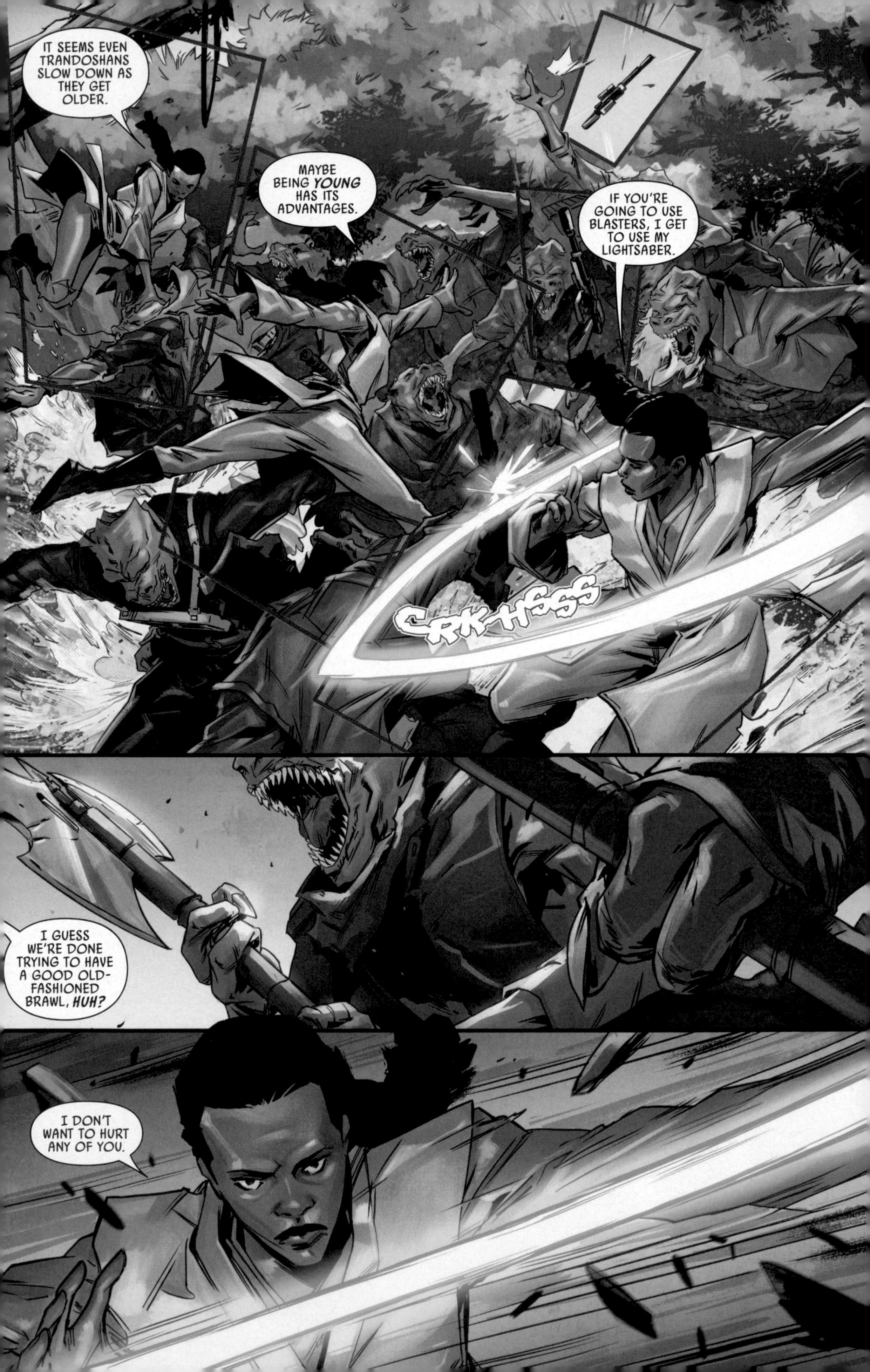
IT SEEMS EVEN TRANDOSHANS SLOW DOWN AS THEY GET OLDER.
MAYBE BEING *YOUNG* HAS ITS ADVANTAGES.
IF YOU'RE GOING TO USE BLASTERS, I GET TO USE MY LIGHTSABER.
CRK-HSSS
I GUESS WE'RE DONE TRYING TO HAVE A GOOD OLD-FASHIONED BRAWL, *HUH?*
I DON'T WANT TO HURT ANY OF YOU.

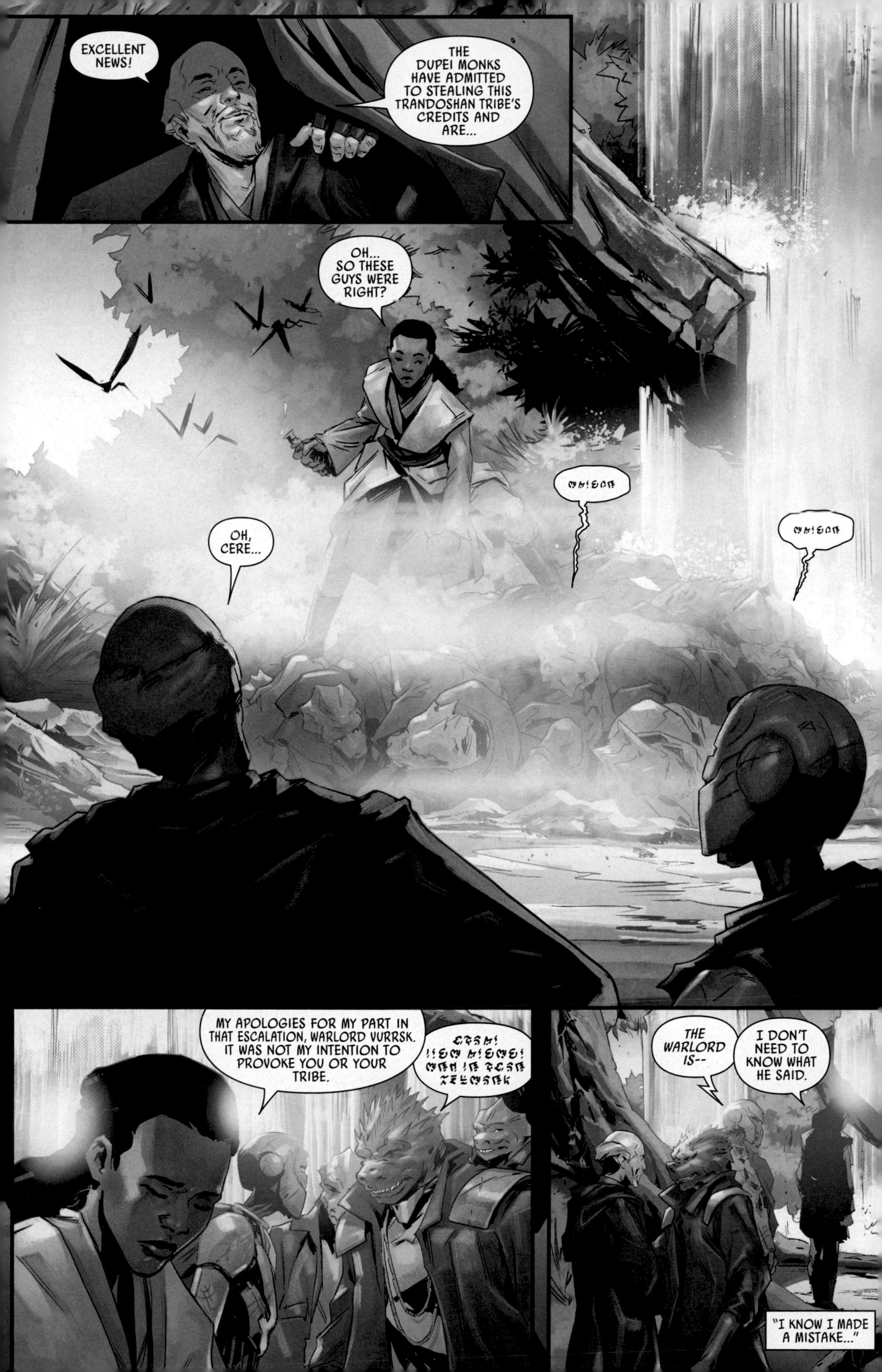
EXCELLENT NEWS!
THE DUPEI MONKS HAVE ADMITTED TO STEALING THIS TRANDOSHAN TRIBE'S CREDITS AND ARE...
OH... SO THESE GUYS WERE RIGHT?
OH, CERE...
MY APOLOGIES FOR MY PART IN THAT ESCALATION, WARLORD VURRSK. IT WAS NOT MY INTENTION TO PROVOKE YOU OR YOUR TRIBE.
THE WARLORD IS--
I DON'T NEED TO KNOW WHAT HE SAID.
"I KNOW I MADE A MISTAKE..."

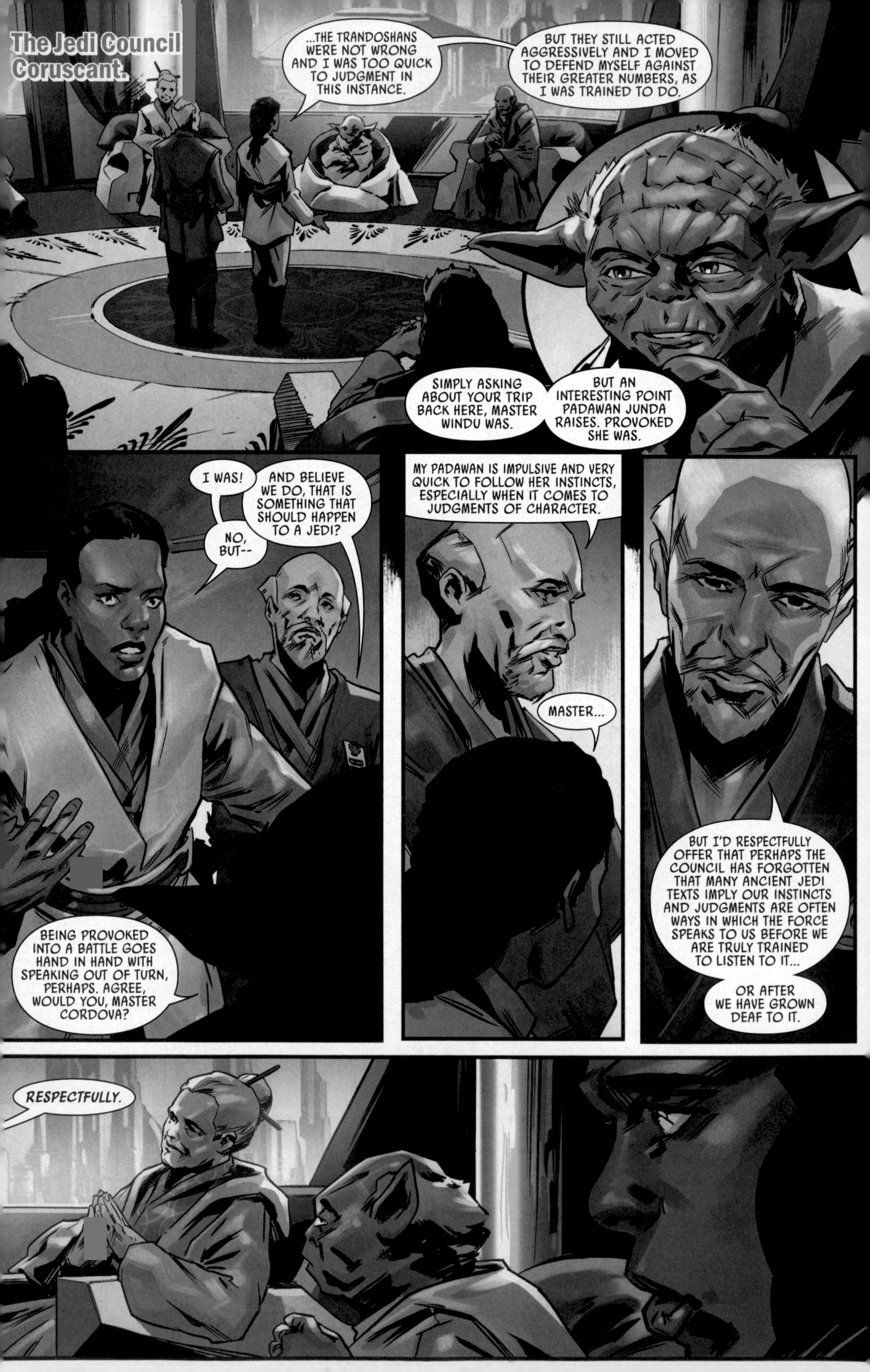
The Jedi Council
Coruscant.
...THE TRANDOSHANS WERE NOT WRONG AND I WAS TOO QUICK TO JUDGMENT IN THIS INSTANCE.
BUT THEY STILL ACTED AGGRESSIVELY AND I MOVED TO DEFEND MYSELF AGAINST THEIR GREATER NUMBERS, AS I WAS TRAINED TO DO.
SIMPLY ASKING ABOUT YOUR TRIP BACK HERE, MASTER WINDU WAS.
BUT AN INTERESTING POINT PADAWAN JUNDA RAISES. PROVOKED SHE WAS.
I WAS!
AND BELIEVE WE DO, THAT IS SOMETHING THAT SHOULD HAPPEN TO A JEDI?
NO, BUT--
BEING PROVOKED INTO A BATTLE GOES HAND IN HAND WITH SPEAKING OUT OF TURN, PERHAPS. AGREE, WOULD YOU, MASTER CORDOVA?
MY PADAWAN IS IMPULSIVE AND VERY QUICK TO FOLLOW HER INSTINCTS, ESPECIALLY WHEN IT COMES TO JUDGMENTS OF CHARACTER.
MASTER...
BUT I'D RESPECTFULLY OFFER THAT PERHAPS THE COUNCIL HAS FORGOTTEN THAT MANY ANCIENT JEDI TEXTS IMPLY OUR INSTINCTS AND JUDGMENTS ARE OFTEN WAYS IN WHICH THE FORCE SPEAKS TO US BEFORE WE ARE TRULY TRAINED TO LISTEN TO IT...
OR AFTER WE HAVE GROWN DEAF TO IT.
RESPECTFULLY.

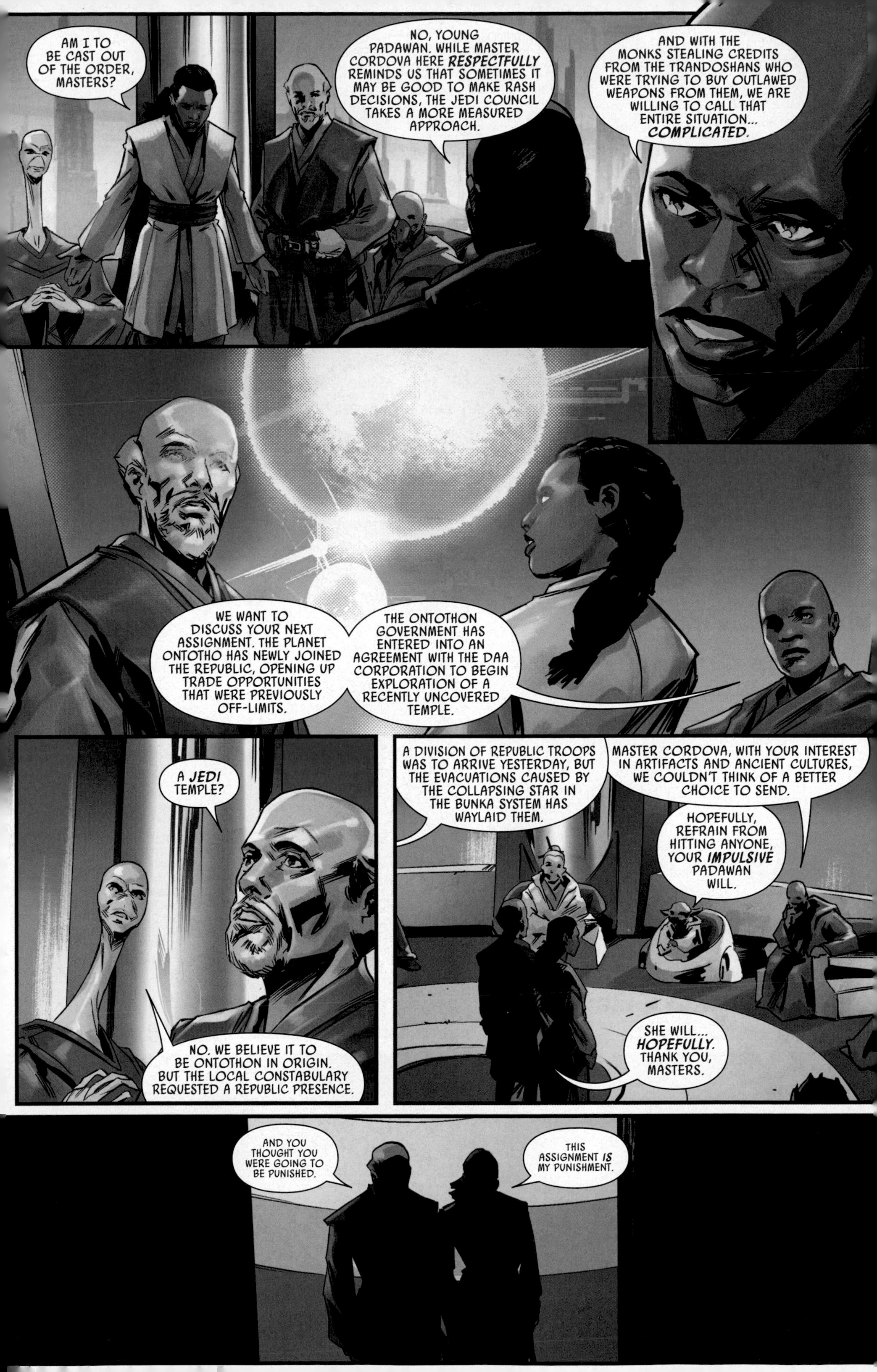
AM I TO BE CAST OUT OF THE ORDER, MASTERS?
NO, YOUNG PADAWAN. WHILE MASTER CORDOVA HERE ***RESPECTFULLY*** REMINDS US THAT SOMETIMES IT MAY BE GOOD TO MAKE RASH DECISIONS, THE JEDI COUNCIL TAKES A MORE MEASURED APPROACH.
AND WITH THE MONKS STEALING CREDITS FROM THE TRANDOSHANS WHO WERE TRYING TO BUY OUTLAWED WEAPONS FROM THEM, WE ARE WILLING TO CALL THAT ENTIRE SITUATION... ***COMPLICATED.***
WE WANT TO DISCUSS YOUR NEXT ASSIGNMENT. THE PLANET ONTOTHO HAS NEWLY JOINED THE REPUBLIC, OPENING UP TRADE OPPORTUNITIES THAT WERE PREVIOUSLY OFF-LIMITS.
THE ONTOTHON GOVERNMENT HAS ENTERED INTO AN AGREEMENT WITH THE DAA CORPORATION TO BEGIN EXPLORATION OF A RECENTLY UNCOVERED TEMPLE.
A ***JEDI*** TEMPLE?
NO. WE BELIEVE IT TO BE ONTOTHON IN ORIGIN. BUT THE LOCAL CONSTABULARY REQUESTED A REPUBLIC PRESENCE.
A DIVISION OF REPUBLIC TROOPS WAS TO ARRIVE YESTERDAY, BUT THE EVACUATIONS CAUSED BY THE COLLAPSING STAR IN THE BUNKA SYSTEM HAS WAYLAID THEM.
MASTER CORDOVA, WITH YOUR INTEREST IN ARTIFACTS AND ANCIENT CULTURES, WE COULDN'T THINK OF A BETTER CHOICE TO SEND.
HOPEFULLY, REFRAIN FROM HITTING ANYONE, YOUR ***IMPULSIVE*** PADAWAN WILL.
SHE WILL... ***HOPEFULLY.*** THANK YOU, MASTERS.
AND YOU THOUGHT YOU WERE GOING TO BE PUNISHED.
THIS ASSIGNMENT ***IS*** MY PUNISHMENT.

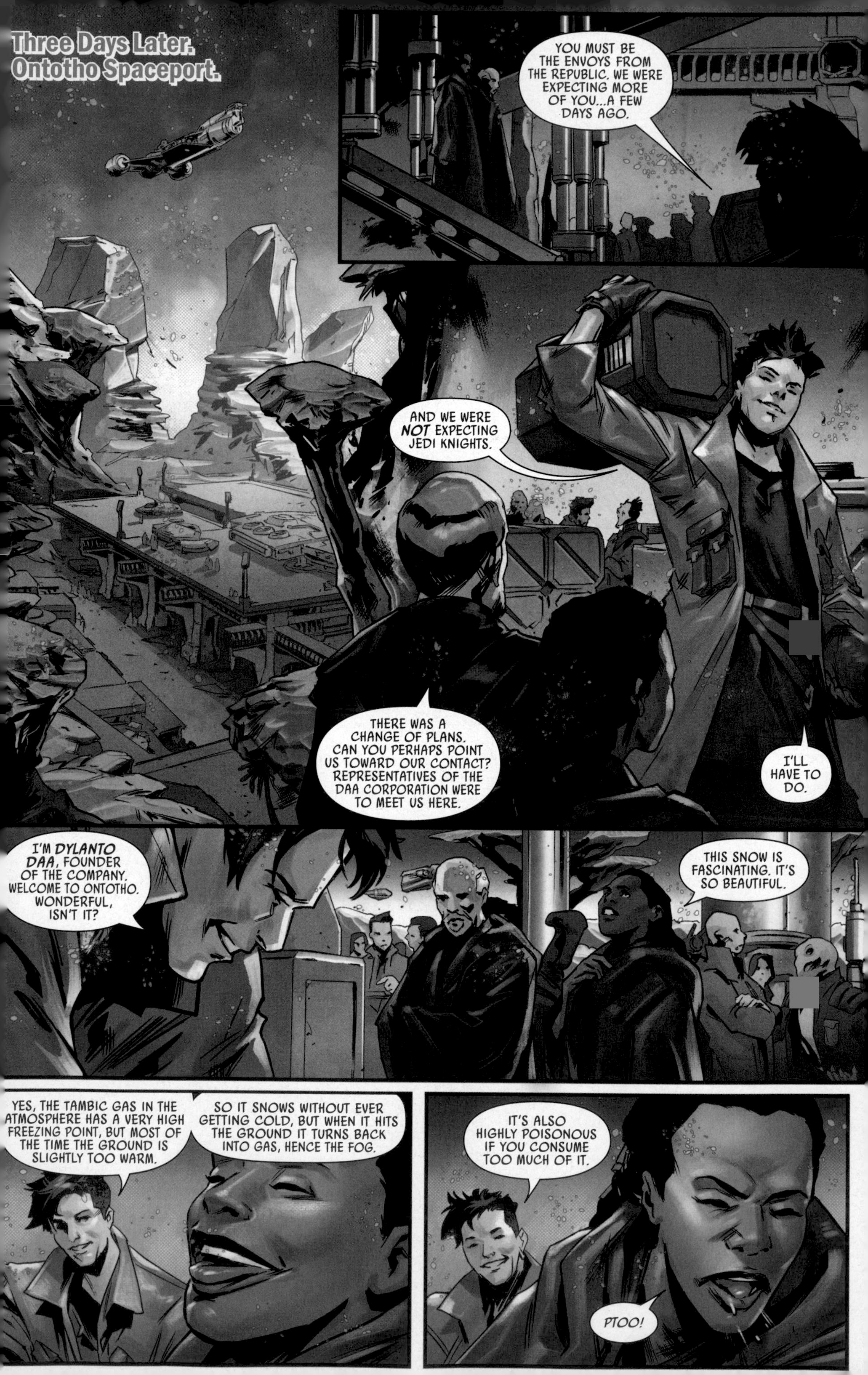
Three Days Later.
Ontotho Spaceport.
YOU MUST BE THE ENVOYS FROM THE REPUBLIC. WE WERE EXPECTING MORE OF YOU...A FEW DAYS AGO.
AND WE WERE NOT EXPECTING JEDI KNIGHTS.
THERE WAS A CHANGE OF PLANS. CAN YOU PERHAPS POINT US TOWARD OUR CONTACT? REPRESENTATIVES OF THE DAA CORPORATION WERE TO MEET US HERE.
I'LL HAVE TO DO.
I'M DYLANTO DAA, FOUNDER OF THE COMPANY. WELCOME TO ONTOTHO. WONDERFUL, ISN'T IT?
THIS SNOW IS FASCINATING. IT'S SO BEAUTIFUL.
YES, THE TAMBIC GAS IN THE ATMOSPHERE HAS A VERY HIGH FREEZING POINT, BUT MOST OF THE TIME THE GROUND IS SLIGHTLY TOO WARM.
SO IT SNOWS WITHOUT EVER GETTING COLD, BUT WHEN IT HITS THE GROUND IT TURNS BACK INTO GAS, HENCE THE FOG.
IT'S ALSO HIGHLY POISONOUS IF YOU CONSUME TOO MUCH OF IT.
PTOO!

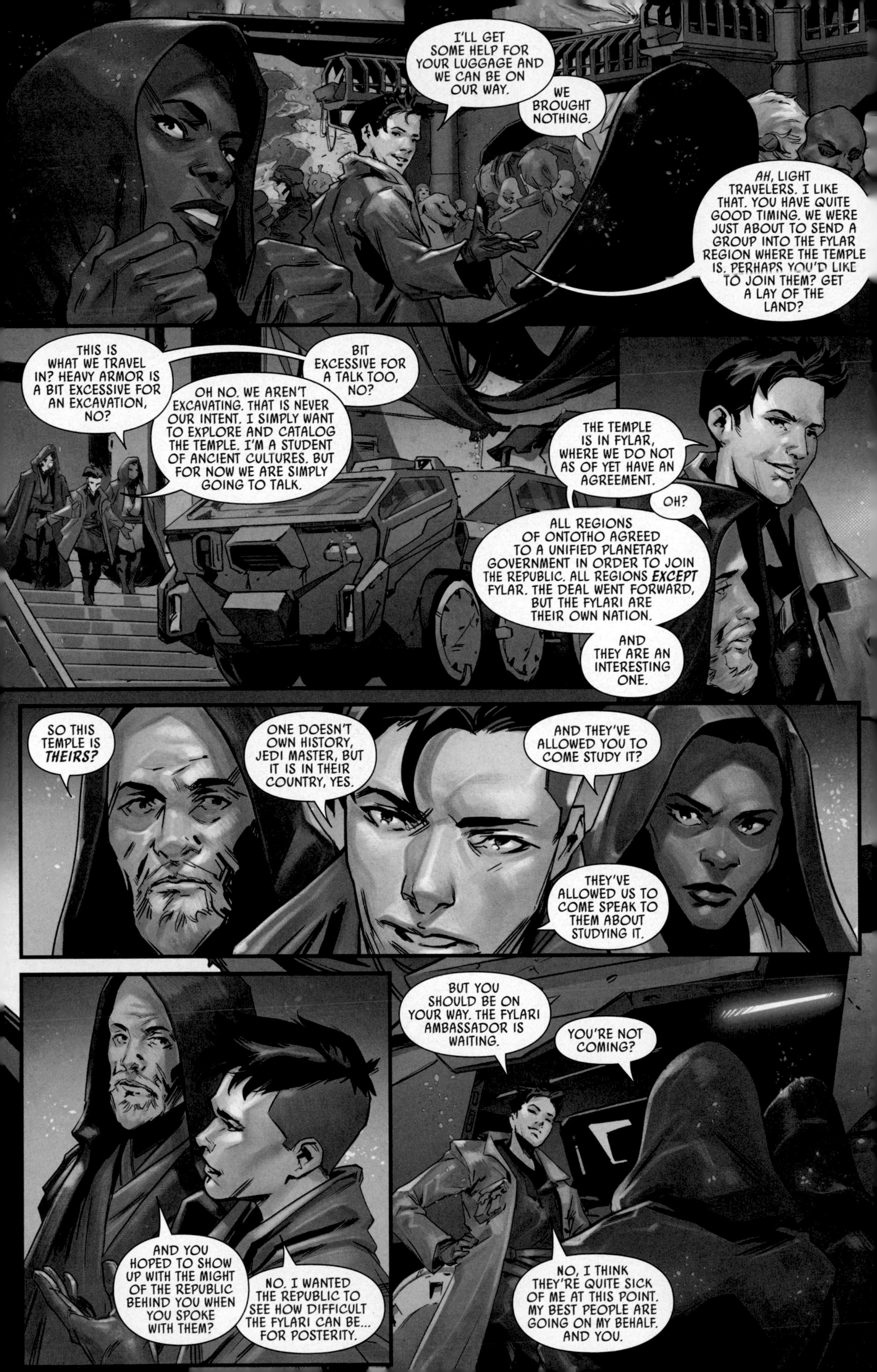
I'LL GET SOME HELP FOR YOUR LUGGAGE AND WE CAN BE ON OUR WAY.
WE BROUGHT NOTHING.
AH, LIGHT TRAVELERS. I LIKE THAT. YOU HAVE QUITE GOOD TIMING. WE WERE JUST ABOUT TO SEND A GROUP INTO THE FYLAR REGION WHERE THE TEMPLE IS. PERHAPS YOU'D LIKE TO JOIN THEM? GET A LAY OF THE LAND?
THIS IS WHAT WE TRAVEL IN? HEAVY ARMOR IS A BIT EXCESSIVE FOR AN EXCAVATION, NO?
OH NO. WE AREN'T EXCAVATING. THAT IS NEVER OUR INTENT. I SIMPLY WANT TO EXPLORE AND CATALOG THE TEMPLE. I'M A STUDENT OF ANCIENT CULTURES. BUT FOR NOW WE ARE SIMPLY GOING TO TALK.
BIT EXCESSIVE FOR A TALK TOO, NO?
THE TEMPLE IS IN FYLAR, WHERE WE DO NOT AS OF YET HAVE AN AGREEMENT.
OH?
ALL REGIONS OF ONTOTHO AGREED TO A UNIFIED PLANETARY GOVERNMENT IN ORDER TO JOIN THE REPUBLIC. ALL REGIONS *EXCEPT* FYLAR. THE DEAL WENT FORWARD, BUT THE FYLARI ARE THEIR OWN NATION.
AND THEY ARE AN INTERESTING ONE.
SO THIS TEMPLE IS *THEIRS?*
ONE DOESN'T OWN HISTORY, JEDI MASTER, BUT IT IS IN THEIR COUNTRY, YES.
AND THEY'VE ALLOWED YOU TO COME STUDY IT?
THEY'VE ALLOWED US TO COME SPEAK TO THEM ABOUT STUDYING IT.
AND YOU HOPED TO SHOW UP WITH THE MIGHT OF THE REPUBLIC BEHIND YOU WHEN YOU SPOKE WITH THEM?
NO. I WANTED THE REPUBLIC TO SEE HOW DIFFICULT THE FYLARI CAN BE... FOR POSTERITY.
BUT YOU SHOULD BE ON YOUR WAY. THE FYLARI AMBASSADOR IS WAITING.
YOU'RE NOT COMING?
NO, I THINK THEY'RE QUITE SICK OF ME AT THIS POINT. MY BEST PEOPLE ARE GOING ON MY BEHALF. AND YOU.

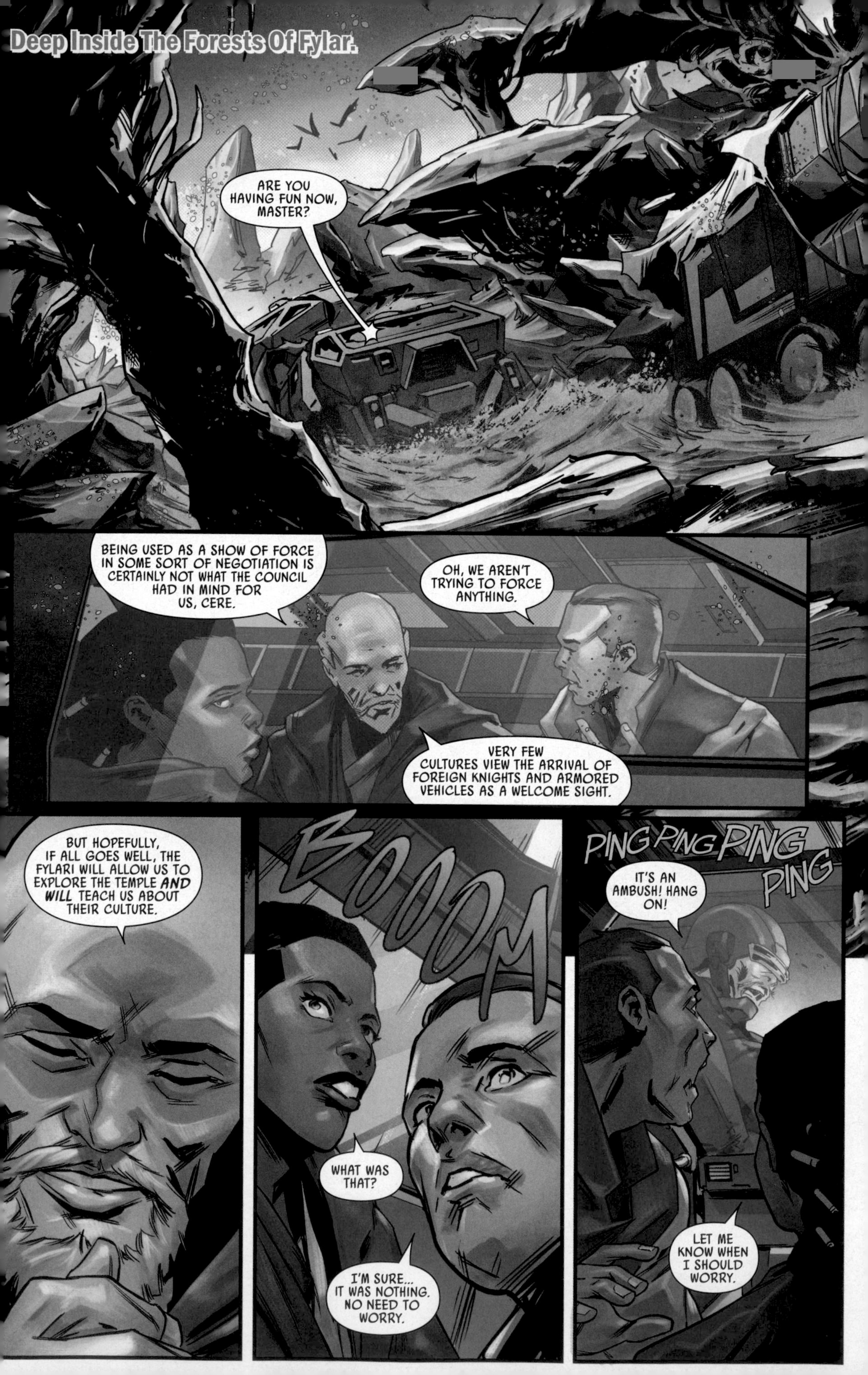

Deep Inside The Forests Of Fylar.
ARE YOU HAVING FUN NOW, MASTER?
BEING USED AS A SHOW OF FORCE IN SOME SORT OF NEGOTIATION IS CERTAINLY NOT WHAT THE COUNCIL HAD IN MIND FOR US, CERE.
OH, WE AREN'T TRYING TO FORCE ANYTHING.
VERY FEW CULTURES VIEW THE ARRIVAL OF FOREIGN KNIGHTS AND ARMORED VEHICLES AS A WELCOME SIGHT.
BUT HOPEFULLY, IF ALL GOES WELL, THE FYLARI WILL ALLOW US TO EXPLORE THE TEMPLE **AND** **WILL** TEACH US ABOUT THEIR CULTURE.
BOOOOM
WHAT WAS THAT?
I'M SURE... IT WAS NOTHING. NO NEED TO WORRY.
PING PING PING PING
IT'S AN AMBUSH! HANG ON!
LET ME KNOW WHEN I SHOULD WORRY.

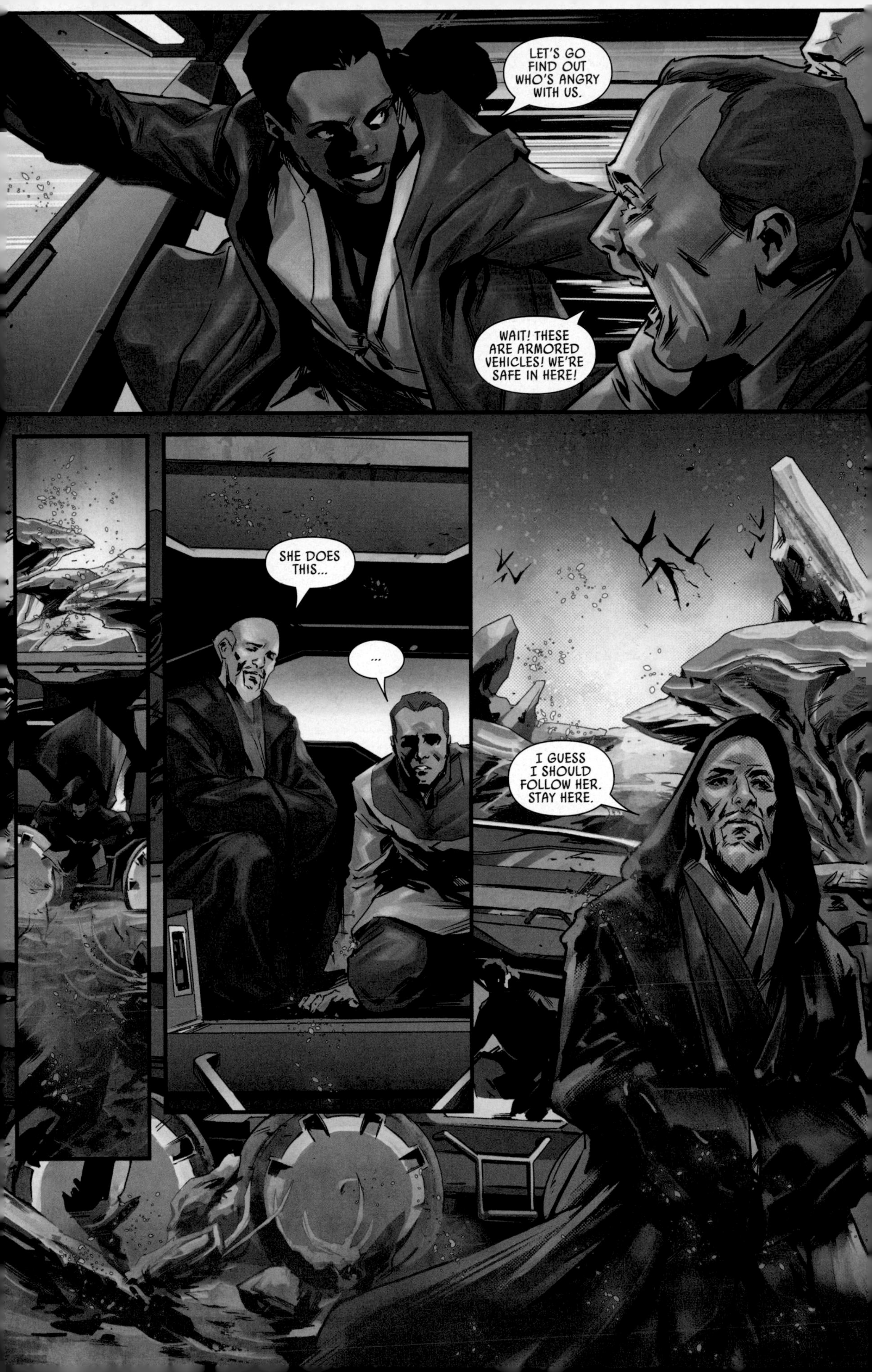
LET'S GO FIND OUT WHO'S ANGRY WITH US.
WAIT! THESE ARE ARMORED VEHICLES! WE'RE SAFE IN HERE!
SHE DOES THIS...
...
I GUESS I SHOULD FOLLOW HER. STAY HERE.

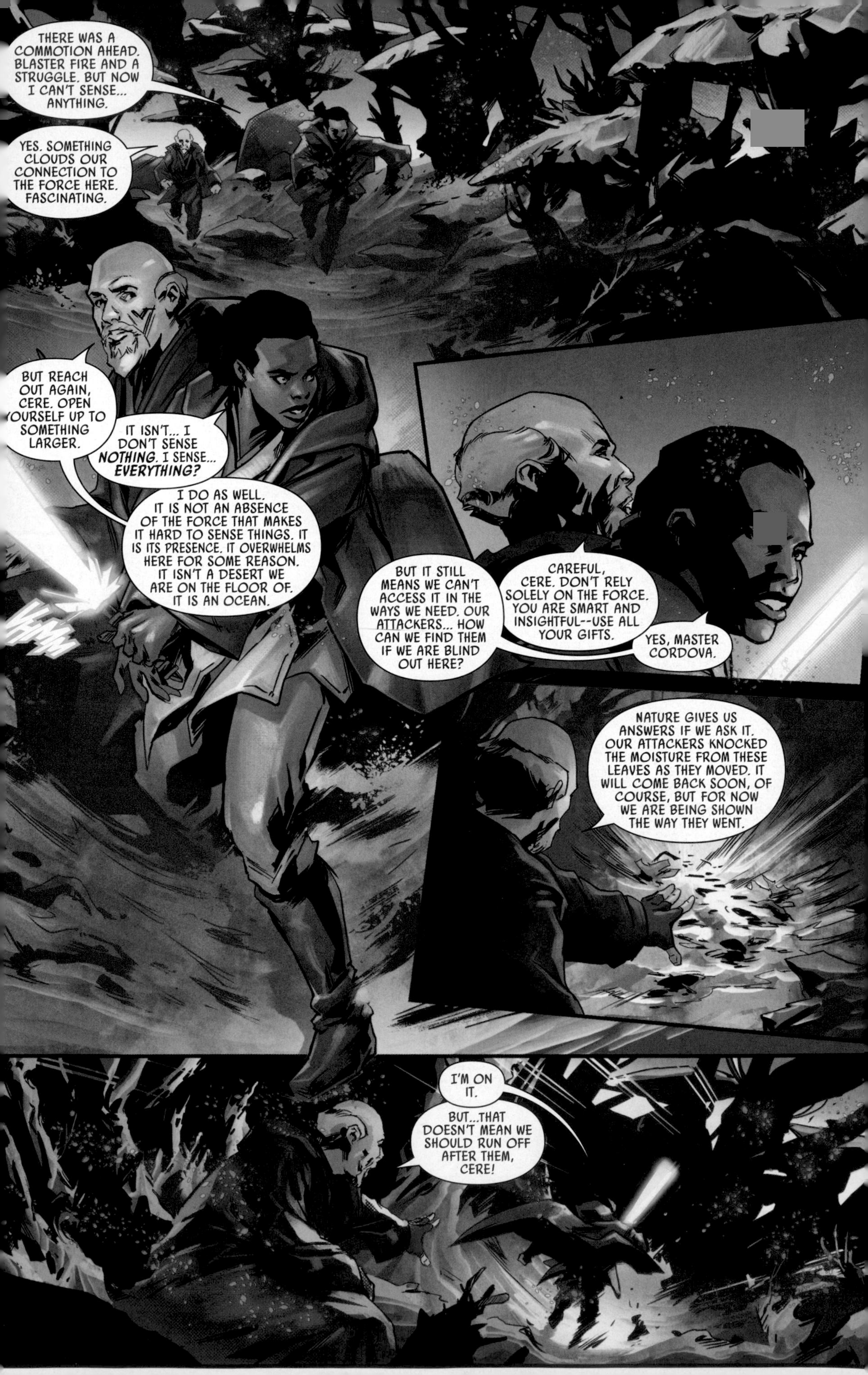
THERE WAS A COMMOTION AHEAD. BLASTER FIRE AND A STRUGGLE. BUT NOW I CAN'T SENSE... ANYTHING.
YES. SOMETHING CLOUDS OUR CONNECTION TO THE FORCE HERE. FASCINATING.
BUT REACH OUT AGAIN, CERE. OPEN YOURSELF UP TO SOMETHING LARGER.
IT ISN'T... I DON'T SENSE *NOTHING*. I SENSE... *EVERYTHING?*
I DO AS WELL. IT IS NOT AN ABSENCE OF THE FORCE THAT MAKES IT HARD TO SENSE THINGS. IT IS ITS PRESENCE. IT OVERWHELMS HERE FOR SOME REASON. IT ISN'T A DESERT WE ARE ON THE FLOOR OF. IT IS AN OCEAN.
VMMM
BUT IT STILL MEANS WE CAN'T ACCESS IT IN THE WAYS WE NEED. OUR ATTACKERS... HOW CAN WE FIND THEM IF WE ARE BLIND OUT HERE?
CAREFUL, CERE. DON'T RELY SOLELY ON THE FORCE. YOU ARE SMART AND INSIGHTFUL--USE ALL YOUR GIFTS.
YES, MASTER CORDOVA.
NATURE GIVES US ANSWERS IF WE ASK IT. OUR ATTACKERS KNOCKED THE MOISTURE FROM THESE LEAVES AS THEY MOVED. IT WILL COME BACK SOON, OF COURSE, BUT FOR NOW WE ARE BEING SHOWN THE WAY THEY WENT.
I'M ON IT.
BUT...THAT DOESN'T MEAN WE SHOULD RUN OFF AFTER THEM, CERE!

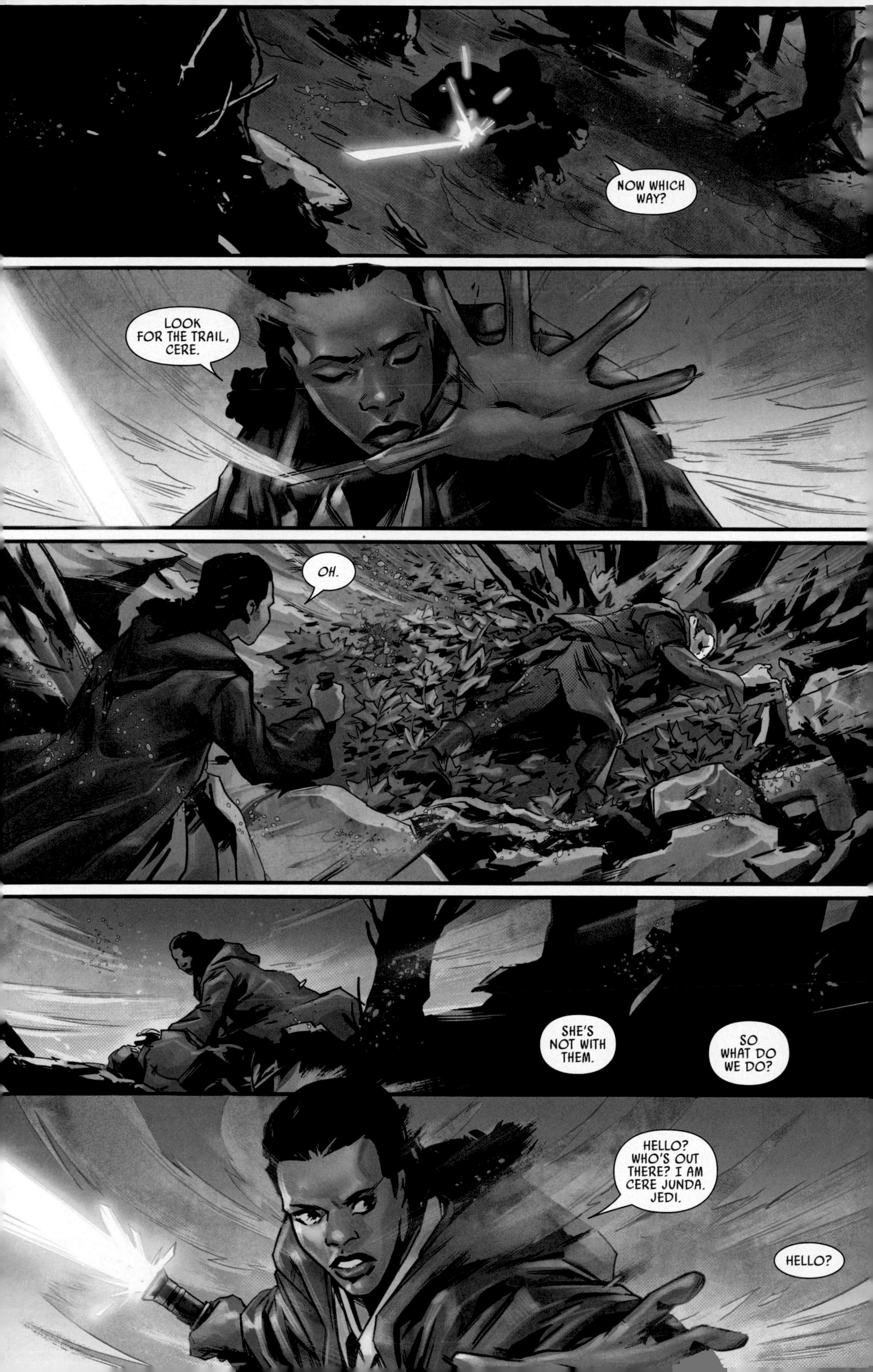
NOW WHICH WAY?
LOOK FOR THE TRAIL, CERE.
OH.
SHE'S NOT WITH THEM.
SO WHAT DO WE DO?
HELLO? WHO'S OUT THERE? I AM CERE JUNDA. JEDI.
HELLO?

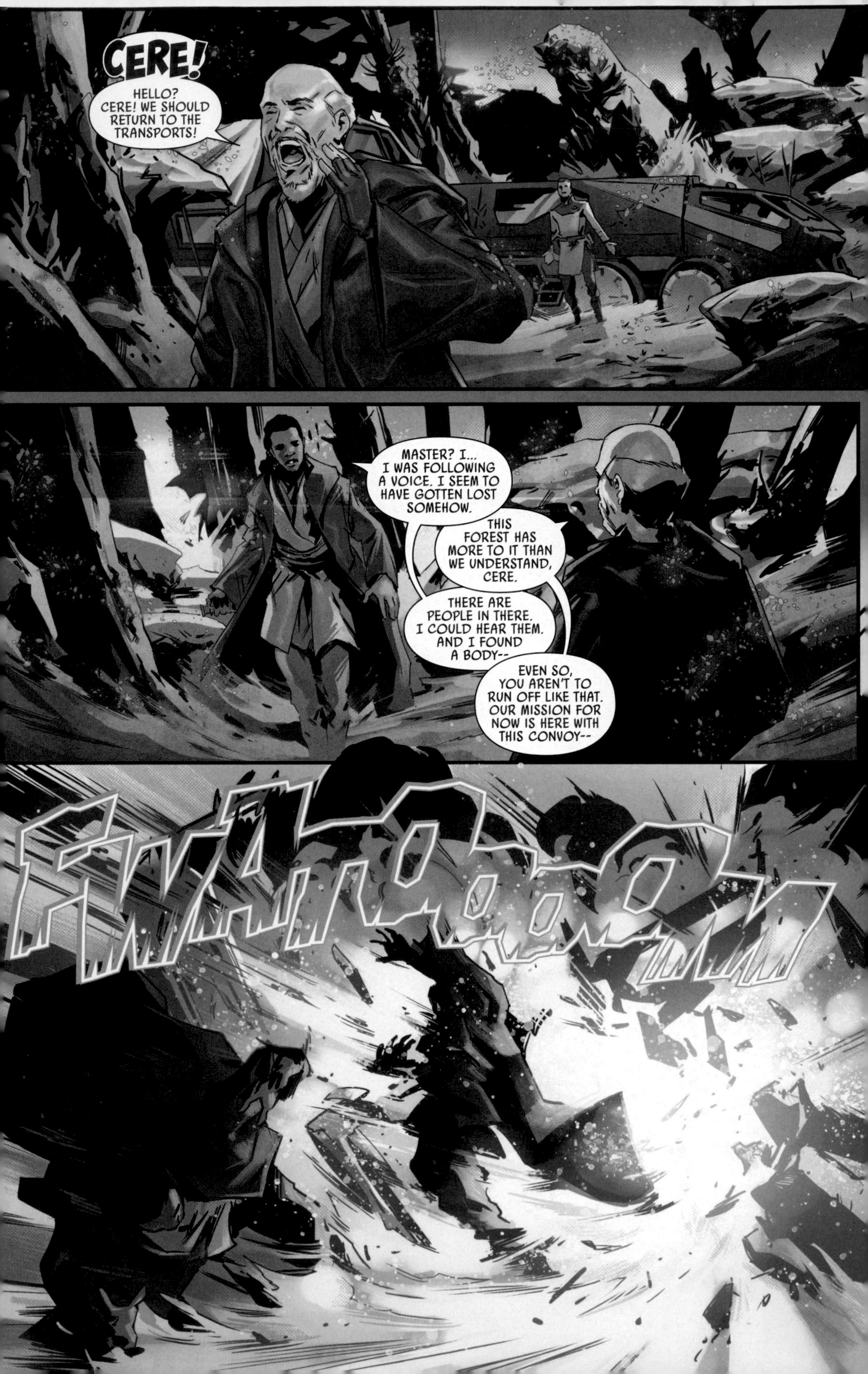
CERE!
HELLO? CERE! WE SHOULD RETURN TO THE TRANSPORTS!
MASTER? I... I WAS FOLLOWING A VOICE. I SEEM TO HAVE GOTTEN LOST SOMEHOW.
THIS FOREST HAS MORE TO IT THAN WE UNDERSTAND, CERE.
THERE ARE PEOPLE IN THERE. I COULD HEAR THEM. AND I FOUND A BODY--
EVEN SO, YOU AREN'T TO RUN OFF LIKE THAT. OUR MISSION FOR NOW IS HERE WITH THIS CONVOY--
FWHOOOOM

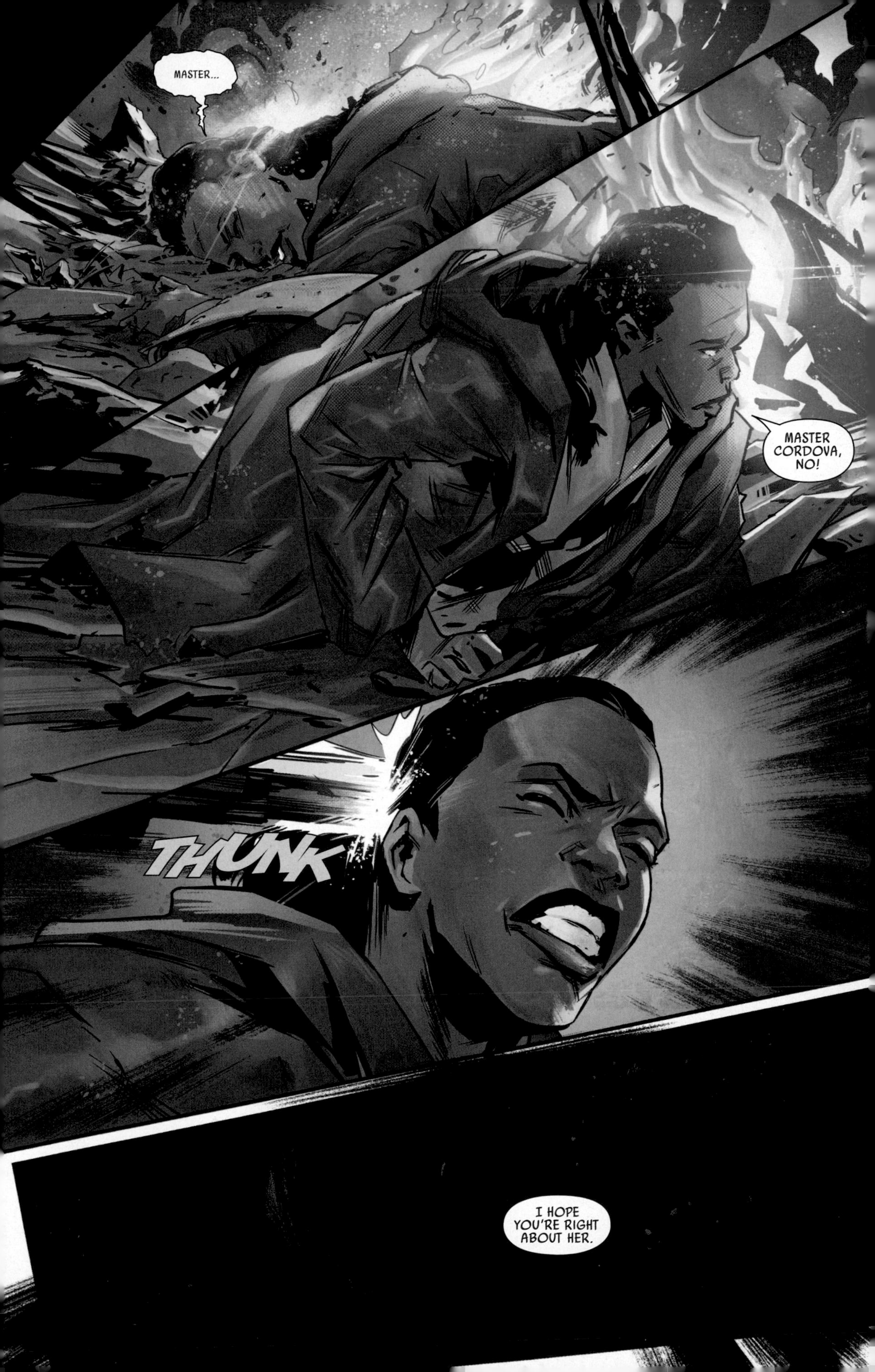
MASTER...
MASTER CORDOVA, NO!
THUNK
I HOPE YOU'RE RIGHT ABOUT HER.

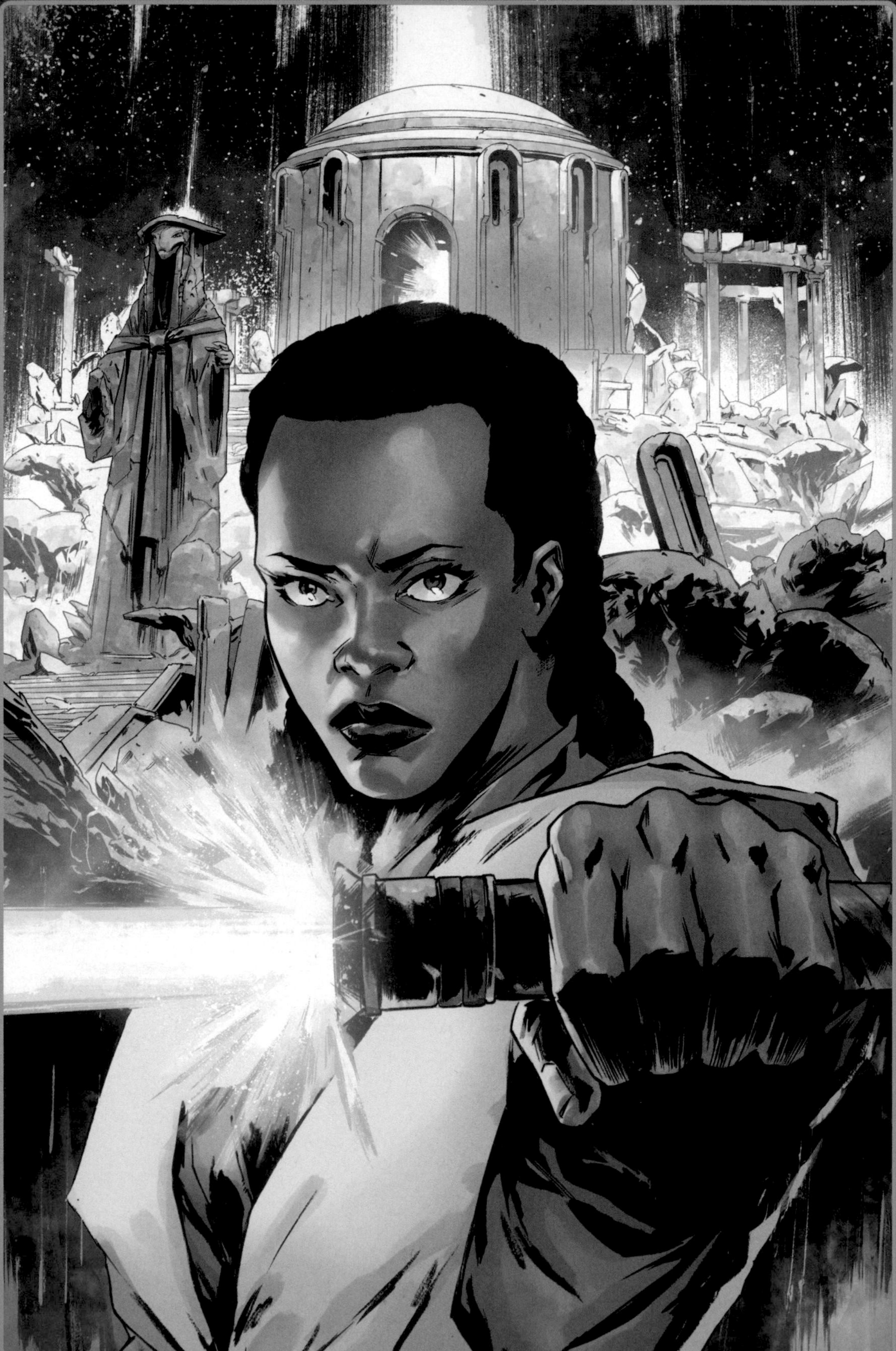

2 – TRAPPED ON ONTOTHO

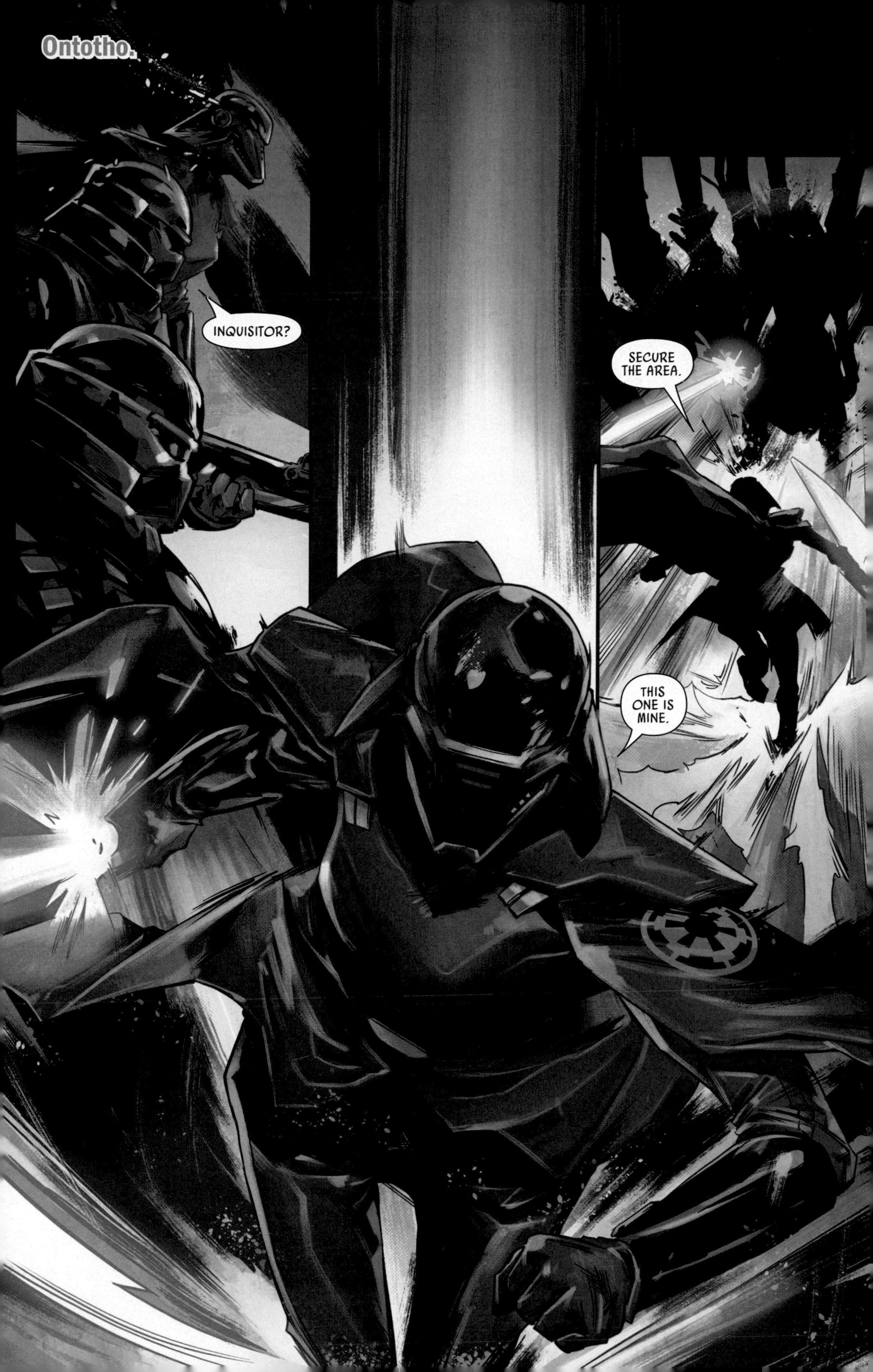
Ontotho.
INQUISITOR?
SECURE THE AREA.
THIS ONE IS MINE.

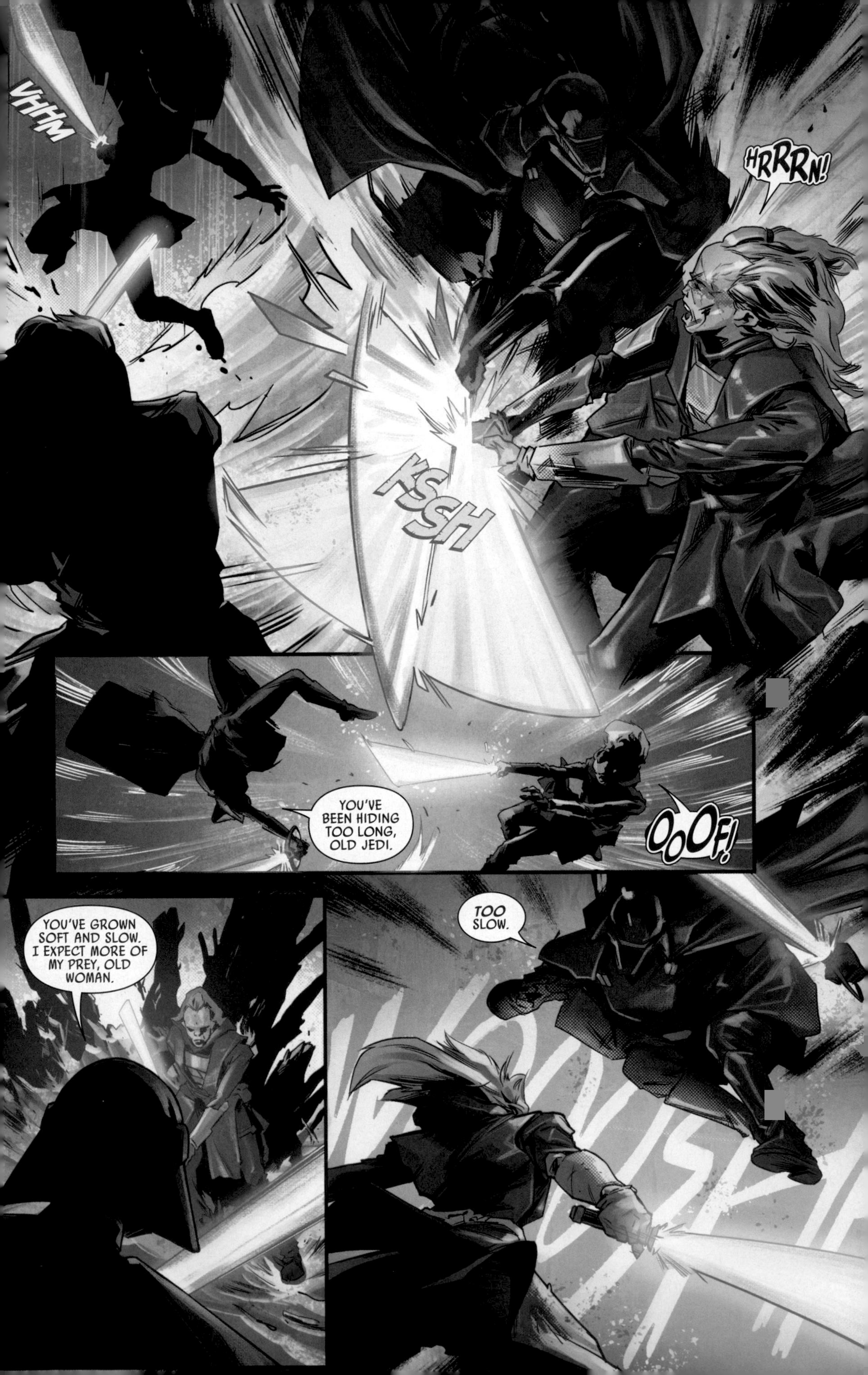
VHHM
HRRRN!
KSSH
YOU'VE BEEN HIDING TOO LONG, OLD JEDI.
OOOF!
YOU'VE GROWN SOFT AND SLOW. I EXPECT MORE OF MY PREY, OLD WOMAN.
TOO SLOW.

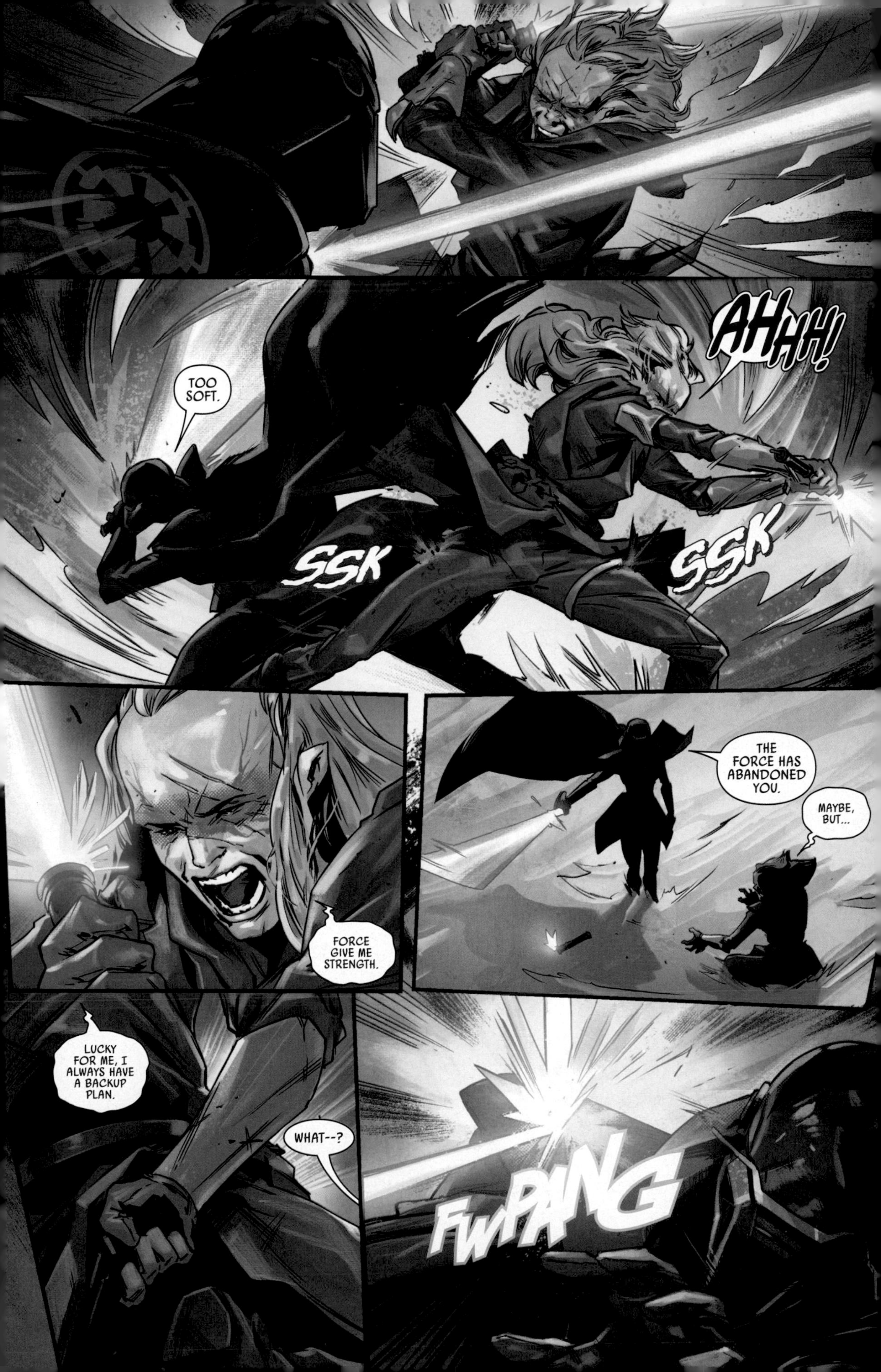
AHHH!
TOO SOFT.
SSK
SSK
FORCE GIVE ME STRENGTH.
THE FORCE HAS ABANDONED YOU.
MAYBE, BUT...
LUCKY FOR ME, I ALWAYS HAVE A BACKUP PLAN.
WHAT--?
FWPANG

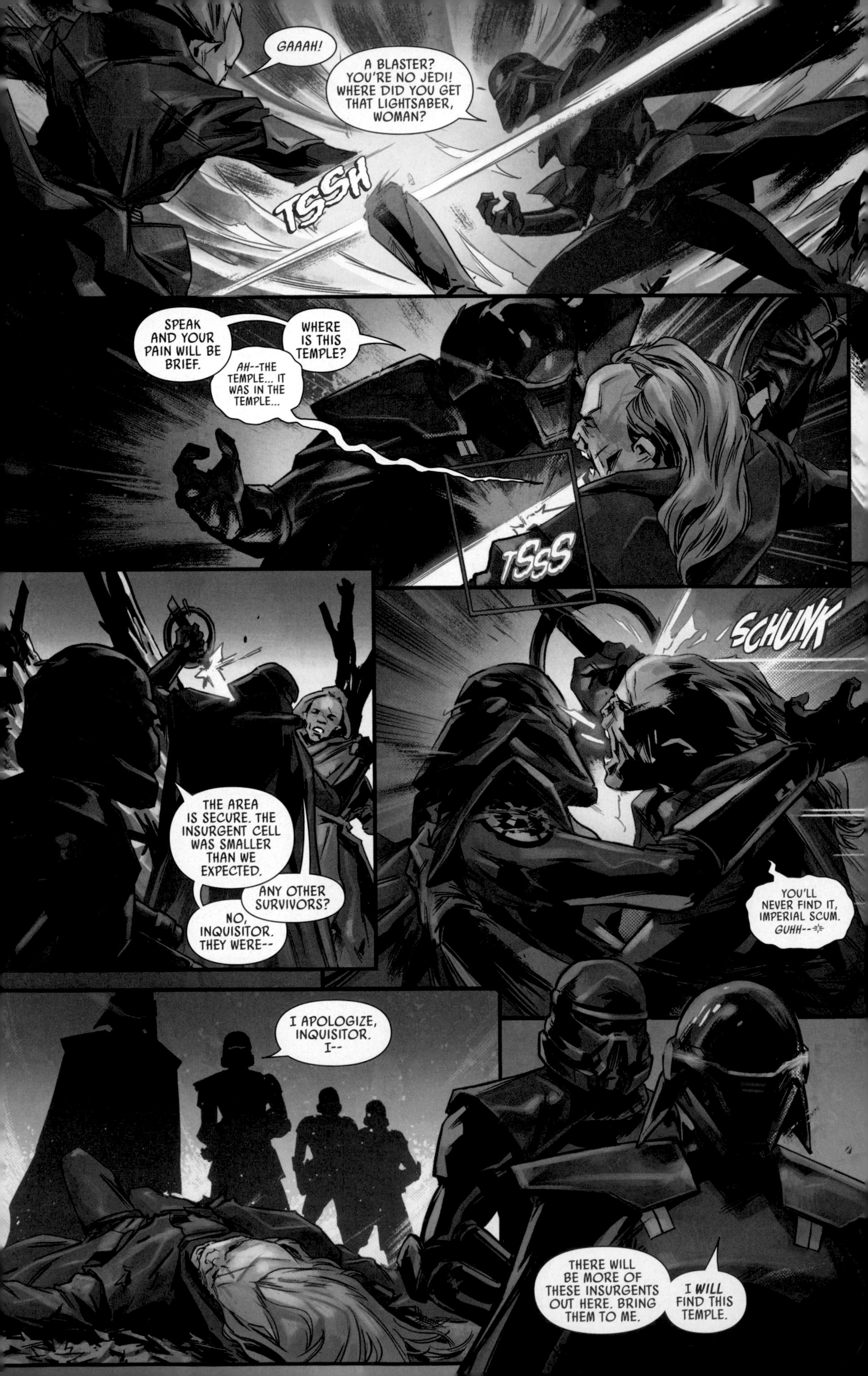
GAAAH!
A BLASTER? YOU'RE NO JEDI! WHERE DID YOU GET THAT LIGHTSABER, WOMAN?
TSSH
SPEAK AND YOUR PAIN WILL BE BRIEF.
WHERE IS THIS TEMPLE?
AH--THE TEMPLE... IT WAS IN THE TEMPLE...
TSSS
SCHUNK
YOU'LL NEVER FIND IT, IMPERIAL SCUM. GUHH--
THE AREA IS SECURE. THE INSURGENT CELL WAS SMALLER THAN WE EXPECTED.
ANY OTHER SURVIVORS?
NO, INQUISITOR. THEY WERE--
I APOLOGIZE, INQUISITOR. I--
THERE WILL BE MORE OF THESE INSURGENTS OUT HERE. BRING THEM TO ME.
I WILL FIND THIS TEMPLE.

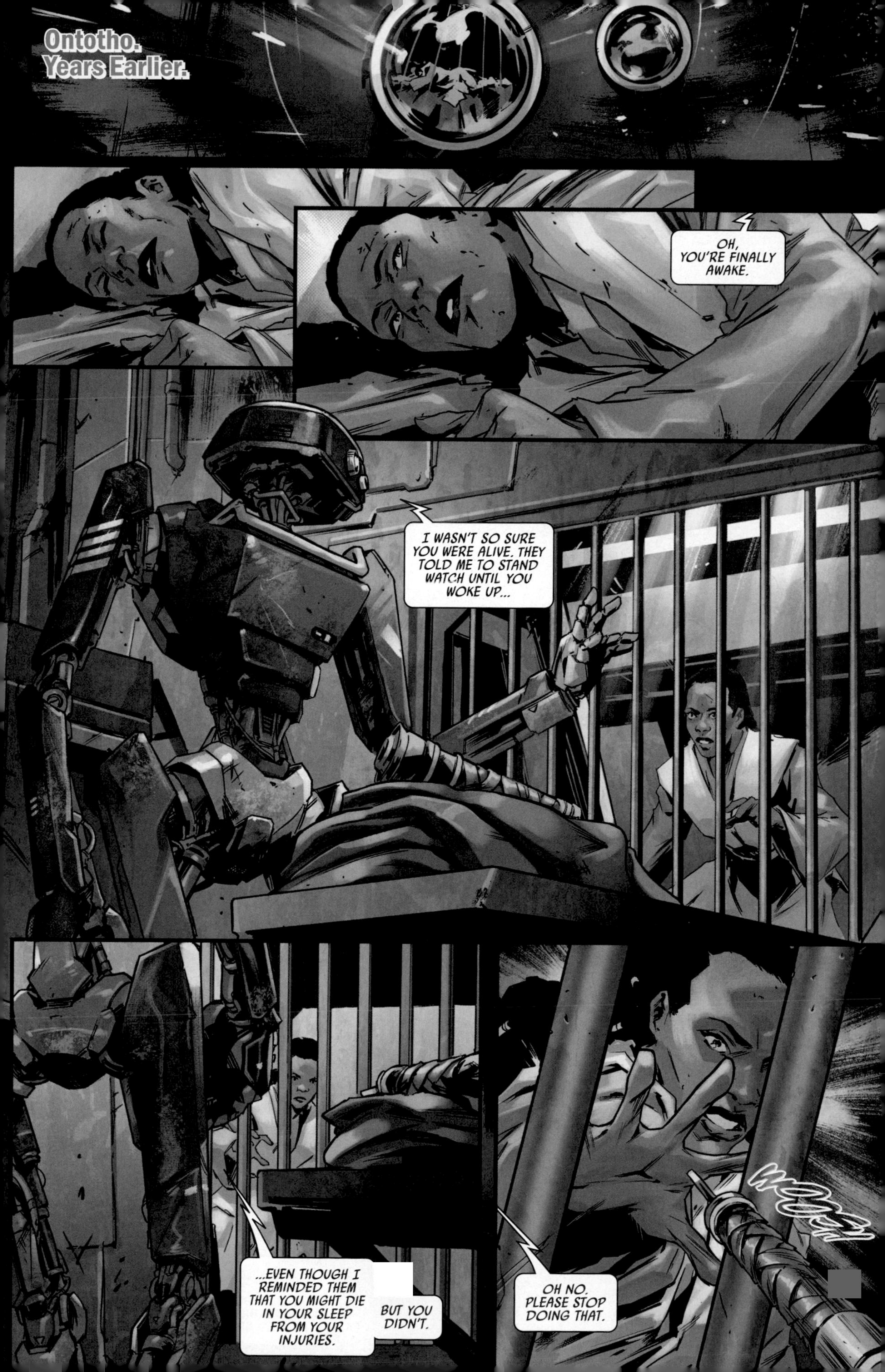
Ontotho.
Years Earlier.
OH, YOU'RE FINALLY AWAKE.
I WASN'T SO SURE YOU WERE ALIVE. THEY TOLD ME TO STAND WATCH UNTIL YOU WOKE UP...
...EVEN THOUGH I REMINDED THEM THAT YOU MIGHT DIE IN YOUR SLEEP FROM YOUR INJURIES.
BUT YOU DIDN'T.
OH NO. PLEASE STOP DOING THAT.

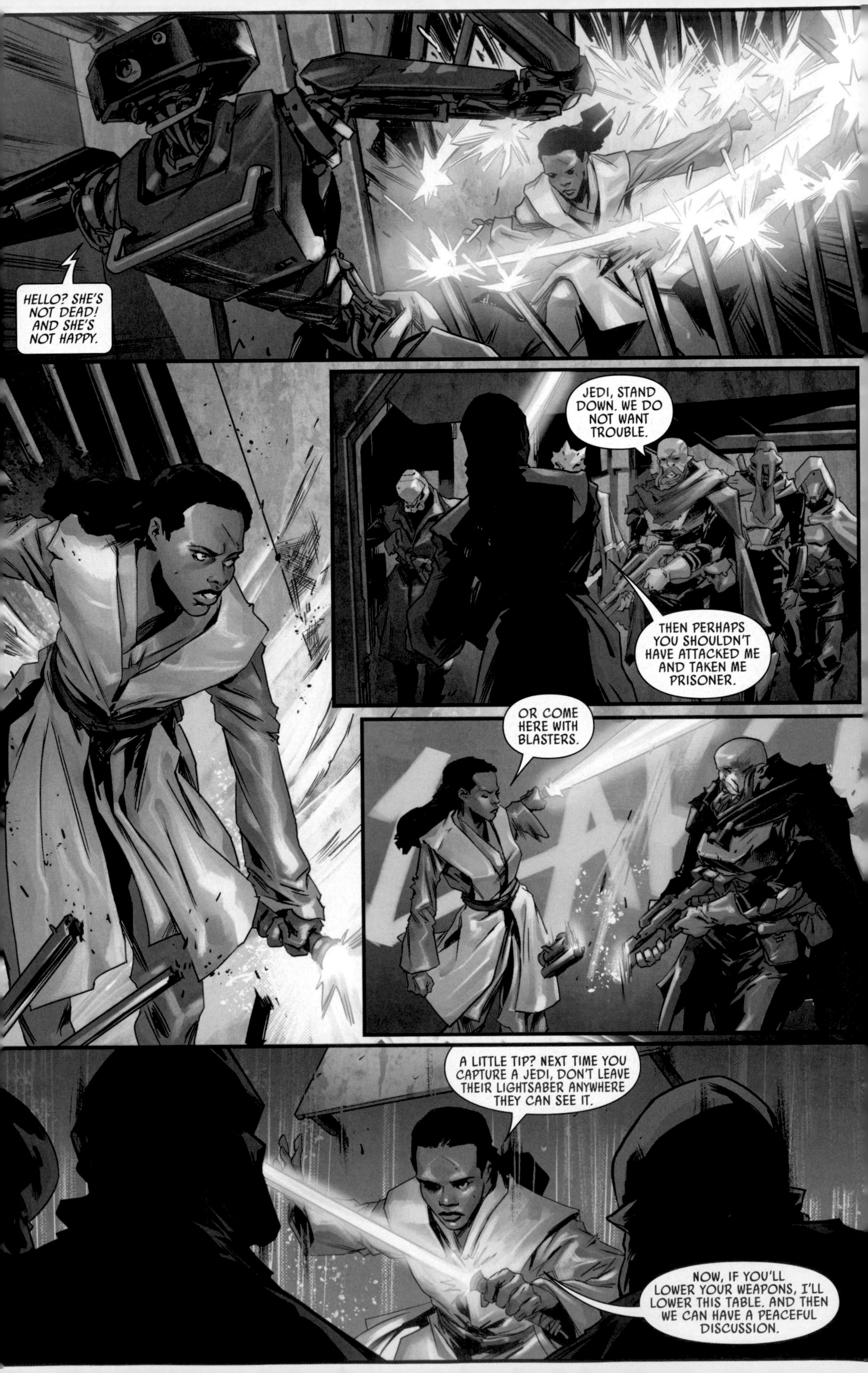
HELLO? SHE'S NOT DEAD! AND SHE'S NOT HAPPY.
JEDI, STAND DOWN. WE DO NOT WANT TROUBLE.
THEN PERHAPS YOU SHOULDN'T HAVE ATTACKED ME AND TAKEN ME PRISONER.
OR COME HERE WITH BLASTERS.
A LITTLE TIP? NEXT TIME YOU CAPTURE A JEDI, DON'T LEAVE THEIR LIGHTSABER ANYWHERE THEY CAN SEE IT.
NOW, IF YOU'LL LOWER YOUR WEAPONS, I'LL LOWER THIS TABLE. AND THEN WE CAN HAVE A PEACEFUL DISCUSSION.

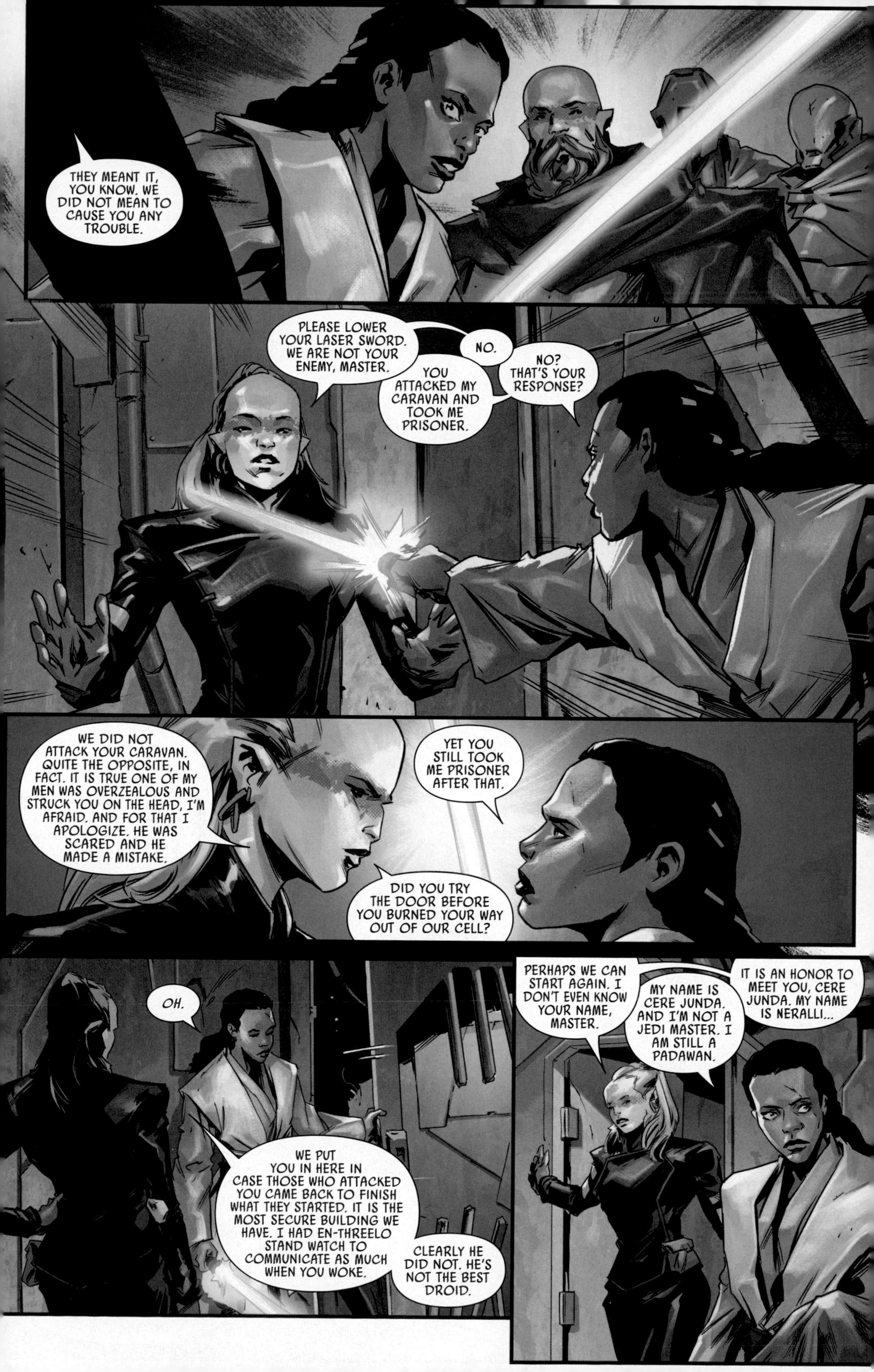
THEY MEANT IT, YOU KNOW. WE DID NOT MEAN TO CAUSE YOU ANY TROUBLE.
PLEASE LOWER YOUR LASER SWORD. WE ARE NOT YOUR ENEMY, MASTER.
NO.
YOU ATTACKED MY CARAVAN AND TOOK ME PRISONER.
NO? THAT'S YOUR RESPONSE?
WE DID NOT ATTACK YOUR CARAVAN. QUITE THE OPPOSITE, IN FACT. IT IS TRUE ONE OF MY MEN WAS OVERZEALOUS AND STRUCK YOU ON THE HEAD, I'M AFRAID. AND FOR THAT I APOLOGIZE. HE WAS SCARED AND HE MADE A MISTAKE.
YET YOU STILL TOOK ME PRISONER AFTER THAT.
DID YOU TRY THE DOOR BEFORE YOU BURNED YOUR WAY OUT OF OUR CELL?
OH.
WE PUT YOU IN HERE IN CASE THOSE WHO ATTACKED YOU CAME BACK TO FINISH WHAT THEY STARTED. IT IS THE MOST SECURE BUILDING WE HAVE. I HAD EN-THREELO STAND WATCH TO COMMUNICATE AS MUCH WHEN YOU WOKE.
CLEARLY HE DID NOT. HE'S NOT THE BEST DROID.
PERHAPS WE CAN START AGAIN. I DON'T EVEN KNOW YOUR NAME, MASTER.
MY NAME IS CERE JUNDA. AND I'M NOT A JEDI MASTER. I AM STILL A PADAWAN.
IT IS AN HONOR TO MEET YOU, CERE JUNDA. MY NAME IS NERALLI...

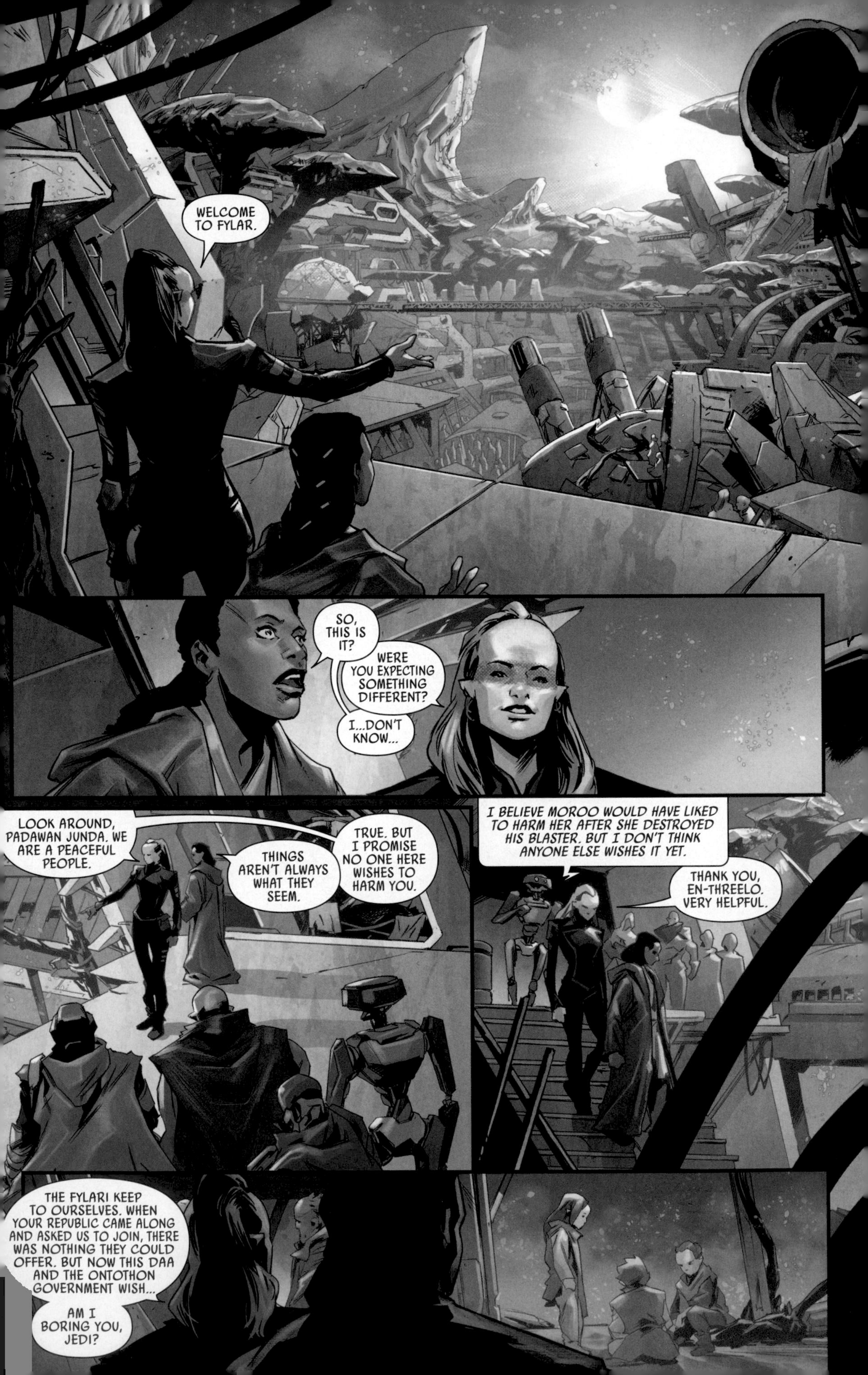
WELCOME TO FYLAR.
SO, THIS IS IT?
WERE YOU EXPECTING SOMETHING DIFFERENT?
I...DON'T KNOW...
LOOK AROUND, PADAWAN JUNDA. WE ARE A PEACEFUL PEOPLE.
THINGS AREN'T ALWAYS WHAT THEY SEEM.
TRUE. BUT I PROMISE NO ONE HERE WISHES TO HARM YOU.
I BELIEVE MOROO WOULD HAVE LIKED TO HARM HER AFTER SHE DESTROYED HIS BLASTER. BUT I DON'T THINK ANYONE ELSE WISHES IT YET.
THANK YOU, EN-THREELO. VERY HELPFUL.
THE FYLARI KEEP TO OURSELVES. WHEN YOUR REPUBLIC CAME ALONG AND ASKED US TO JOIN, THERE WAS NOTHING THEY COULD OFFER. BUT NOW THIS DAA AND THE ONTOTHON GOVERNMENT WISH...
AM I BORING YOU, JEDI?

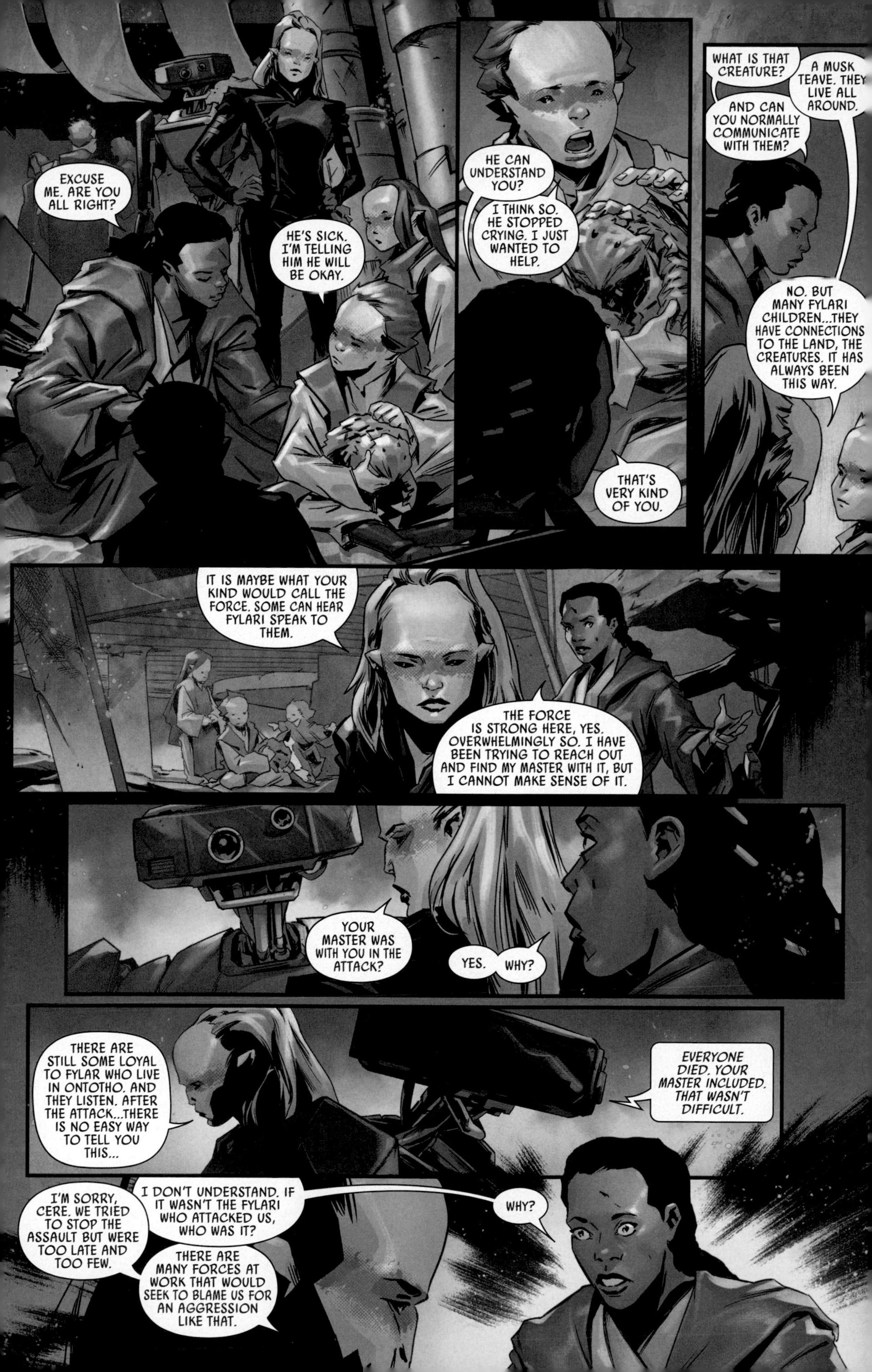
EXCUSE ME. ARE YOU ALL RIGHT?
HE'S SICK. I'M TELLING HIM HE WILL BE OKAY.
HE CAN UNDERSTAND YOU?
I THINK SO. HE STOPPED CRYING. I JUST WANTED TO HELP.
THAT'S VERY KIND OF YOU.
WHAT IS THAT CREATURE?
A MUSK TEAVE. THEY LIVE ALL AROUND.
AND CAN YOU NORMALLY COMMUNICATE WITH THEM?
NO. BUT MANY FYLARI CHILDREN...THEY HAVE CONNECTIONS TO THE LAND, THE CREATURES. IT HAS ALWAYS BEEN THIS WAY.
IT IS MAYBE WHAT YOUR KIND WOULD CALL THE FORCE. SOME CAN HEAR FYLARI SPEAK TO THEM.
THE FORCE IS STRONG HERE, YES. OVERWHELMINGLY SO. I HAVE BEEN TRYING TO REACH OUT AND FIND MY MASTER WITH IT, BUT I CANNOT MAKE SENSE OF IT.
YOUR MASTER WAS WITH YOU IN THE ATTACK?
YES.
WHY?
THERE ARE STILL SOME LOYAL TO FYLAR WHO LIVE IN ONTOTHO. AND THEY LISTEN. AFTER THE ATTACK...THERE IS NO EASY WAY TO TELL YOU THIS...
EVERYONE DIED. YOUR MASTER INCLUDED. THAT WASN'T DIFFICULT.
I'M SORRY, CERE. WE TRIED TO STOP THE ASSAULT BUT WERE TOO LATE AND TOO FEW.
I DON'T UNDERSTAND. IF IT WASN'T THE FYLARI WHO ATTACKED US, WHO WAS IT?
WHY?
THERE ARE MANY FORCES AT WORK THAT WOULD SEEK TO BLAME US FOR AN AGGRESSION LIKE THAT.

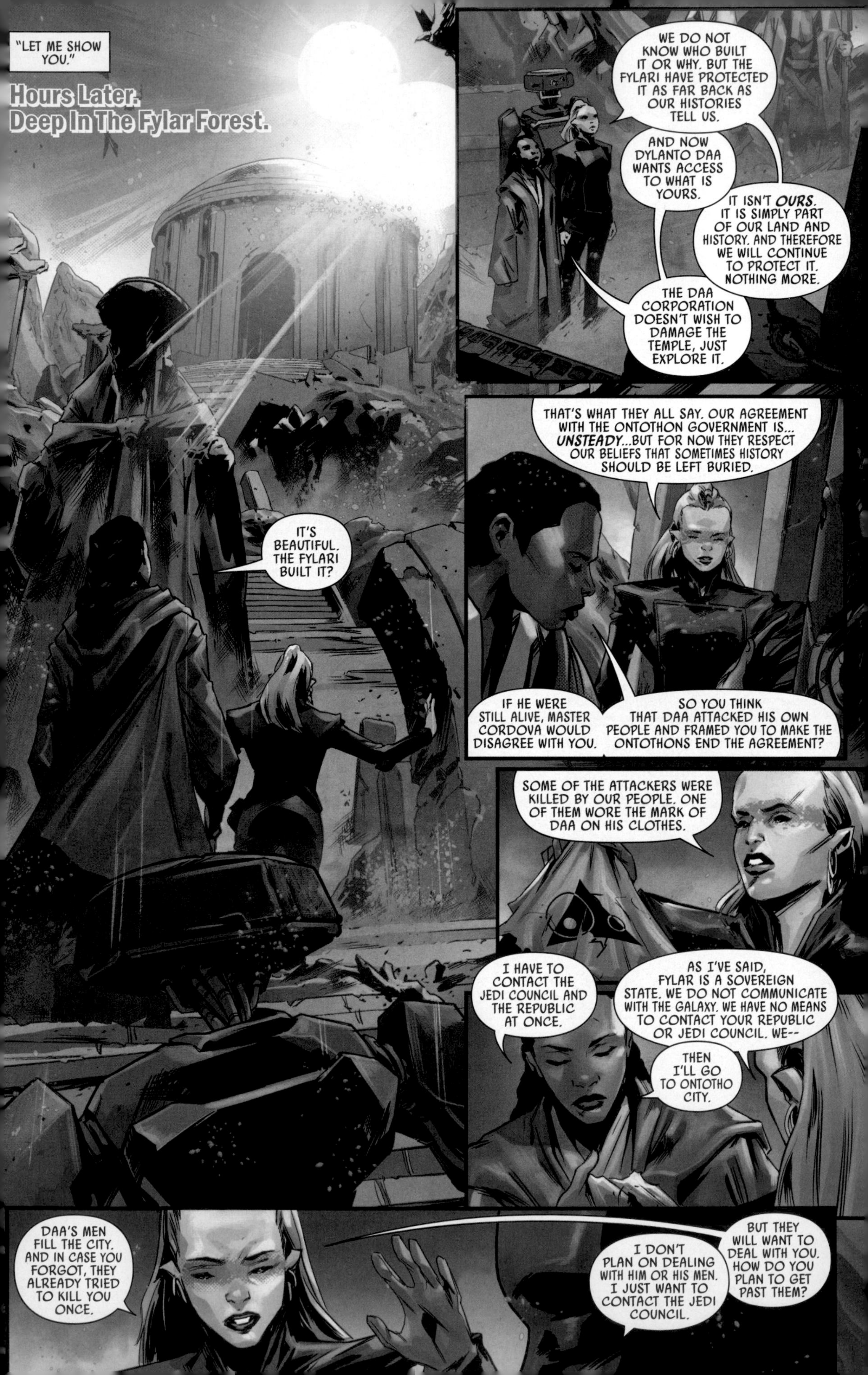
"LET ME SHOW YOU."
Hours Later. Deep In The Fylar Forest.
IT'S BEAUTIFUL. THE FYLARI BUILT IT?
WE DO NOT KNOW WHO BUILT IT OR WHY. BUT THE FYLARI HAVE PROTECTED IT AS FAR BACK AS OUR HISTORIES TELL US.
AND NOW DYLANTO DAA WANTS ACCESS TO WHAT IS YOURS.
IT ISN'T OURS. IT IS SIMPLY PART OF OUR LAND AND HISTORY. AND THEREFORE WE WILL CONTINUE TO PROTECT IT. NOTHING MORE.
THE DAA CORPORATION DOESN'T WISH TO DAMAGE THE TEMPLE, JUST EXPLORE IT.
THAT'S WHAT THEY ALL SAY. OUR AGREEMENT WITH THE ONTOTHON GOVERNMENT IS... UNSTEADY...BUT FOR NOW THEY RESPECT OUR BELIEFS THAT SOMETIMES HISTORY SHOULD BE LEFT BURIED.
SO YOU THINK THAT DAA ATTACKED HIS OWN PEOPLE AND FRAMED YOU TO MAKE THE ONTOTHONS END THE AGREEMENT?
IF HE WERE STILL ALIVE, MASTER CORDOVA WOULD DISAGREE WITH YOU.
SOME OF THE ATTACKERS WERE KILLED BY OUR PEOPLE. ONE OF THEM WORE THE MARK OF DAA ON HIS CLOTHES.
I HAVE TO CONTACT THE JEDI COUNCIL AND THE REPUBLIC AT ONCE.
AS I'VE SAID, FYLAR IS A SOVEREIGN STATE. WE DO NOT COMMUNICATE WITH THE GALAXY. WE HAVE NO MEANS TO CONTACT YOUR REPUBLIC OR JEDI COUNCIL. WE--
THEN I'LL GO TO ONTOTHO CITY.
DAA'S MEN FILL THE CITY. AND IN CASE YOU FORGOT, THEY ALREADY TRIED TO KILL YOU ONCE.
BUT THEY WILL WANT TO DEAL WITH YOU. HOW DO YOU PLAN TO GET PAST THEM?
I DON'T PLAN ON DEALING WITH HIM OR HIS MEN. I JUST WANT TO CONTACT THE JEDI COUNCIL.

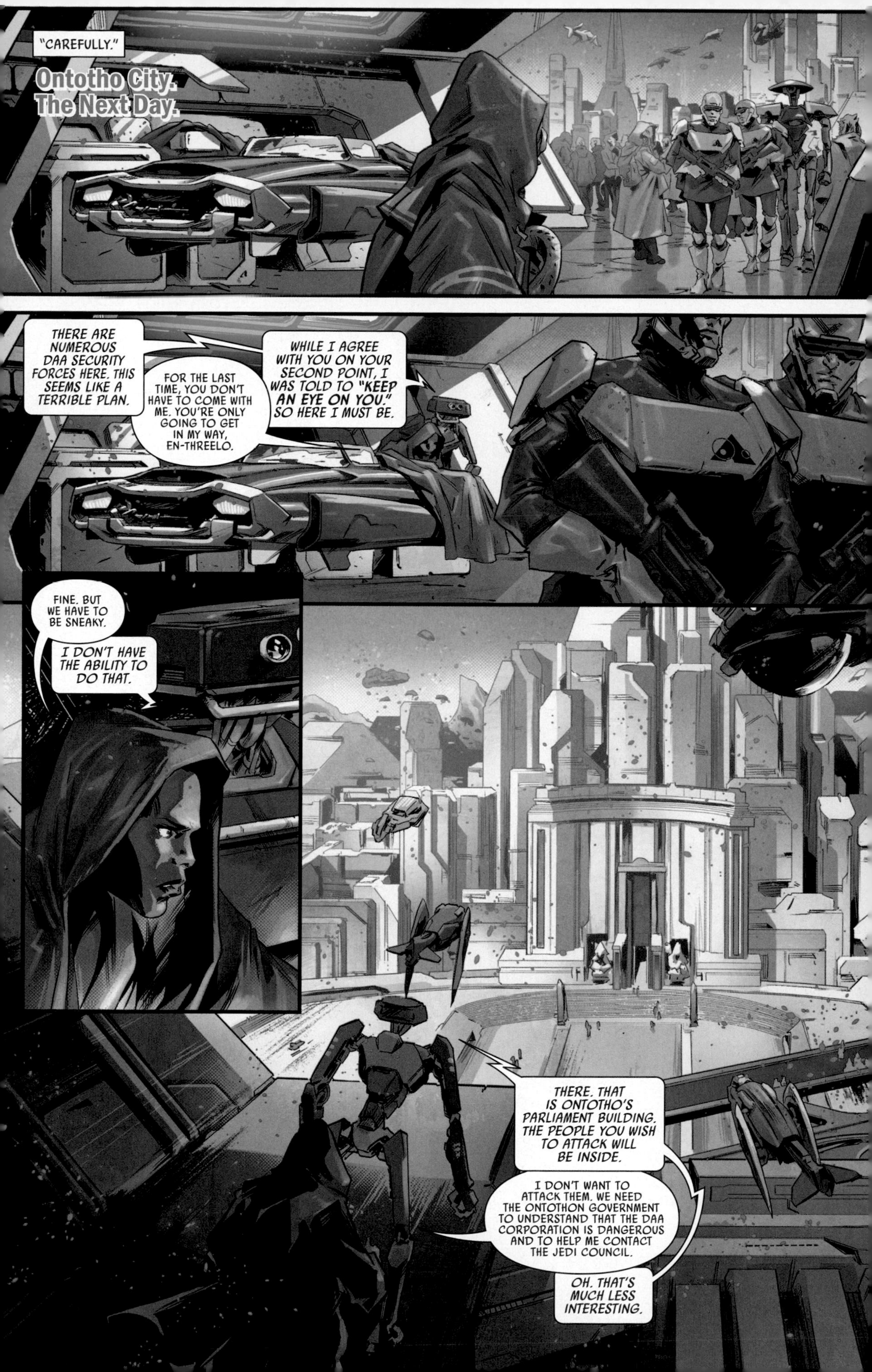
"CAREFULLY."
Ontotho City. The Next Day.
THERE ARE NUMEROUS DAA SECURITY FORCES HERE. THIS SEEMS LIKE A TERRIBLE PLAN.
FOR THE LAST TIME, YOU DON'T HAVE TO COME WITH ME. YOU'RE ONLY GOING TO GET IN MY WAY, EN-THREELO.
WHILE I AGREE WITH YOU ON YOUR SECOND POINT, I WAS TOLD TO "KEEP AN EYE ON YOU." SO HERE I MUST BE.
FINE. BUT WE HAVE TO BE SNEAKY.
I DON'T HAVE THE ABILITY TO DO THAT.
THERE. THAT IS ONTOTHO'S PARLIAMENT BUILDING. THE PEOPLE YOU WISH TO ATTACK WILL BE INSIDE.
I DON'T WANT TO ATTACK THEM. WE NEED THE ONTOTHON GOVERNMENT TO UNDERSTAND THAT THE DAA CORPORATION IS DANGEROUS AND TO HELP ME CONTACT THE JEDI COUNCIL.
OH. THAT'S MUCH LESS INTERESTING.

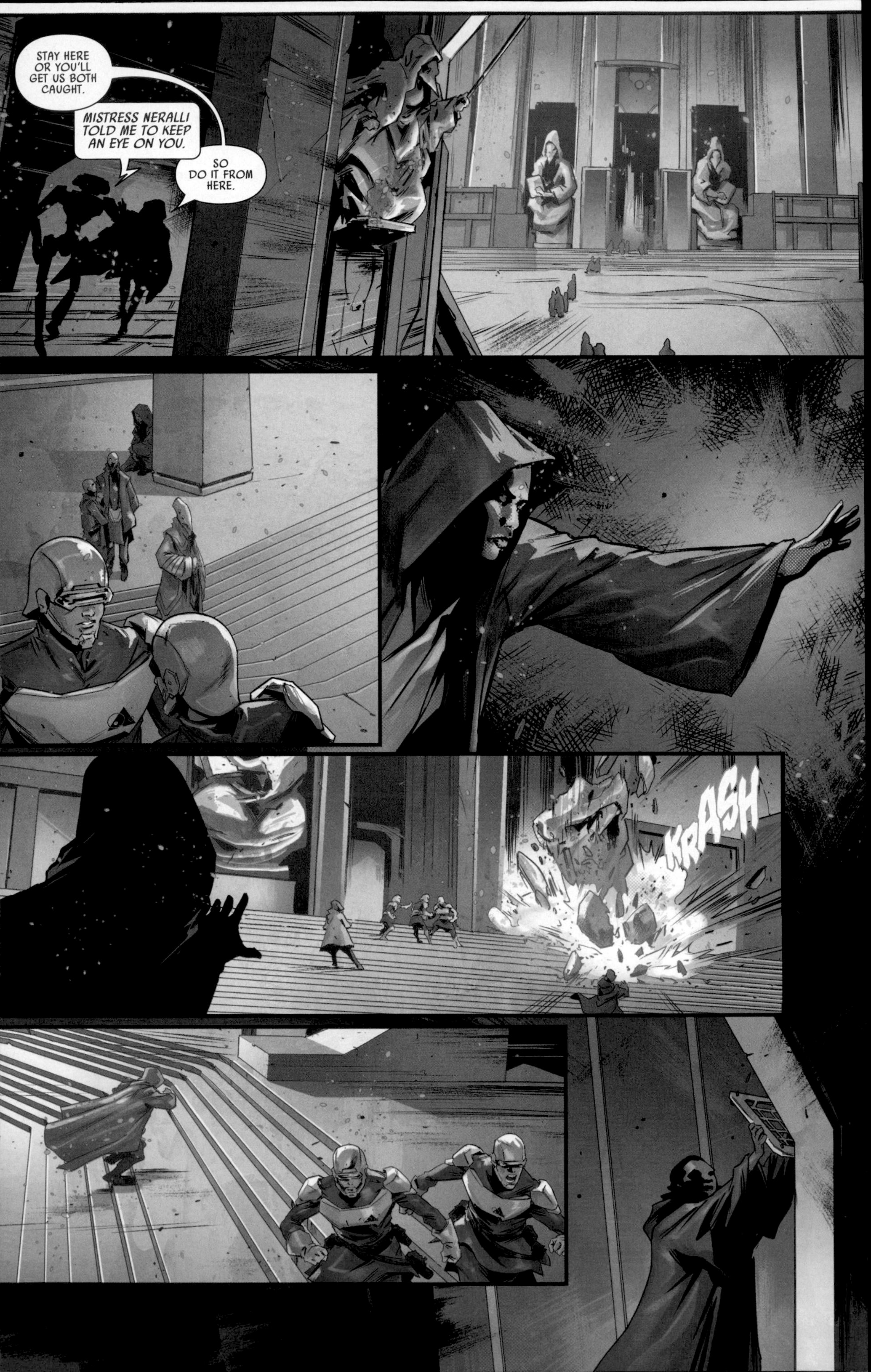
STAY HERE OR YOU'LL GET US BOTH CAUGHT.
MISTRESS NERALLI TOLD ME TO KEEP AN EYE ON YOU.
SO DO IT FROM HERE.
KRASH

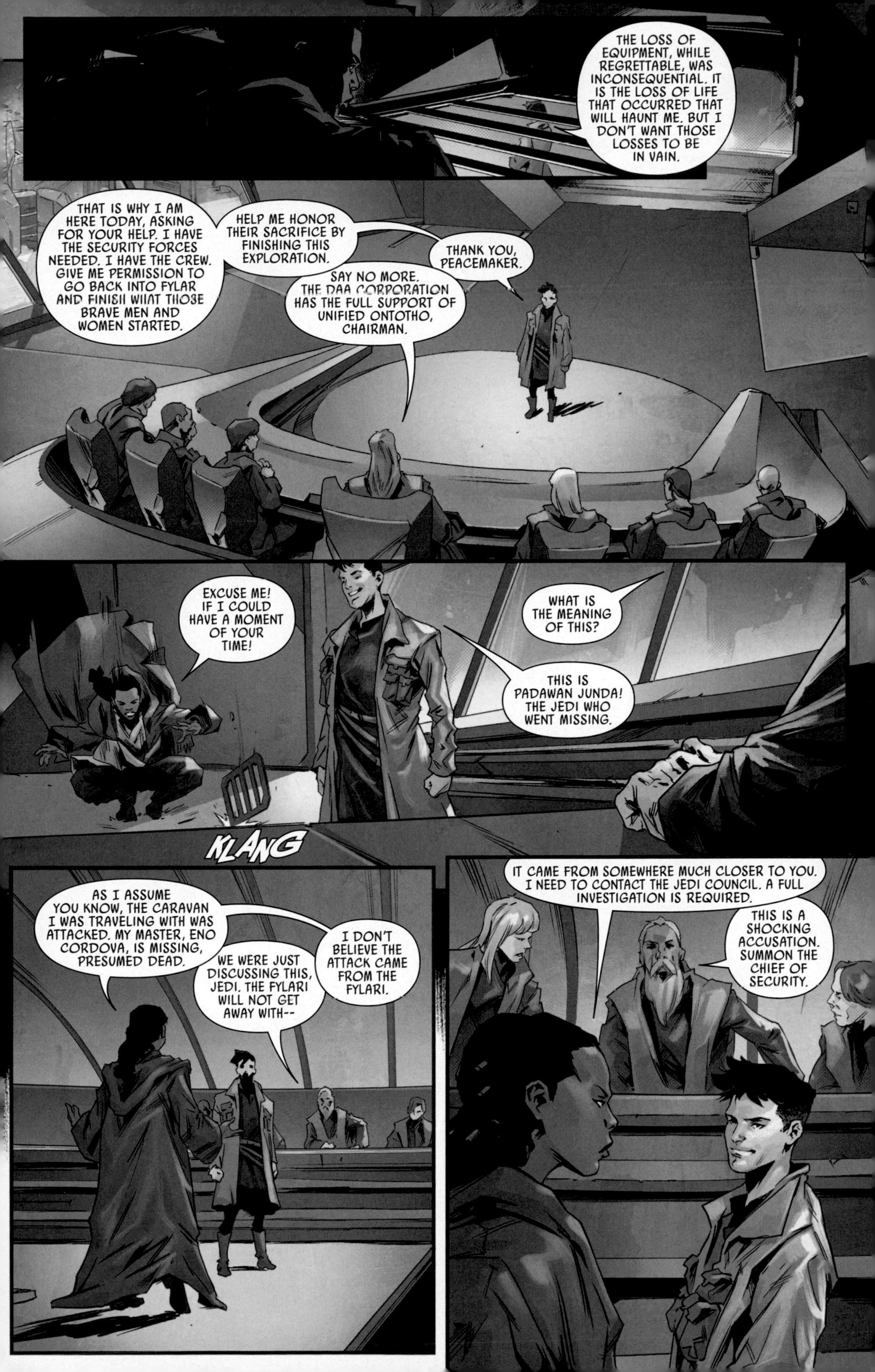
THE LOSS OF EQUIPMENT, WHILE REGRETTABLE, WAS INCONSEQUENTIAL. IT IS THE LOSS OF LIFE THAT OCCURRED THAT WILL HAUNT ME. BUT I DON'T WANT THOSE LOSSES TO BE IN VAIN.
THAT IS WHY I AM HERE TODAY, ASKING FOR YOUR HELP. I HAVE THE SECURITY FORCES NEEDED. I HAVE THE CREW. GIVE ME PERMISSION TO GO BACK INTO FYLAR AND FINISH WHAT THOSE BRAVE MEN AND WOMEN STARTED.
HELP ME HONOR THEIR SACRIFICE BY FINISHING THIS EXPLORATION.
SAY NO MORE. THE DAA CORPORATION HAS THE FULL SUPPORT OF UNIFIED ONTOTHO, CHAIRMAN.
THANK YOU, PEACEMAKER.
EXCUSE ME! IF I COULD HAVE A MOMENT OF YOUR TIME!
WHAT IS THE MEANING OF THIS?
THIS IS PADAWAN JUNDA! THE JEDI WHO WENT MISSING.
KLANG
AS I ASSUME YOU KNOW, THE CARAVAN I WAS TRAVELING WITH WAS ATTACKED. MY MASTER, ENO CORDOVA, IS MISSING, PRESUMED DEAD.
WE WERE JUST DISCUSSING THIS, JEDI. THE FYLARI WILL NOT GET AWAY WITH--
I DON'T BELIEVE THE ATTACK CAME FROM THE FYLARI.
IT CAME FROM SOMEWHERE MUCH CLOSER TO YOU. I NEED TO CONTACT THE JEDI COUNCIL. A FULL INVESTIGATION IS REQUIRED.
THIS IS A SHOCKING ACCUSATION. SUMMON THE CHIEF OF SECURITY.

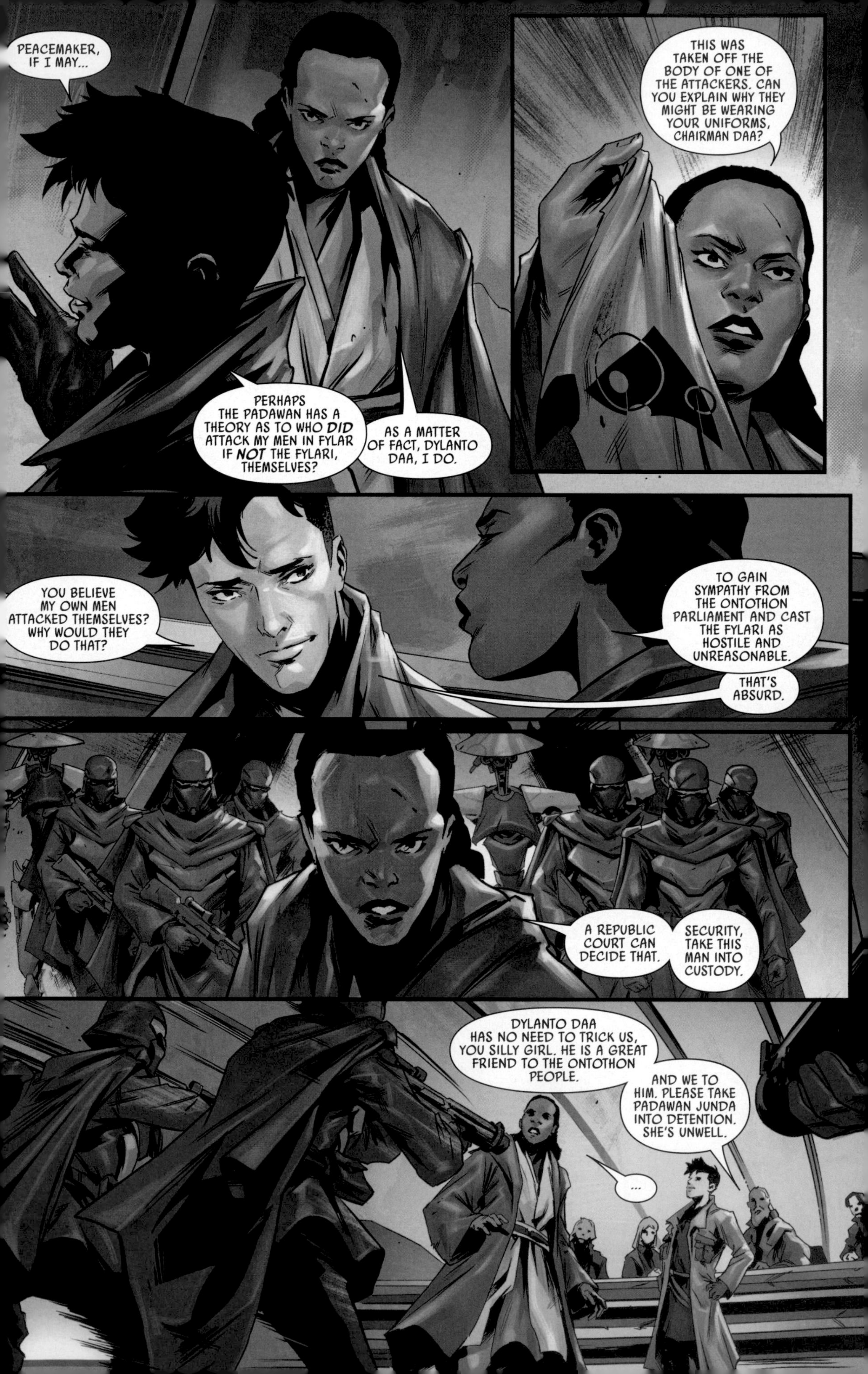
PEACEMAKER, IF I MAY...
THIS WAS TAKEN OFF THE BODY OF ONE OF THE ATTACKERS. CAN YOU EXPLAIN WHY THEY MIGHT BE WEARING YOUR UNIFORMS, CHAIRMAN DAA?
PERHAPS THE PADAWAN HAS A THEORY AS TO WHO *DID* ATTACK MY MEN IN FYLAR IF *NOT* THE FYLARI, THEMSELVES?
AS A MATTER OF FACT, DYLANTO DAA, I DO.
YOU BELIEVE MY OWN MEN ATTACKED THEMSELVES? WHY WOULD THEY DO THAT?
TO GAIN SYMPATHY FROM THE ONTOTHON PARLIAMENT AND CAST THE FYLARI AS HOSTILE AND UNREASONABLE.
THAT'S ABSURD.
A REPUBLIC COURT CAN DECIDE THAT.
SECURITY, TAKE THIS MAN INTO CUSTODY.
DYLANTO DAA HAS NO NEED TO TRICK US, YOU SILLY GIRL. HE IS A GREAT FRIEND TO THE ONTOTHON PEOPLE.
AND WE TO HIM. PLEASE TAKE PADAWAN JUNDA INTO DETENTION. SHE'S UNWELL.
...

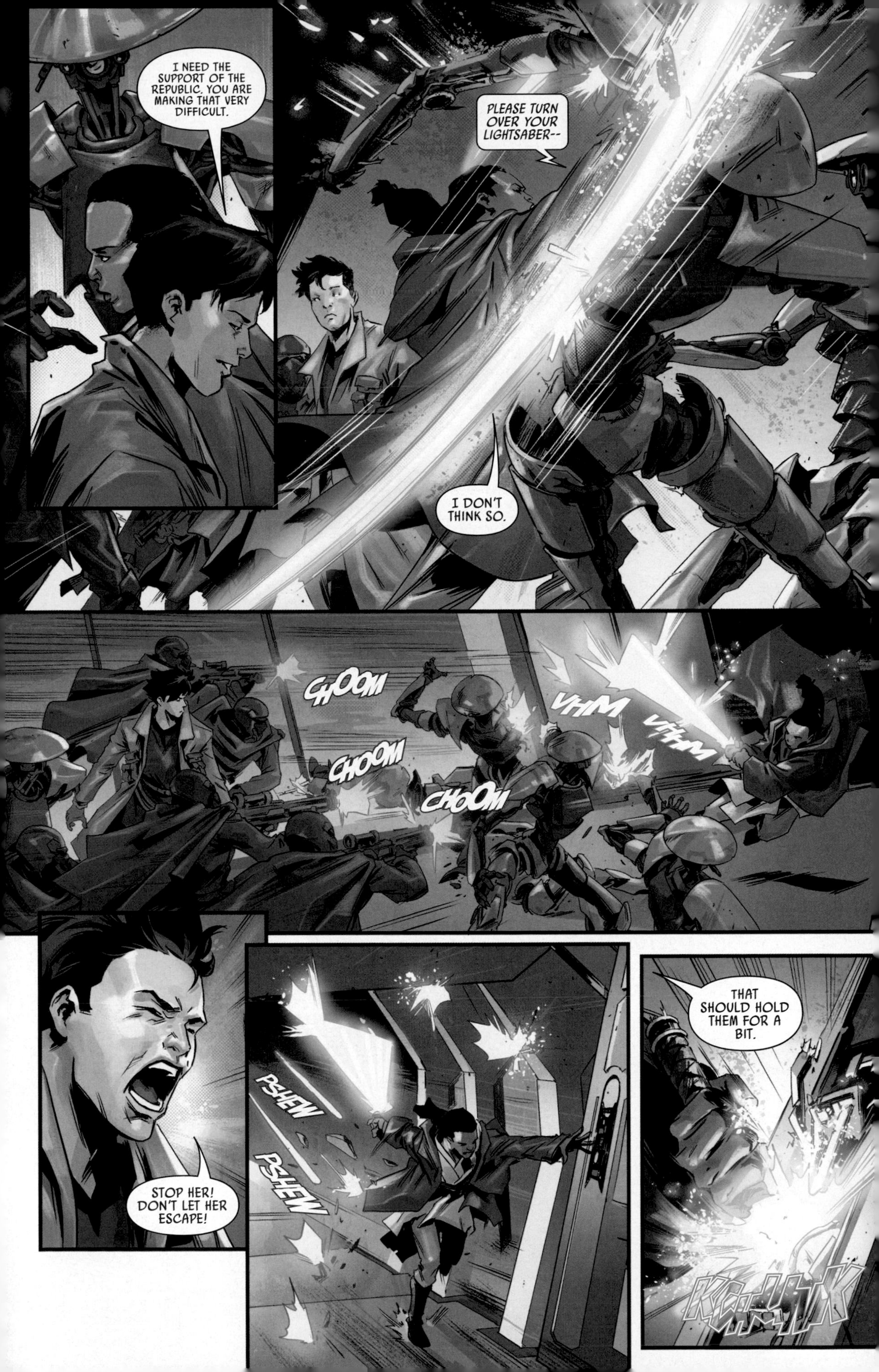
I NEED THE SUPPORT OF THE REPUBLIC. YOU ARE MAKING THAT VERY DIFFICULT.
PLEASE TURN OVER YOUR LIGHTSABER--
I DON'T THINK SO.
CHOOM
CHOOM
CHOOM
VHM
VHM
STOP HER! DON'T LET HER ESCAPE!
PSHEW
PSHEW
THAT SHOULD HOLD THEM FOR A BIT.

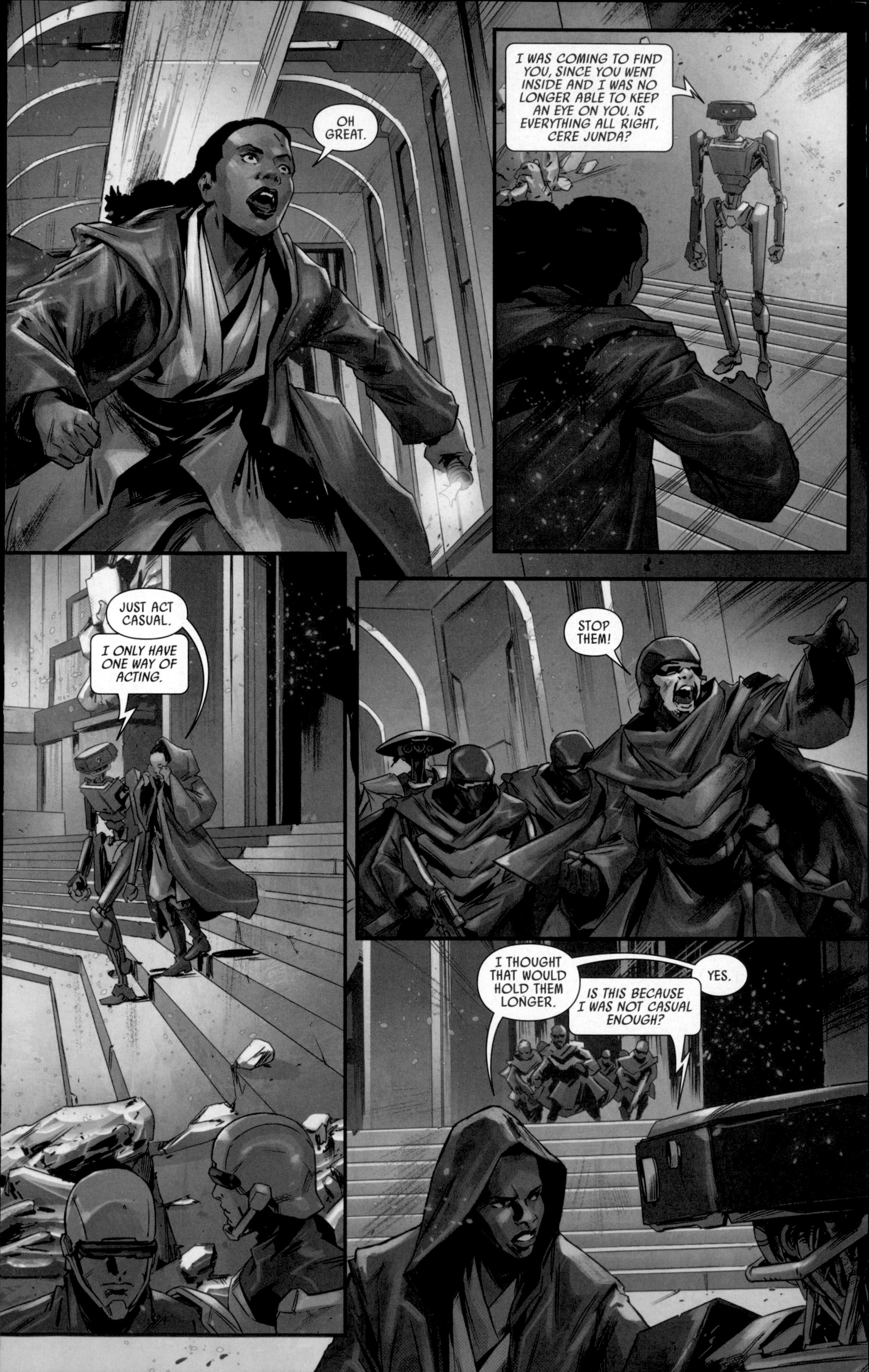
OH GREAT.
I WAS COMING TO FIND YOU, SINCE YOU WENT INSIDE AND I WAS NO LONGER ABLE TO KEEP AN EYE ON YOU. IS EVERYTHING ALL RIGHT, CERE JUNDA?
JUST ACT CASUAL.
I ONLY HAVE ONE WAY OF ACTING.
STOP THEM!
I THOUGHT THAT WOULD HOLD THEM LONGER.
YES.
IS THIS BECAUSE I WAS NOT CASUAL ENOUGH?

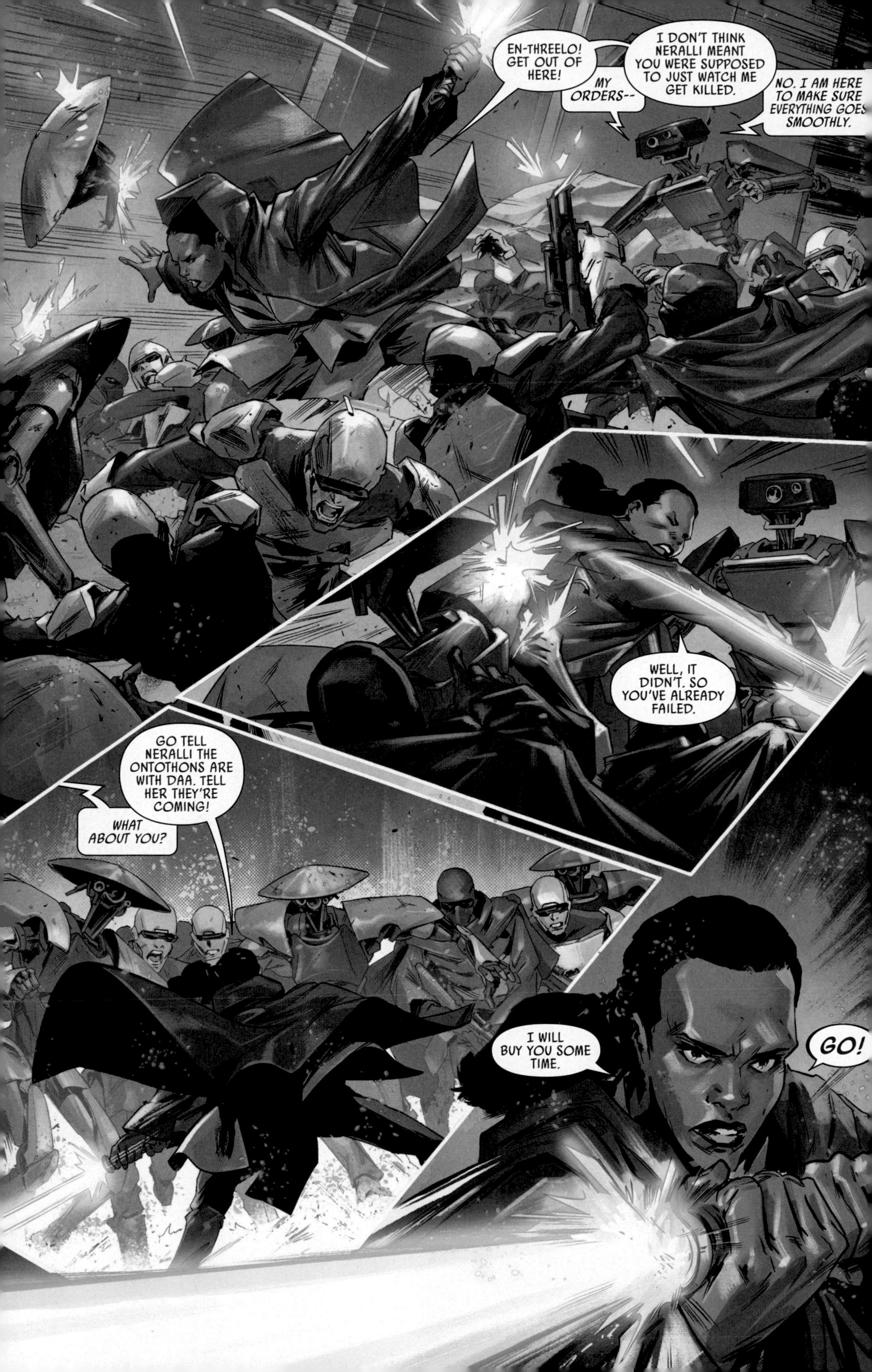
EN-THREELO! GET OUT OF HERE!
MY ORDERS--
I DON'T THINK NERALLI MEANT YOU WERE SUPPOSED TO JUST WATCH ME GET KILLED.
NO. I AM HERE TO MAKE SURE EVERYTHING GOES SMOOTHLY.
WELL, IT DIDN'T. SO YOU'VE ALREADY FAILED.
GO TELL NERALLI THE ONTOTHONS ARE WITH DAA. TELL HER THEY'RE COMING!
WHAT ABOUT YOU?
I WILL BUY YOU SOME TIME.
GO!

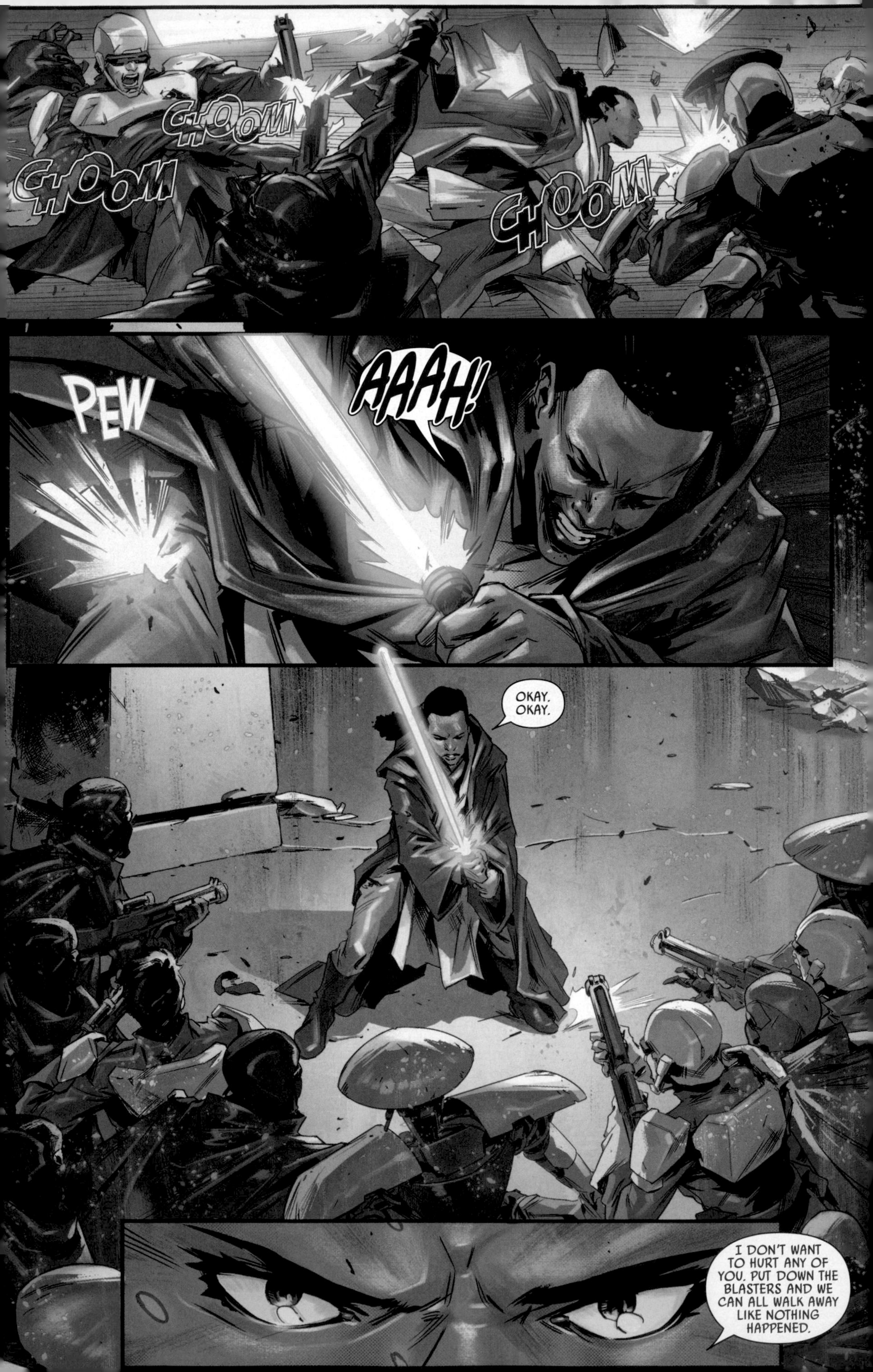
CHOOM
CHOOM
CHOOM
PEW
AAAH!
OKAY. OKAY.
I DON'T WANT TO HURT ANY OF YOU. PUT DOWN THE BLASTERS AND WE CAN ALL WALK AWAY LIKE NOTHING HAPPENED.

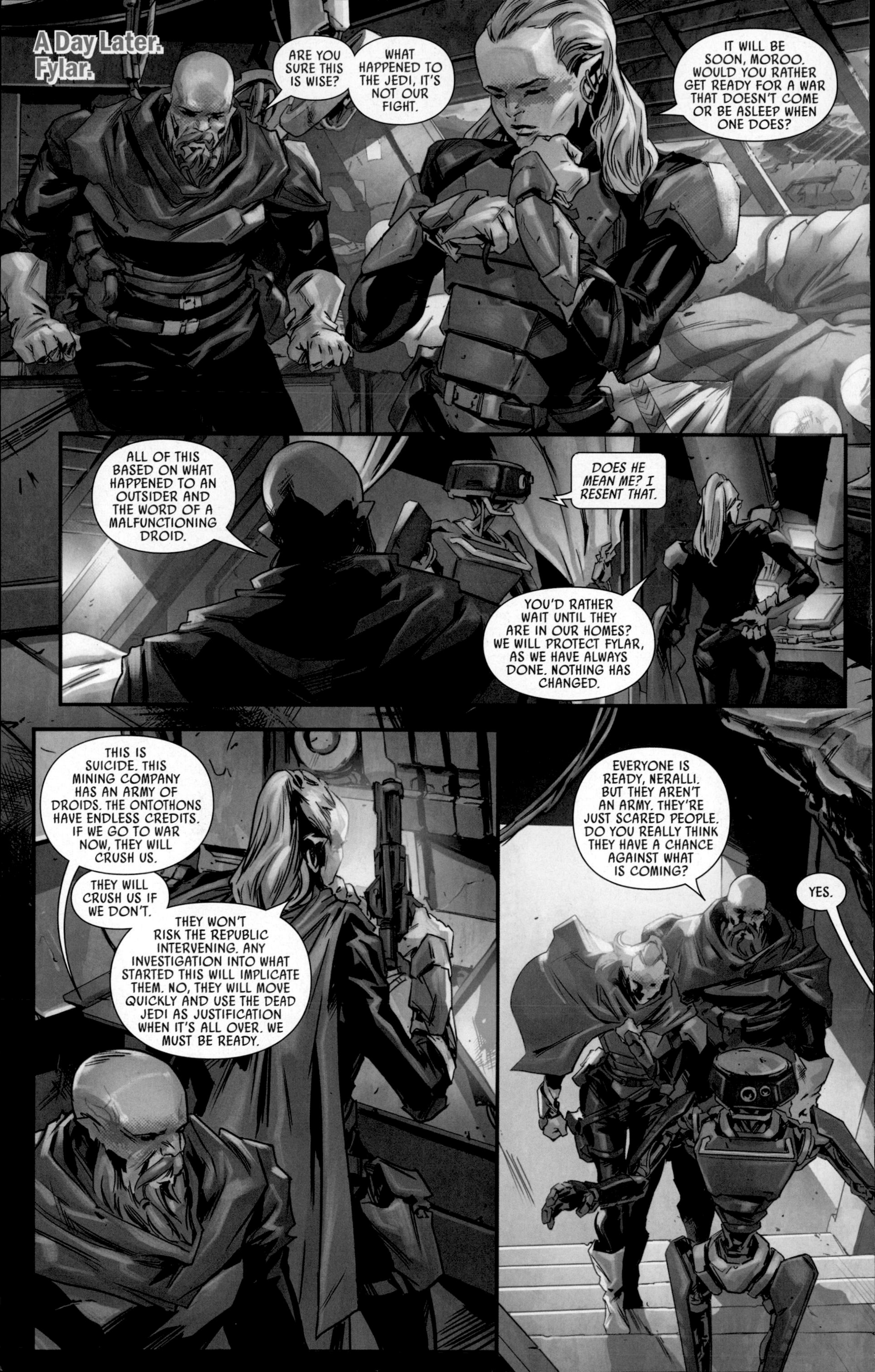
A Day Later.
Fylar.
ARE YOU SURE THIS IS WISE?
WHAT HAPPENED TO THE JEDI, IT'S NOT OUR FIGHT.
IT WILL BE SOON, MOROO. WOULD YOU RATHER GET READY FOR A WAR THAT DOESN'T COME OR BE ASLEEP WHEN ONE DOES?
ALL OF THIS BASED ON WHAT HAPPENED TO AN OUTSIDER AND THE WORD OF A MALFUNCTIONING DROID.
DOES HE MEAN ME? I RESENT THAT.
YOU'D RATHER WAIT UNTIL THEY ARE IN OUR HOMES? WE WILL PROTECT FYLAR, AS WE HAVE ALWAYS DONE. NOTHING HAS CHANGED.
THIS IS SUICIDE. THIS MINING COMPANY HAS AN ARMY OF DROIDS. THE ONTOTHONS HAVE ENDLESS CREDITS. IF WE GO TO WAR NOW, THEY WILL CRUSH US.
THEY WILL CRUSH US IF WE DON'T.
THEY WON'T RISK THE REPUBLIC INTERVENING. ANY INVESTIGATION INTO WHAT STARTED THIS WILL IMPLICATE THEM. NO, THEY WILL MOVE QUICKLY AND USE THE DEAD JEDI AS JUSTIFICATION WHEN IT'S ALL OVER. WE MUST BE READY.
EVERYONE IS READY, NERALLI. BUT THEY AREN'T AN ARMY. THEY'RE JUST SCARED PEOPLE. DO YOU REALLY THINK THEY HAVE A CHANCE AGAINST WHAT IS COMING?
YES.

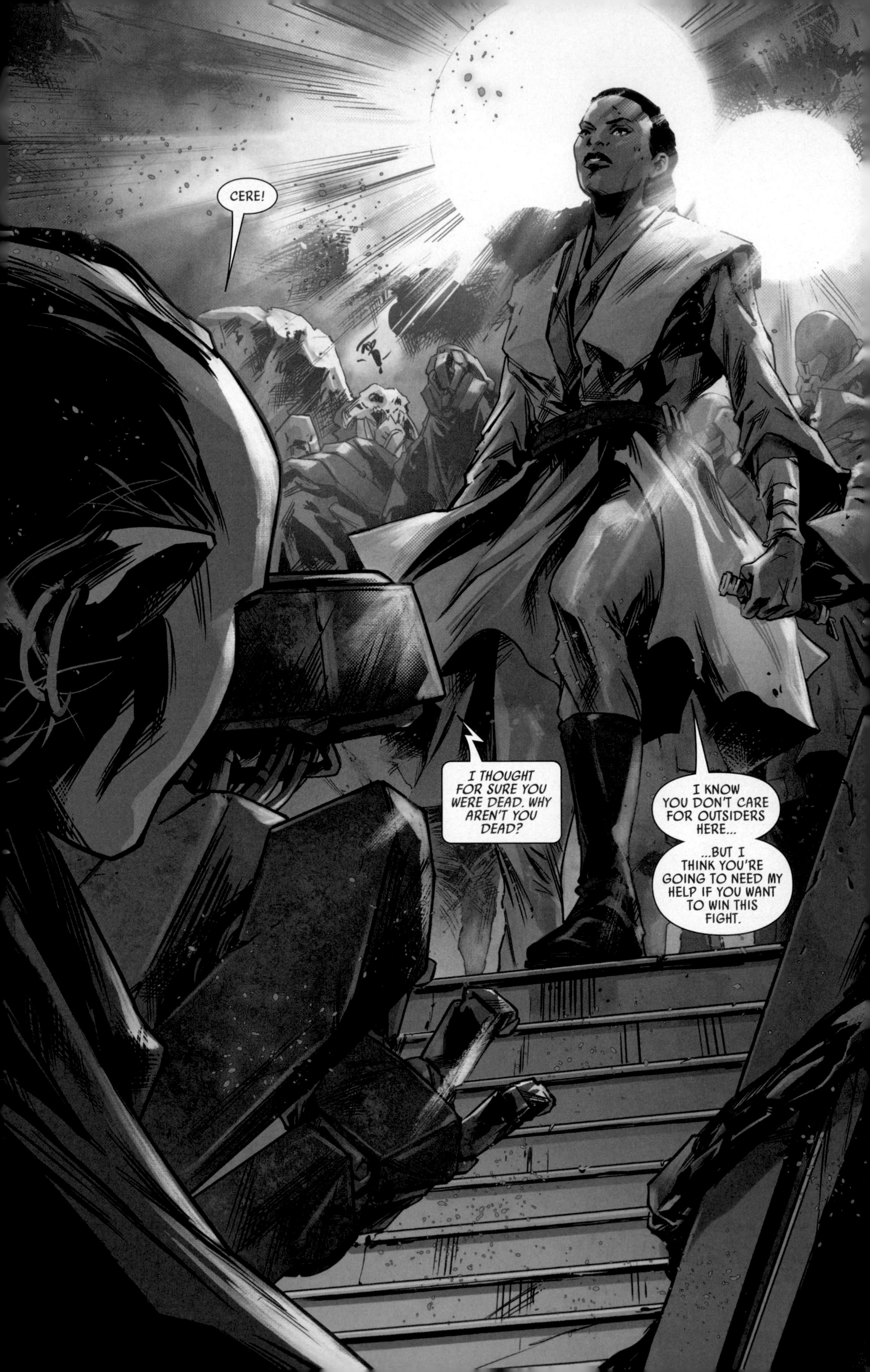
CERE!
I THOUGHT FOR SURE YOU WERE DEAD. WHY AREN'T YOU DEAD?
I KNOW YOU DON'T CARE FOR OUTSIDERS HERE...
...BUT I THINK YOU'RE GOING TO NEED MY HELP IF YOU WANT TO WIN THIS FIGHT.

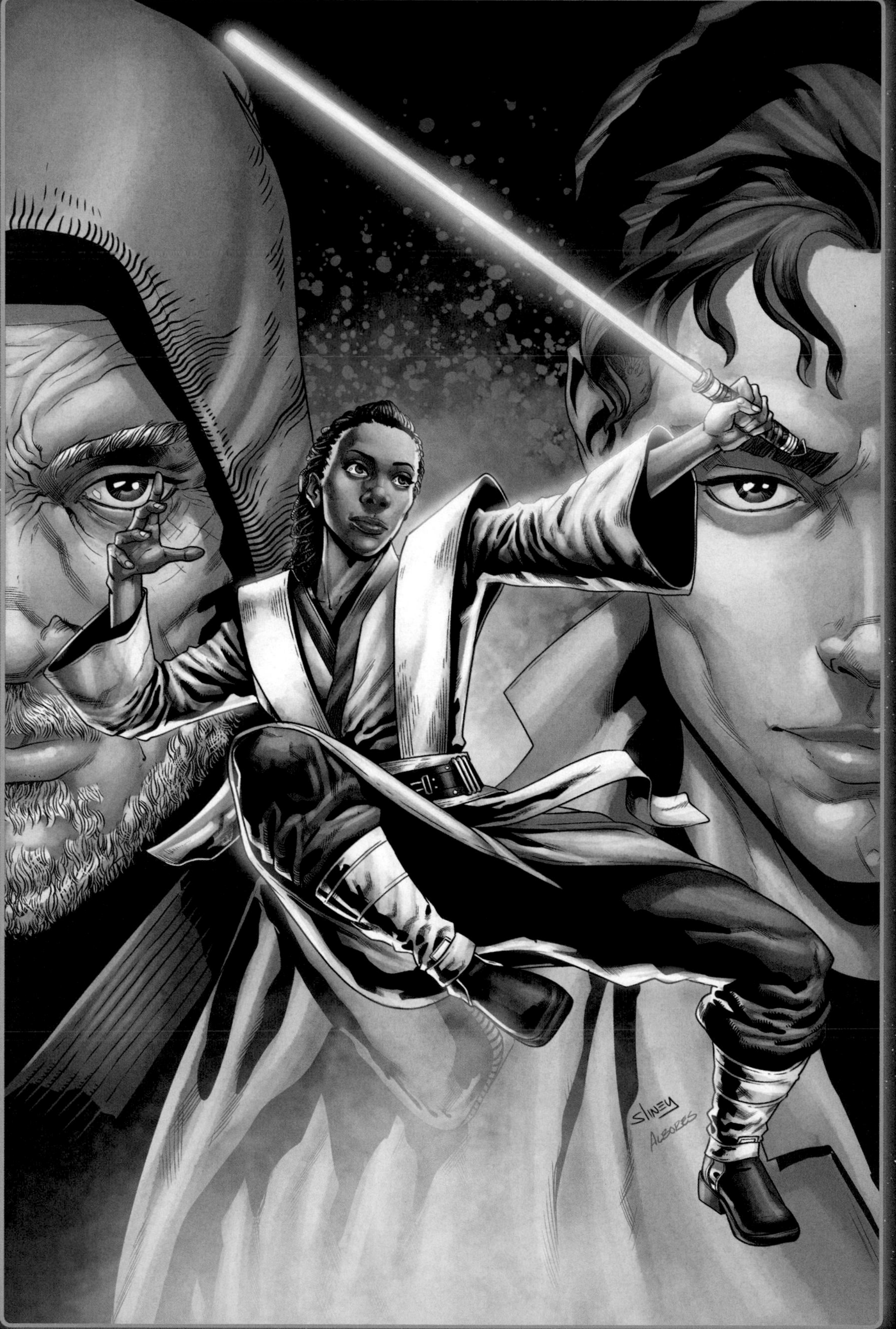
SLINEY
ALBORES

3 – A FRAGILE PEACE

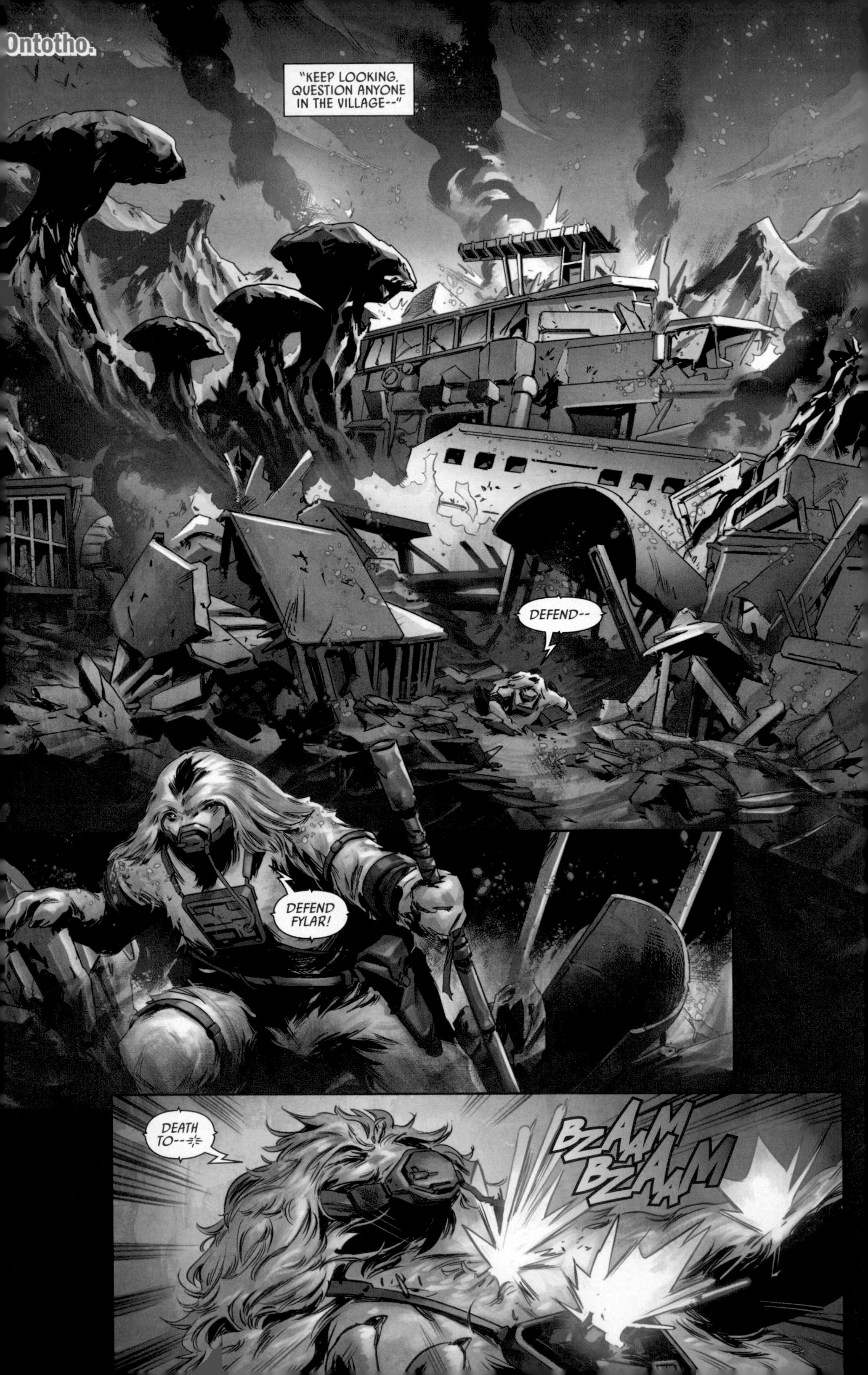
Ontotho.
"KEEP LOOKING. QUESTION ANYONE IN THE VILLAGE--"
DEFEND--
DEFEND FYLAR!
DEATH TO--
BZAAM
BZAAM

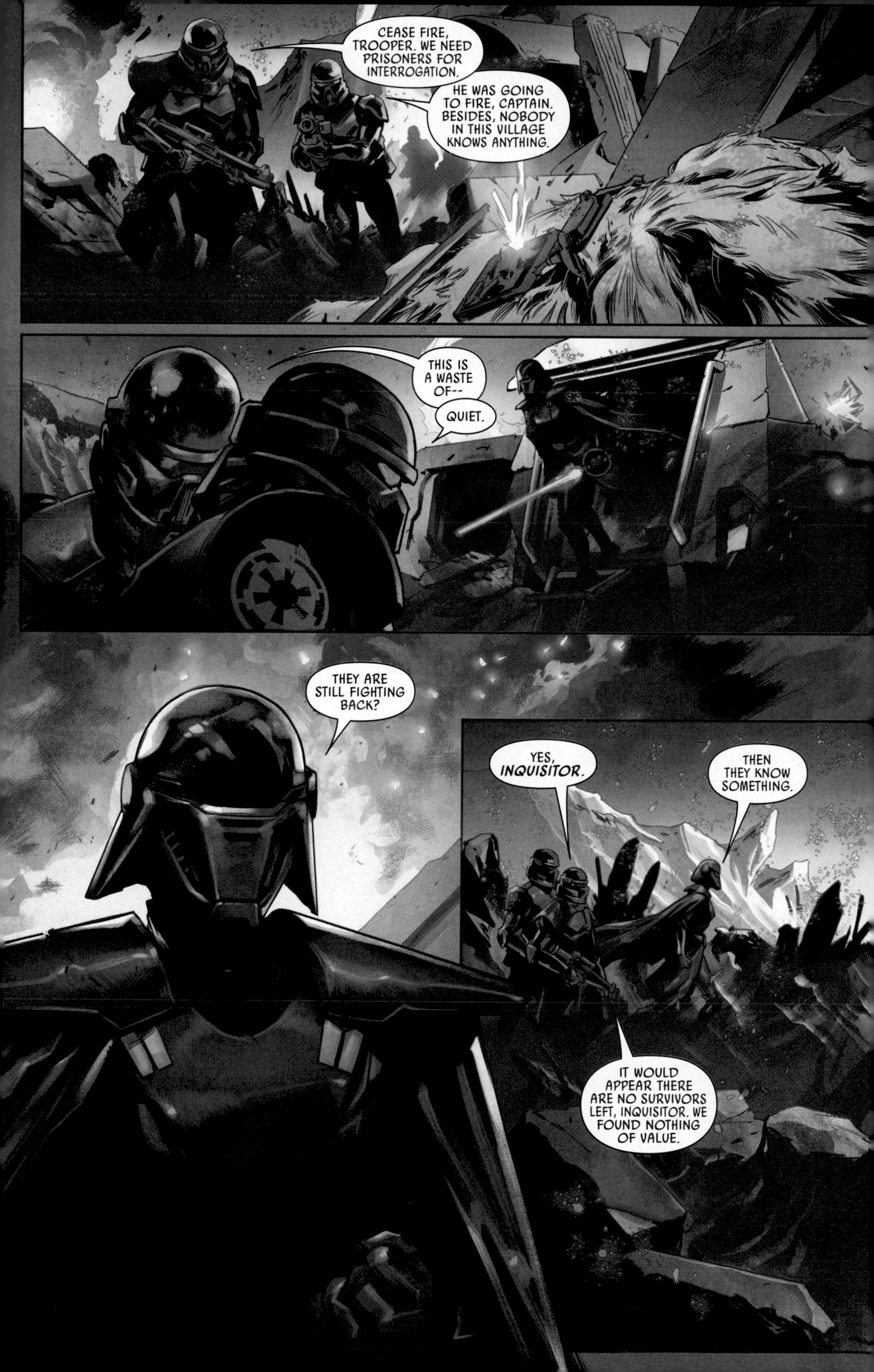
CEASE FIRE, TROOPER. WE NEED PRISONERS FOR INTERROGATION.
HE WAS GOING TO FIRE, CAPTAIN. BESIDES, NOBODY IN THIS VILLAGE KNOWS ANYTHING.
THIS IS A WASTE OF--
QUIET.
THEY ARE STILL FIGHTING BACK?
YES, *INQUISITOR*.
THEN THEY KNOW SOMETHING.
IT WOULD APPEAR THERE ARE NO SURVIVORS LEFT, INQUISITOR. WE FOUND NOTHING OF VALUE.

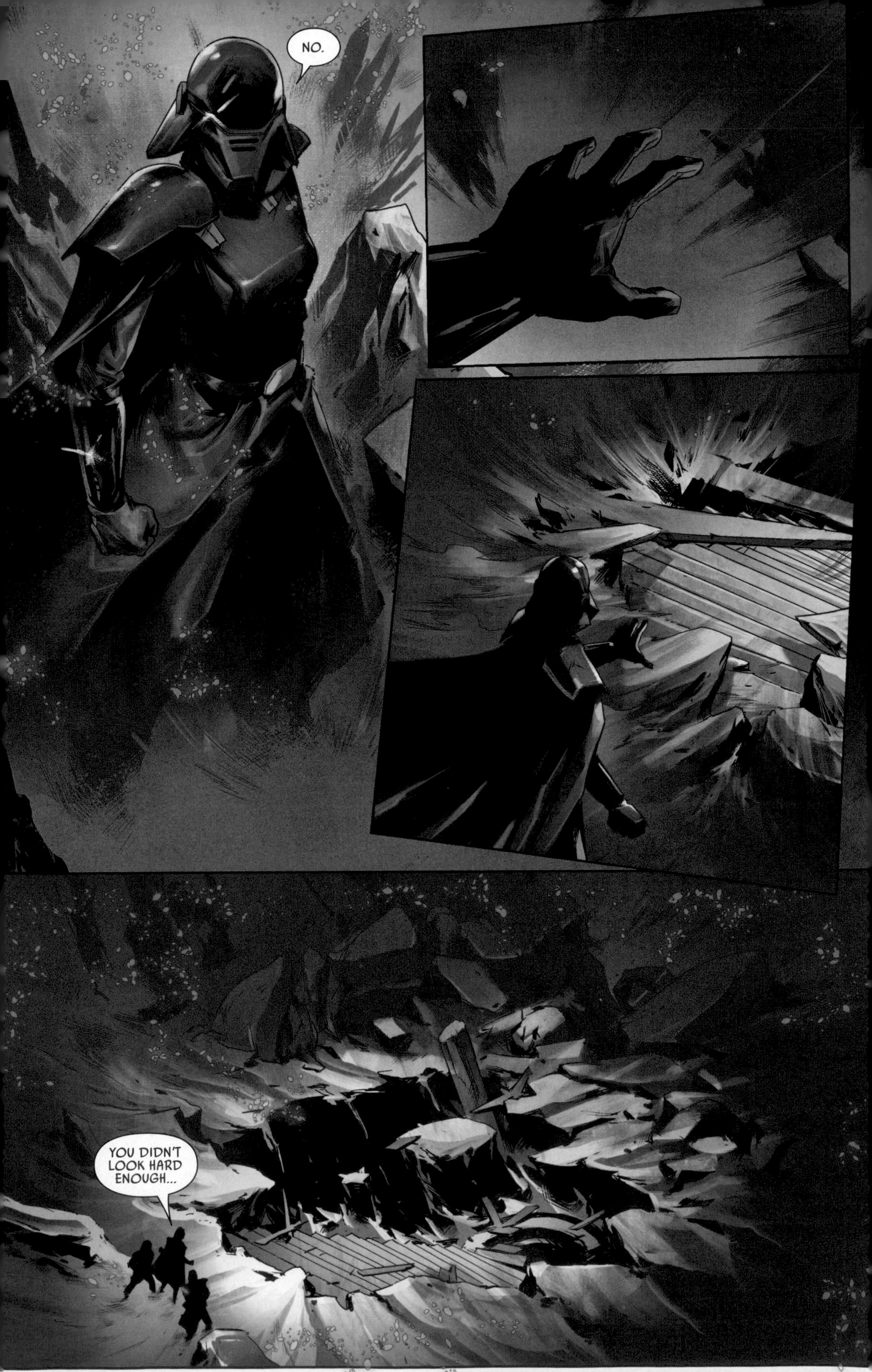
NO.
YOU DIDN'T LOOK HARD ENOUGH...

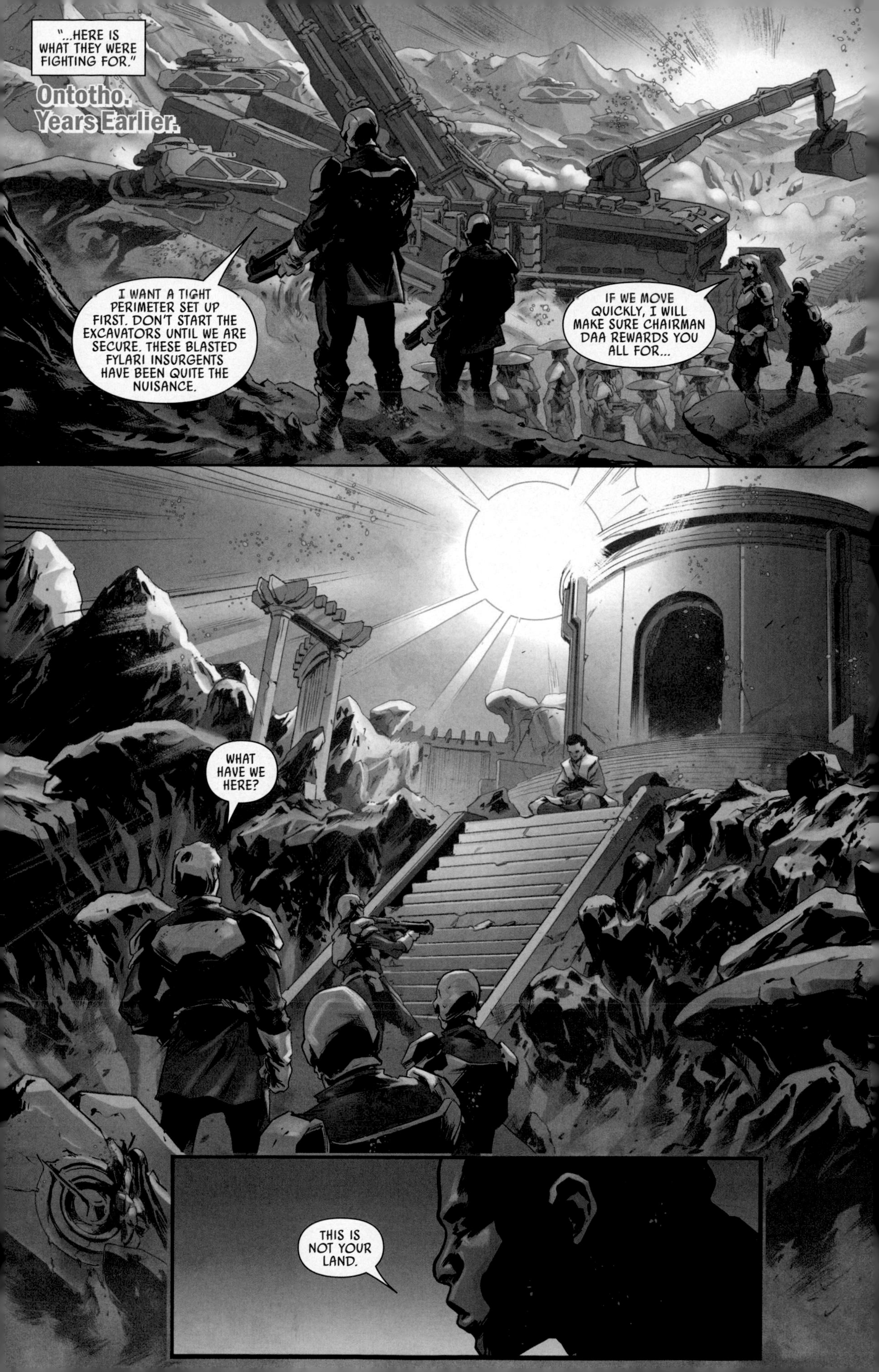
"...HERE IS WHAT THEY WERE FIGHTING FOR."
Ontotho. Years Earlier.
I WANT A TIGHT PERIMETER SET UP FIRST. DON'T START THE EXCAVATORS UNTIL WE ARE SECURE. THESE BLASTED FYLARI INSURGENTS HAVE BEEN QUITE THE NUISANCE.
IF WE MOVE QUICKLY, I WILL MAKE SURE CHAIRMAN DAA REWARDS YOU ALL FOR...
WHAT HAVE WE HERE?
THIS IS NOT YOUR LAND.

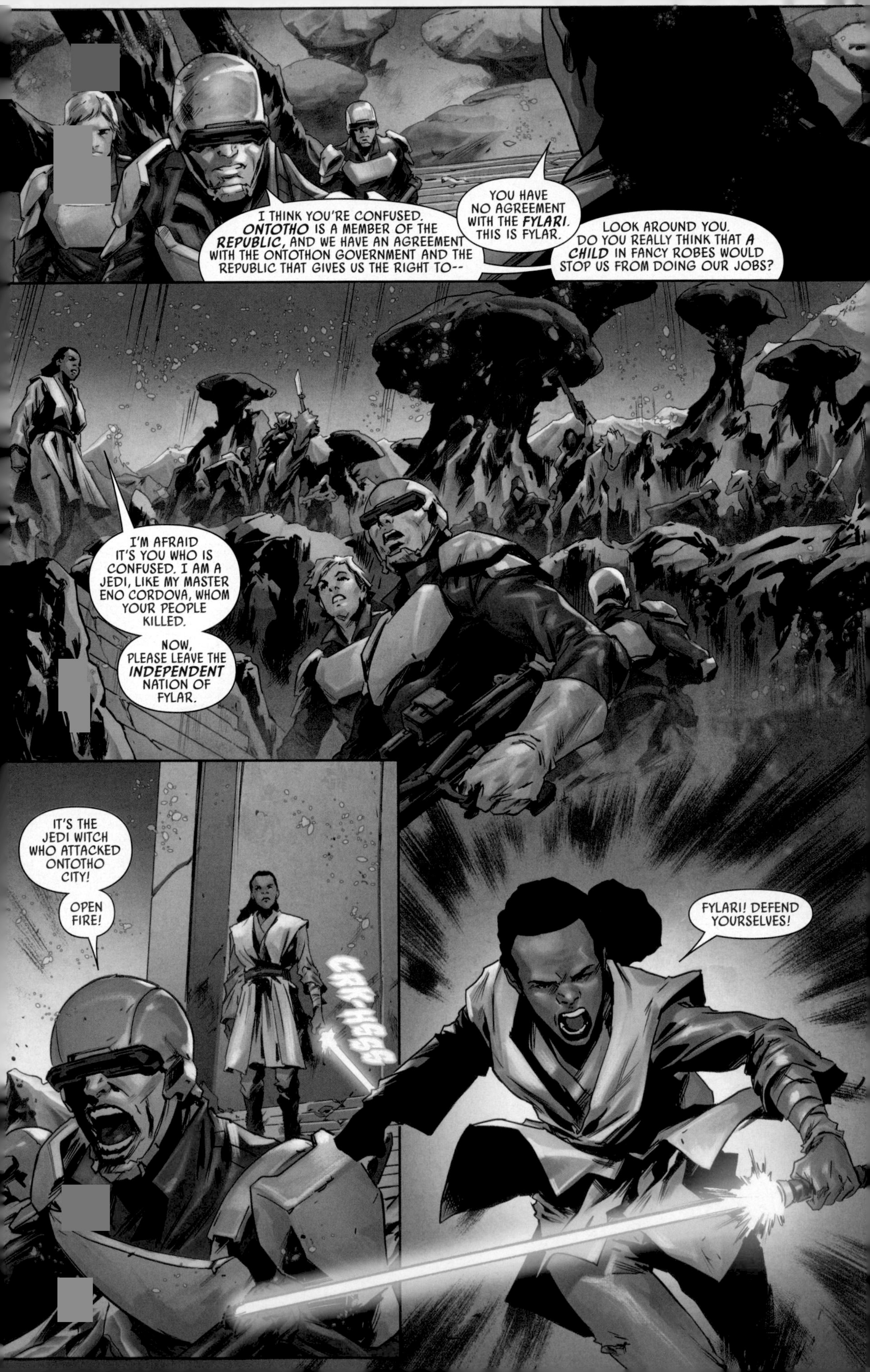
I THINK YOU'RE CONFUSED. ***ONTOTHO*** IS A MEMBER OF THE ***REPUBLIC,*** AND WE HAVE AN AGREEMENT WITH THE ONTOTHON GOVERNMENT AND THE REPUBLIC THAT GIVES US THE RIGHT TO--
YOU HAVE NO AGREEMENT WITH THE ***FYLARI***. THIS IS FYLAR.
LOOK AROUND YOU. DO YOU REALLY THINK THAT ***A CHILD*** IN FANCY ROBES WOULD STOP US FROM DOING OUR JOBS?
I'M AFRAID IT'S YOU WHO IS CONFUSED. I AM A JEDI, LIKE MY MASTER ENO CORDOVA, WHOM YOUR PEOPLE KILLED.
NOW, PLEASE LEAVE THE ***INDEPENDENT*** NATION OF FYLAR.
IT'S THE JEDI WITCH WHO ATTACKED ONTOTHO CITY!
OPEN FIRE!
CRK-HSSS
FYLARI! DEFEND YOURSELVES!

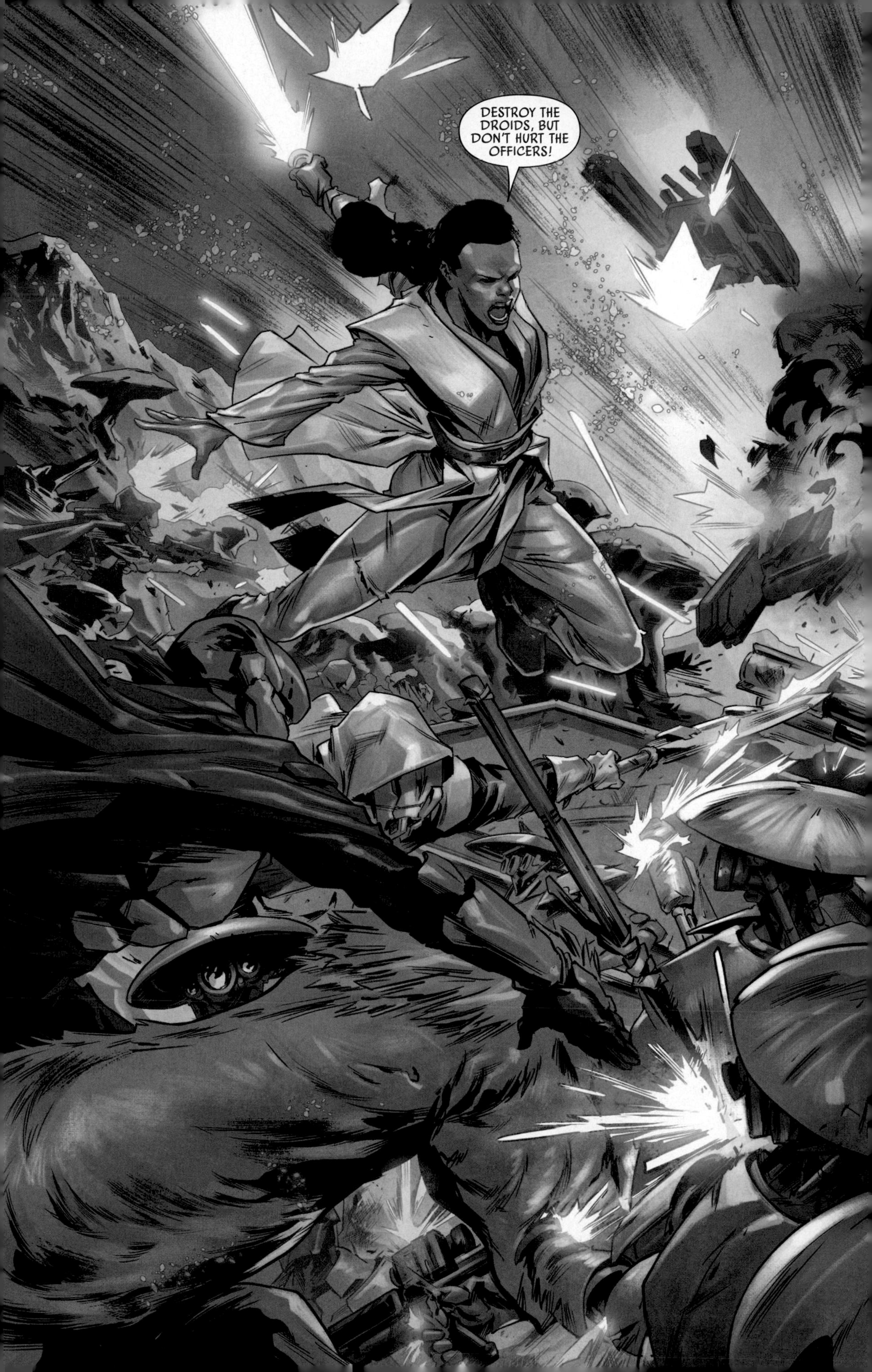
DESTROY THE DROIDS, BUT DON'T HURT THE OFFICERS!

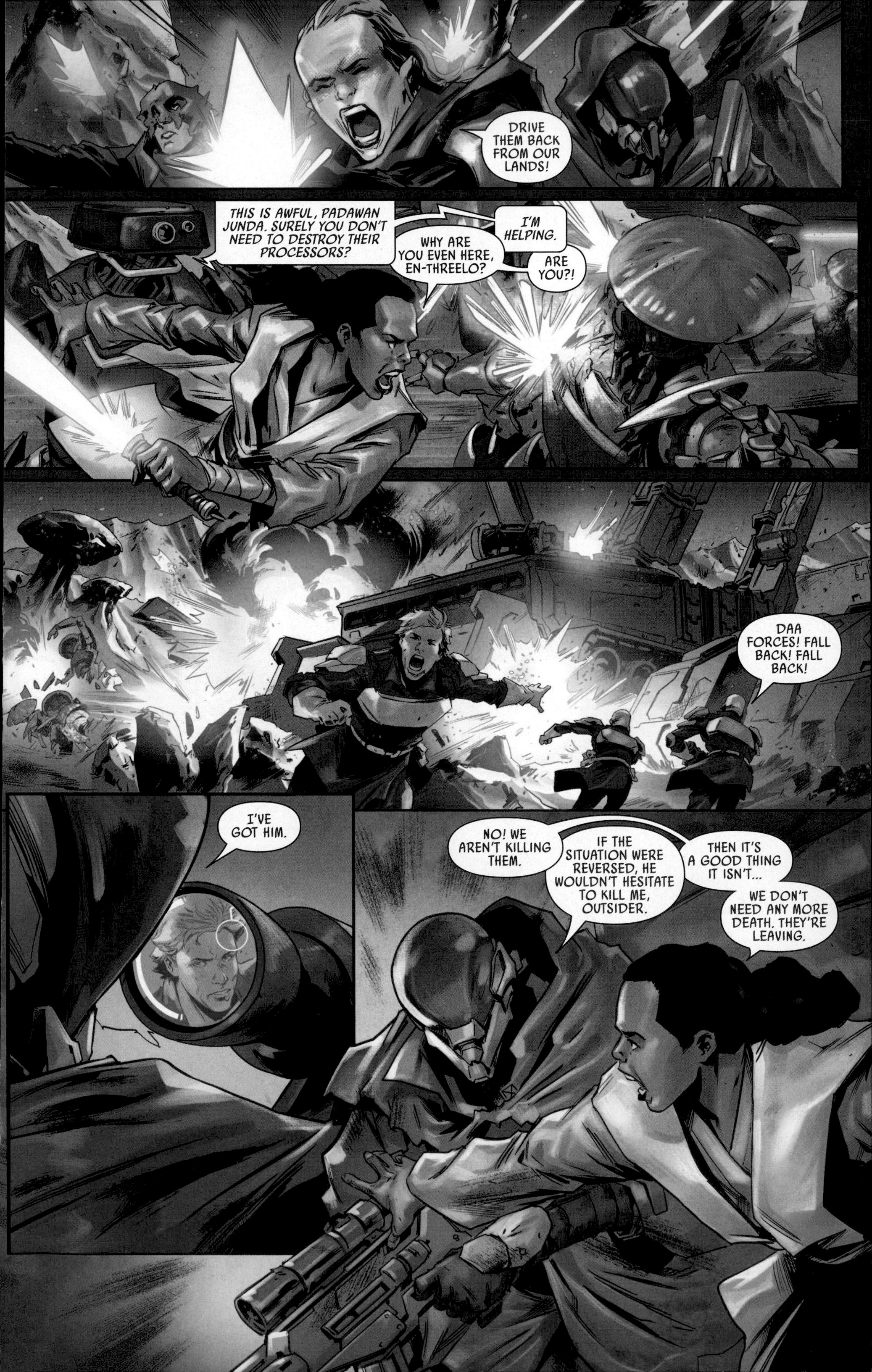
DRIVE THEM BACK FROM OUR LANDS!
THIS IS AWFUL, PADAWAN JUNDA. SURELY YOU DON'T NEED TO DESTROY THEIR PROCESSORS?
I'M HELPING.
WHY ARE YOU EVEN HERE, EN-THREELO?
ARE YOU?!
DAA FORCES! FALL BACK! FALL BACK!
I'VE GOT HIM.
NO! WE AREN'T KILLING THEM.
IF THE SITUATION WERE REVERSED, HE WOULDN'T HESITATE TO KILL ME, OUTSIDER.
THEN IT'S A GOOD THING IT ISN'T...
WE DON'T NEED ANY MORE DEATH. THEY'RE LEAVING.

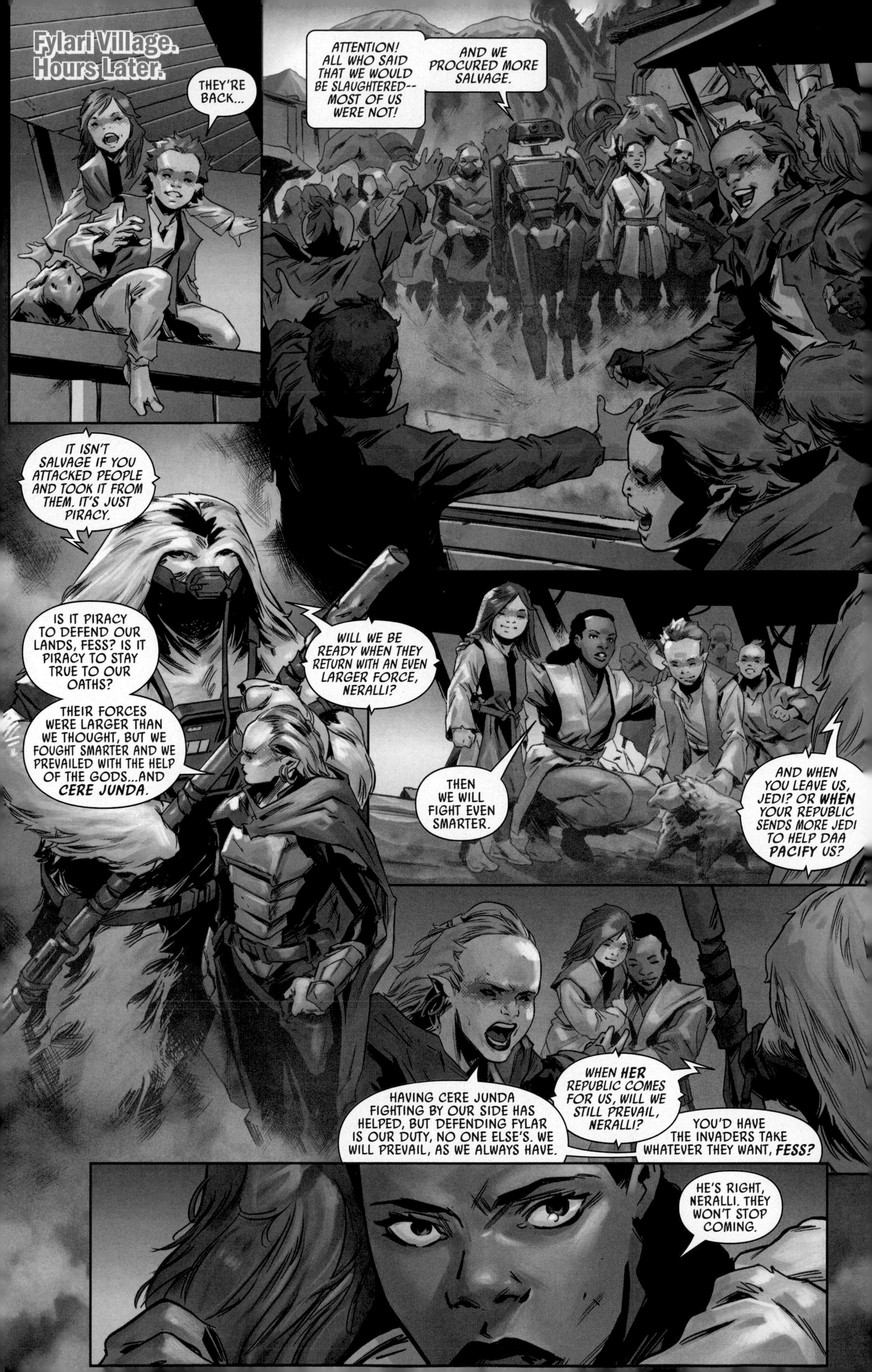
Fylari Village. Hours Later.
THEY'RE BACK...
ATTENTION! ALL WHO SAID THAT WE WOULD BE SLAUGHTERED-- MOST OF US WERE NOT!
AND WE PROCURED MORE SALVAGE.
IT ISN'T SALVAGE IF YOU ATTACKED PEOPLE AND TOOK IT FROM THEM. IT'S JUST PIRACY.
IS IT PIRACY TO DEFEND OUR LANDS, FESS? IS IT PIRACY TO STAY TRUE TO OUR OATHS?
THEIR FORCES WERE LARGER THAN WE THOUGHT, BUT WE FOUGHT SMARTER AND WE PREVAILED WITH THE HELP OF THE GODS...AND CERE JUNDA.
WILL WE BE READY WHEN THEY RETURN WITH AN EVEN LARGER FORCE, NERALLI?
THEN WE WILL FIGHT EVEN SMARTER.
AND WHEN YOU LEAVE US, JEDI? OR WHEN YOUR REPUBLIC SENDS MORE JEDI TO HELP DAA PACIFY US?
HAVING CERE JUNDA FIGHTING BY OUR SIDE HAS HELPED, BUT DEFENDING FYLAR IS OUR DUTY, NO ONE ELSE'S. WE WILL PREVAIL, AS WE ALWAYS HAVE.
WHEN HER REPUBLIC COMES FOR US, WILL WE STILL PREVAIL, NERALLI?
YOU'D HAVE THE INVADERS TAKE WHATEVER THEY WANT, FESS?
HE'S RIGHT, NERALLI. THEY WON'T STOP COMING.

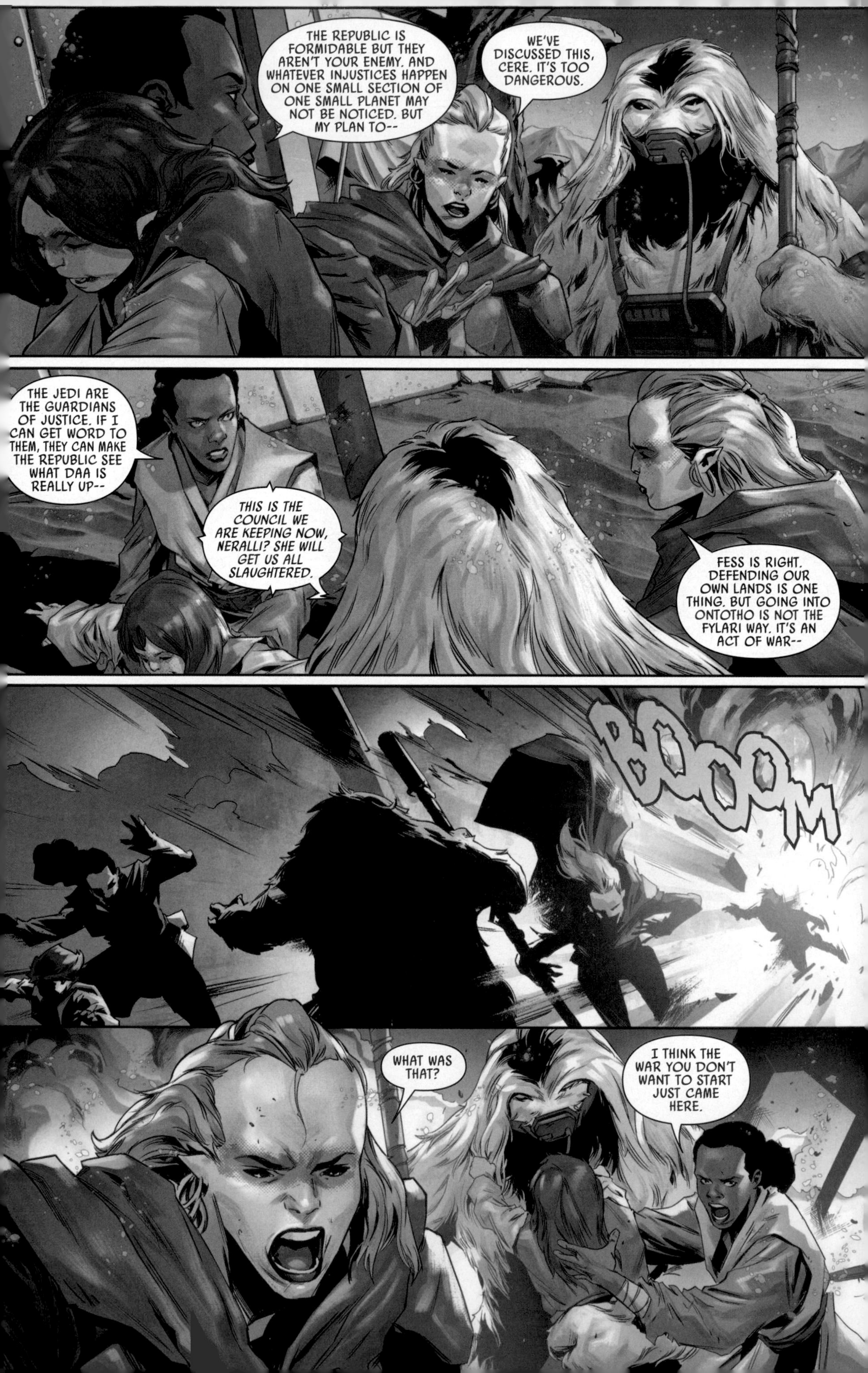
THE REPUBLIC IS FORMIDABLE BUT THEY AREN'T YOUR ENEMY. AND WHATEVER INJUSTICES HAPPEN ON ONE SMALL SECTION OF ONE SMALL PLANET MAY NOT BE NOTICED. BUT MY PLAN TO--
WE'VE DISCUSSED THIS, CERE. IT'S TOO DANGEROUS.
THE JEDI ARE THE GUARDIANS OF JUSTICE. IF I CAN GET WORD TO THEM, THEY CAN MAKE THE REPUBLIC SEE WHAT DAA IS REALLY UP--
THIS IS THE COUNCIL WE ARE KEEPING NOW, NERALLI? SHE WILL GET US ALL SLAUGHTERED.
FESS IS RIGHT. DEFENDING OUR OWN LANDS IS ONE THING. BUT GOING INTO ONTOTHO IS NOT THE FYLARI WAY. IT'S AN ACT OF WAR--
BOOOM
WHAT WAS THAT?
I THINK THE WAR YOU DON'T WANT TO START JUST CAME HERE.

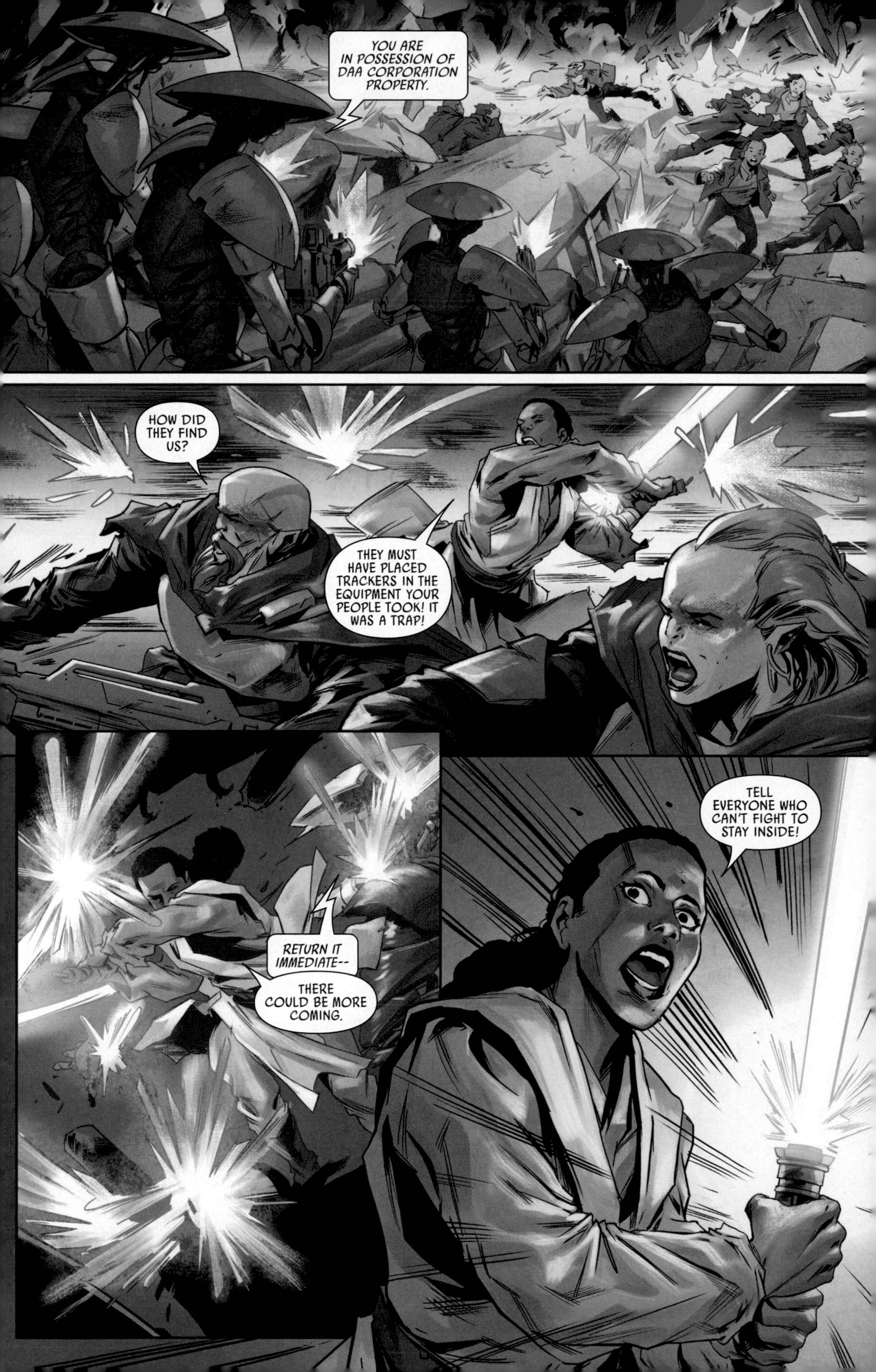
YOU ARE IN POSSESSION OF DAA CORPORATION PROPERTY.
HOW DID THEY FIND US?
THEY MUST HAVE PLACED TRACKERS IN THE EQUIPMENT YOUR PEOPLE TOOK! IT WAS A TRAP!
RETURN IT IMMEDIATE--
THERE COULD BE MORE COMING.
TELL EVERYONE WHO CAN'T FIGHT TO STAY INSIDE!

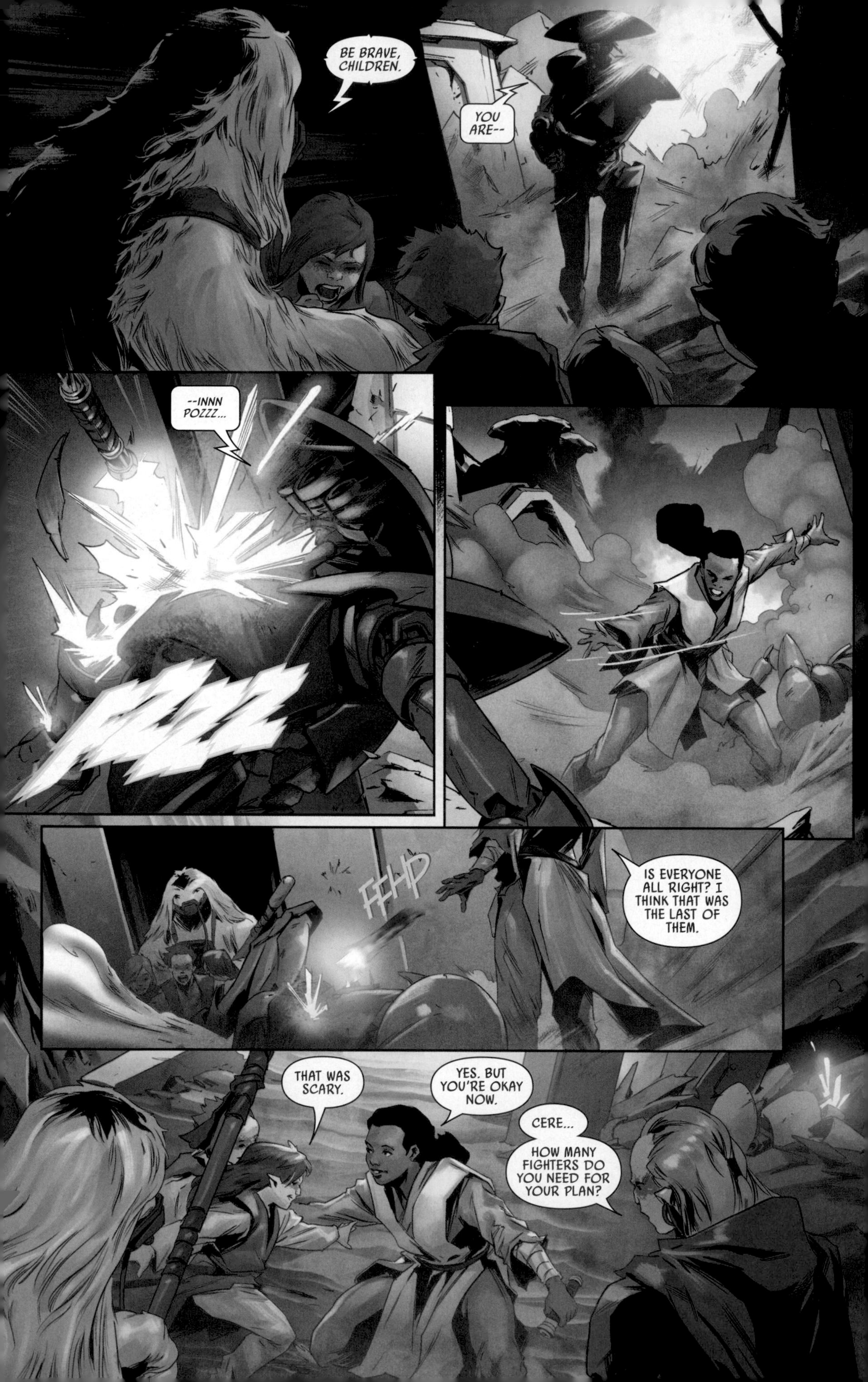
BE BRAVE, CHILDREN.
YOU ARE--
--INNN POZZZ...
FZZZ
IS EVERYONE ALL RIGHT? I THINK THAT WAS THE LAST OF THEM.
FFHP
THAT WAS SCARY.
YES. BUT YOU'RE OKAY NOW.
CERE...
HOW MANY FIGHTERS DO YOU NEED FOR YOUR PLAN?

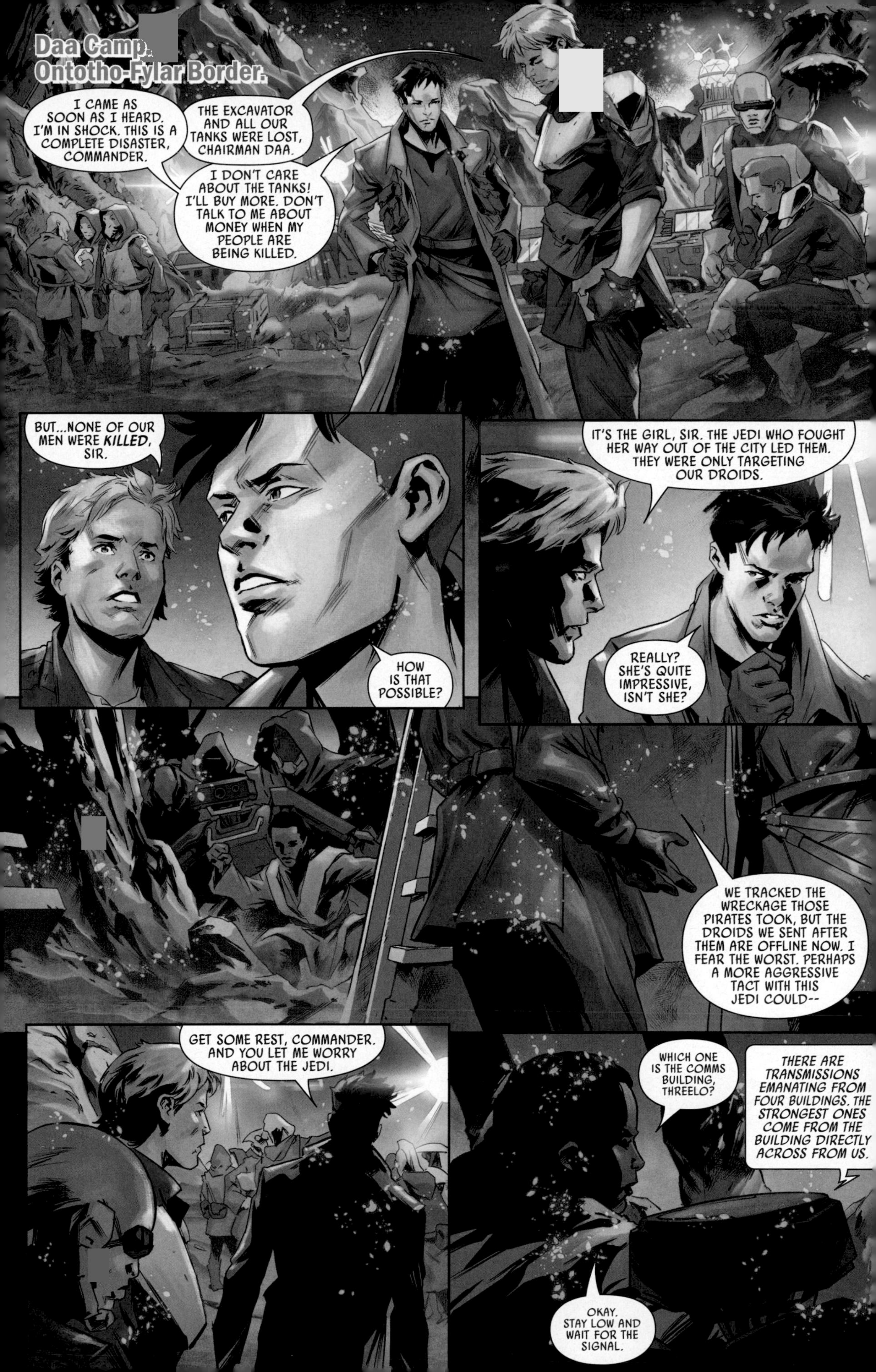
Daa Camp
Ontotho-Fylar Border.
I CAME AS SOON AS I HEARD. I'M IN SHOCK. THIS IS A COMPLETE DISASTER, COMMANDER.
THE EXCAVATOR AND ALL OUR TANKS WERE LOST, CHAIRMAN DAA.
I DON'T CARE ABOUT THE TANKS! I'LL BUY MORE. DON'T TALK TO ME ABOUT MONEY WHEN MY PEOPLE ARE BEING KILLED.
BUT...NONE OF OUR MEN WERE *KILLED*, SIR.
HOW IS THAT POSSIBLE?
IT'S THE GIRL, SIR. THE JEDI WHO FOUGHT HER WAY OUT OF THE CITY LED THEM. THEY WERE ONLY TARGETING OUR DROIDS.
REALLY? SHE'S QUITE IMPRESSIVE, ISN'T SHE?
WE TRACKED THE WRECKAGE THOSE PIRATES TOOK, BUT THE DROIDS WE SENT AFTER THEM ARE OFFLINE NOW. I FEAR THE WORST. PERHAPS A MORE AGGRESSIVE TACT WITH THIS JEDI COULD--
GET SOME REST, COMMANDER. AND YOU LET ME WORRY ABOUT THE JEDI.
WHICH ONE IS THE COMMS BUILDING, THREELO?
THERE ARE TRANSMISSIONS EMANATING FROM FOUR BUILDINGS. THE STRONGEST ONES COME FROM THE BUILDING DIRECTLY ACROSS FROM US.
OKAY. STAY LOW AND WAIT FOR THE SIGNAL.

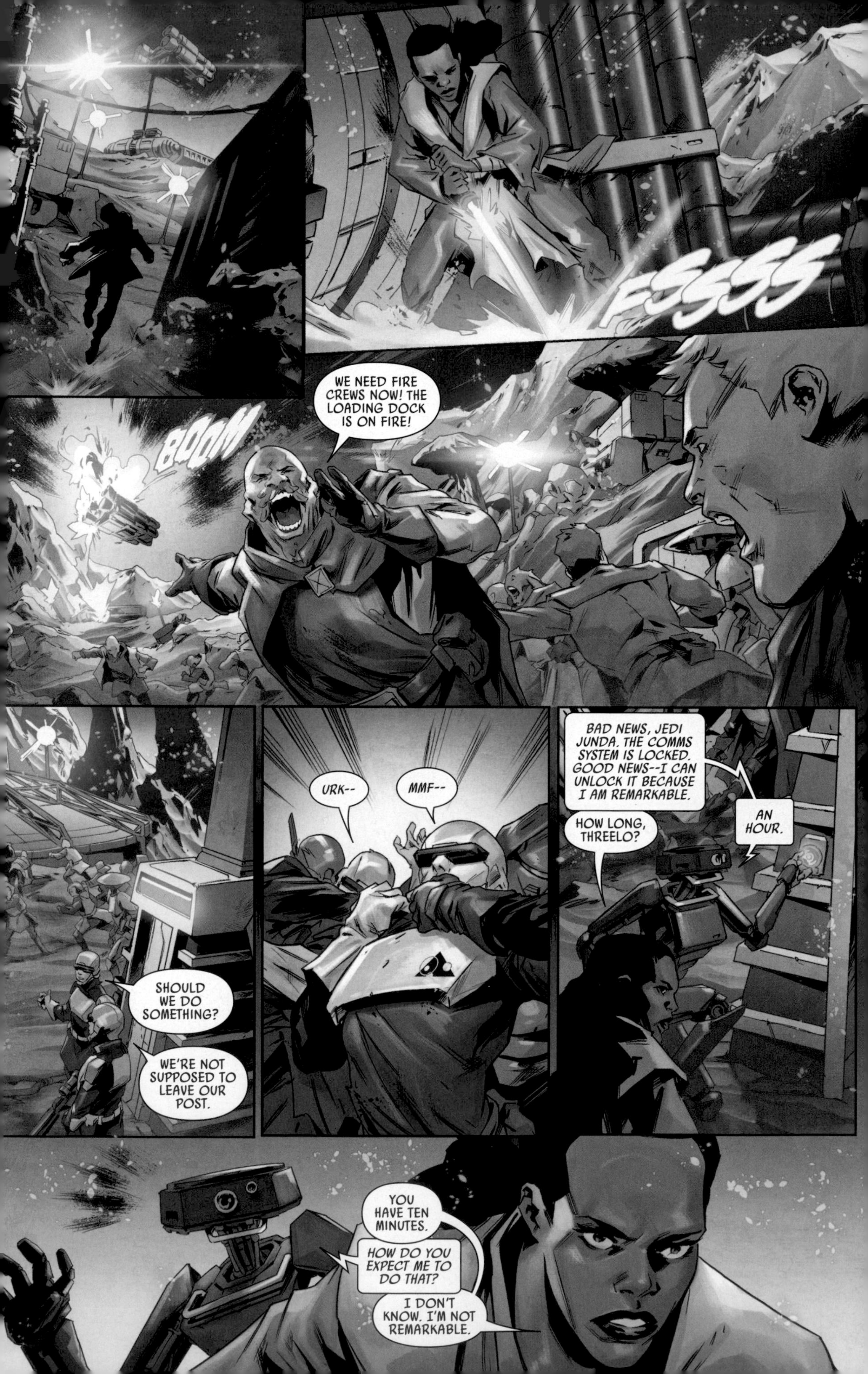
FSSSS
WE NEED FIRE CREWS NOW! THE LOADING DOCK IS ON FIRE!
BOOM
SHOULD WE DO SOMETHING?
WE'RE NOT SUPPOSED TO LEAVE OUR POST.
URK--
MMF--
BAD NEWS, JEDI JUNDA. THE COMMS SYSTEM IS LOCKED. GOOD NEWS--I CAN UNLOCK IT BECAUSE I AM REMARKABLE.
HOW LONG, THREELO?
AN HOUR.
YOU HAVE TEN MINUTES.
HOW DO YOU EXPECT ME TO DO THAT?
I DON'T KNOW. I'M NOT REMARKABLE.

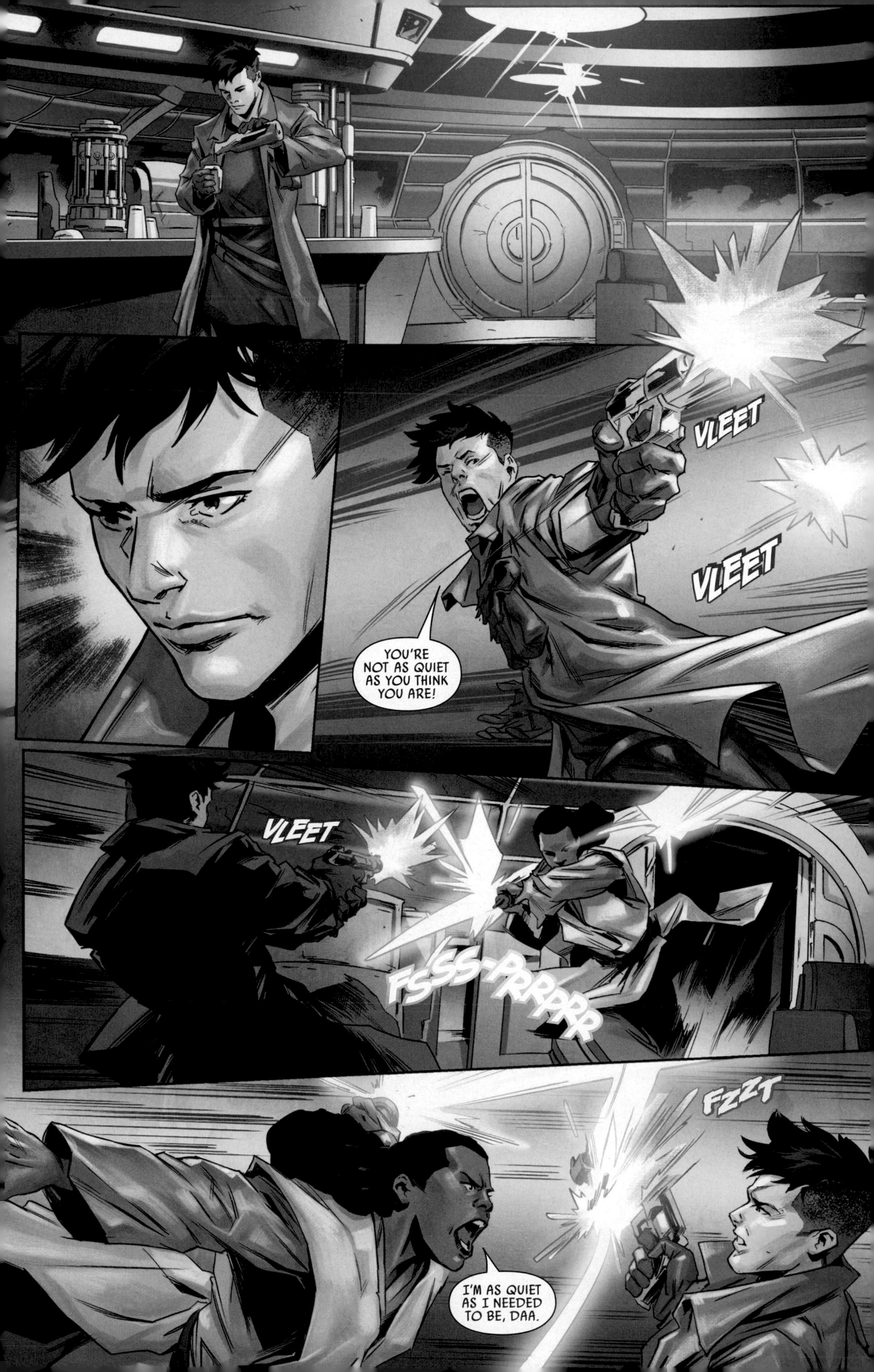
VLEET
VLEET
YOU'RE NOT AS QUIET AS YOU THINK YOU ARE!
VLEET
FSSS-PRRPRR
FZZT
I'M AS QUIET AS I NEEDED TO BE, DAA.

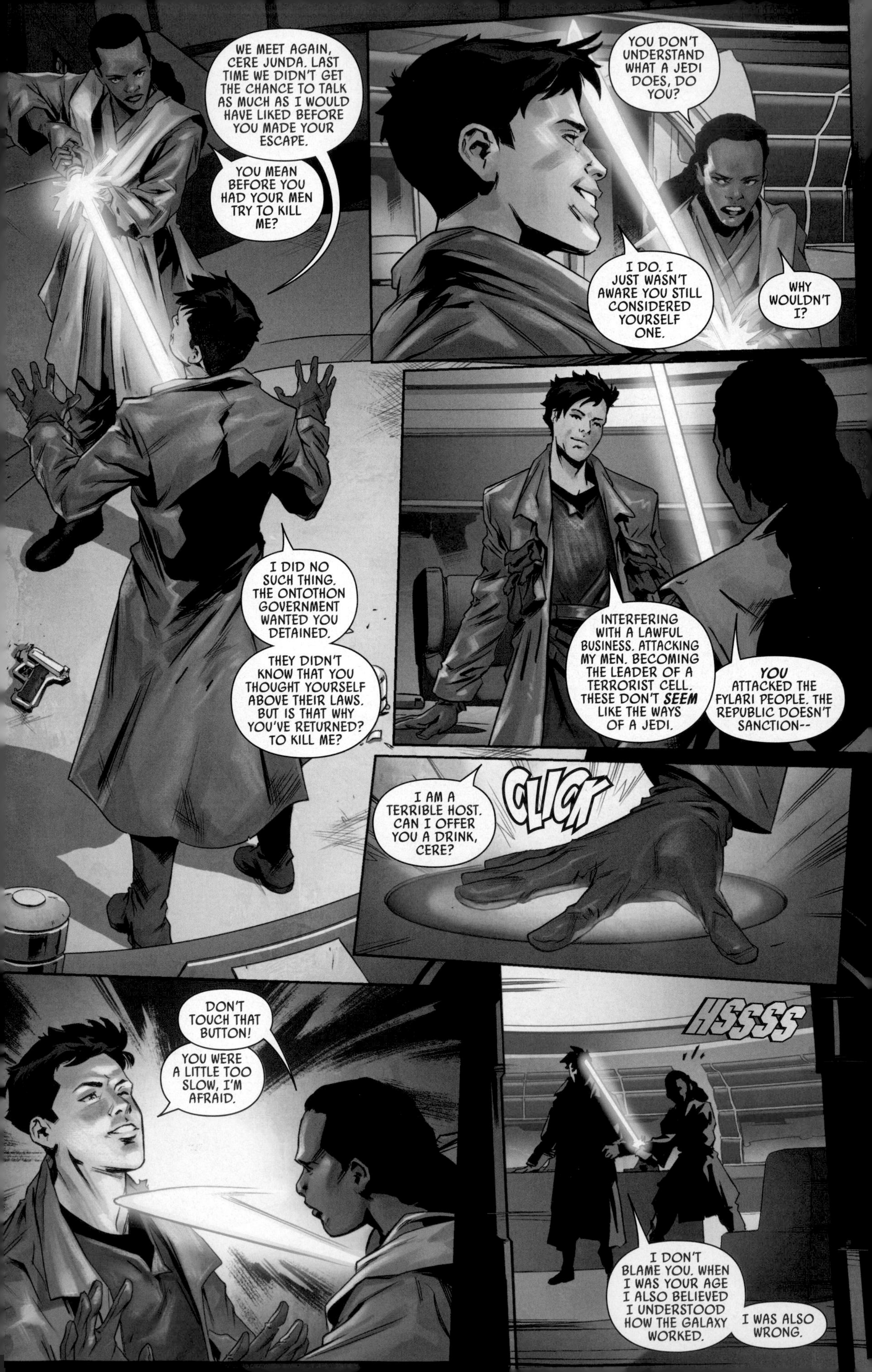
WE MEET AGAIN, CERE JUNDA. LAST TIME WE DIDN'T GET THE CHANCE TO TALK AS MUCH AS I WOULD HAVE LIKED BEFORE YOU MADE YOUR ESCAPE.
YOU MEAN BEFORE YOU HAD YOUR MEN TRY TO KILL ME?
YOU DON'T UNDERSTAND WHAT A JEDI DOES, DO YOU?
I DO. I JUST WASN'T AWARE YOU STILL CONSIDERED YOURSELF ONE.
WHY WOULDN'T I?
I DID NO SUCH THING. THE ONTOTHON GOVERNMENT WANTED YOU DETAINED.
THEY DIDN'T KNOW THAT YOU THOUGHT YOURSELF ABOVE THEIR LAWS. BUT IS THAT WHY YOU'VE RETURNED? TO KILL ME?
INTERFERING WITH A LAWFUL BUSINESS. ATTACKING MY MEN. BECOMING THE LEADER OF A TERRORIST CELL. THESE DON'T **SEEM** LIKE THE WAYS OF A JEDI.
YOU ATTACKED THE FYLARI PEOPLE. THE REPUBLIC DOESN'T SANCTION--
I AM A TERRIBLE HOST. CAN I OFFER YOU A DRINK, CERE?
CLICK
DON'T TOUCH THAT BUTTON!
YOU WERE A LITTLE TOO SLOW, I'M AFRAID.
HSSSS
I DON'T BLAME YOU. WHEN I WAS YOUR AGE I ALSO BELIEVED I UNDERSTOOD HOW THE GALAXY WORKED.
I WAS ALSO WRONG.

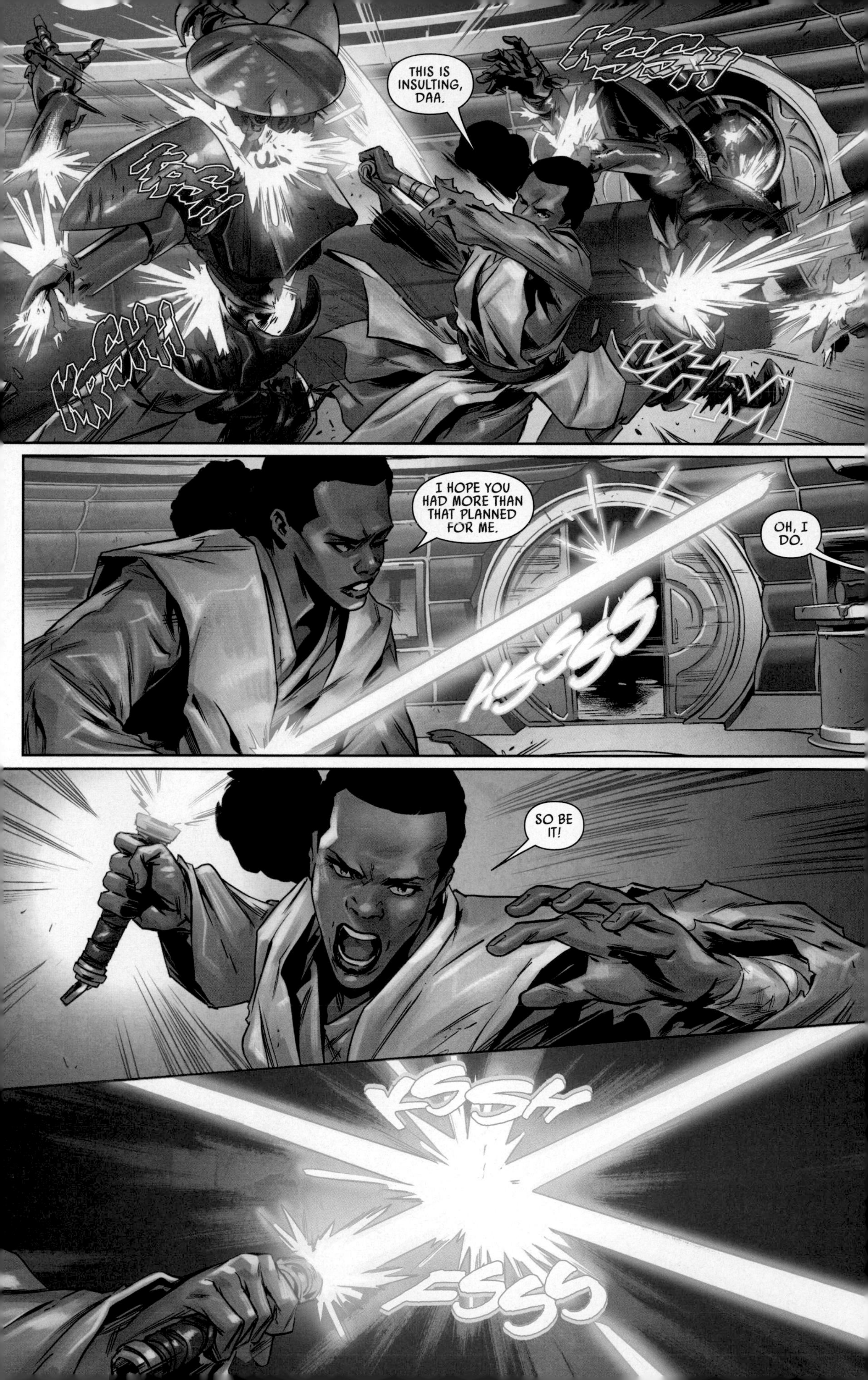
KRSSH
THIS IS INSULTING, DAA.
KRSSH
KRRSSHH
VHMM
I HOPE YOU HAD MORE THAN THAT PLANNED FOR ME.
OH, I DO.
KSSSS
SO BE IT!
KSSH
ZSSS

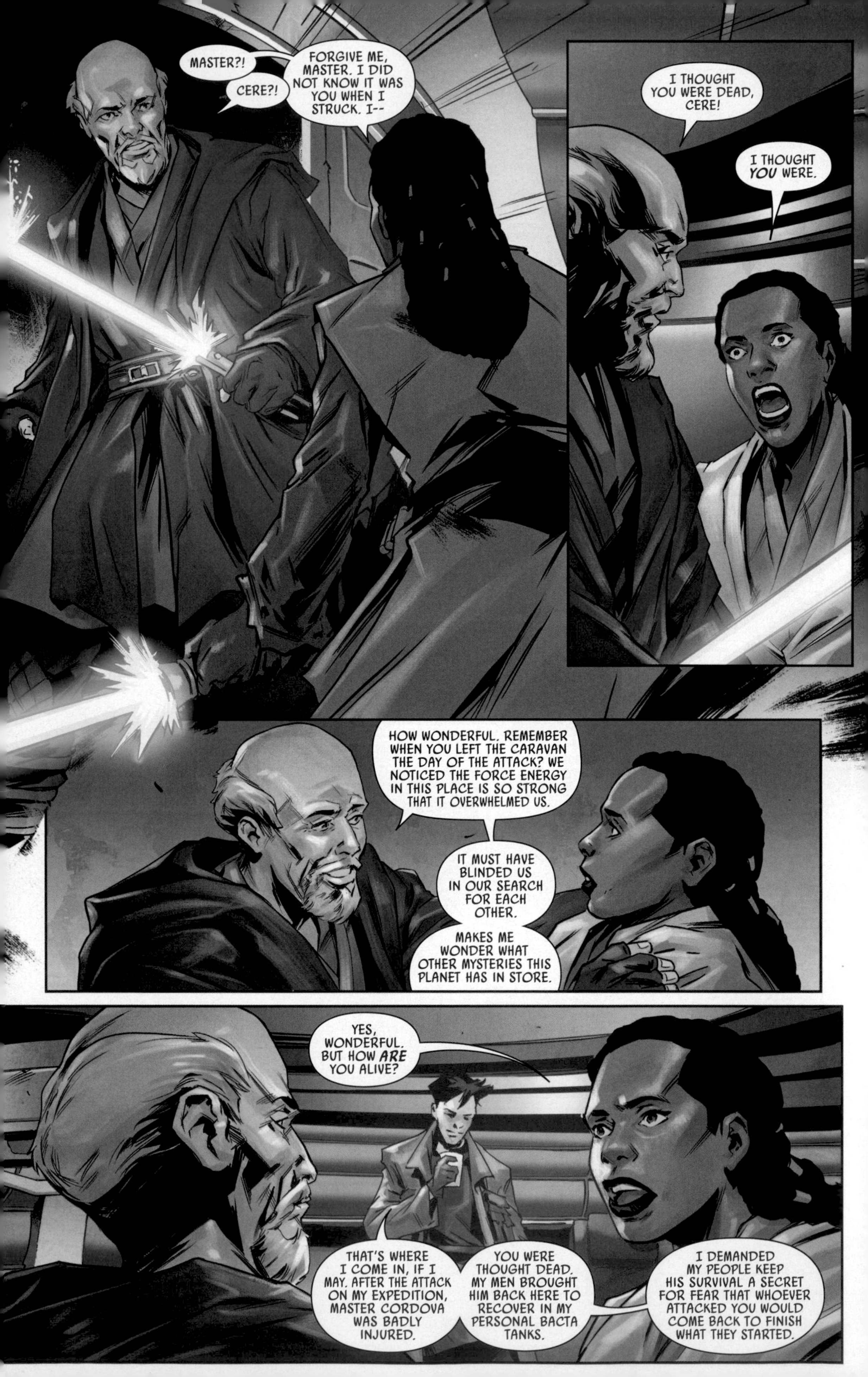
MASTER?!
CERE?!
FORGIVE ME, MASTER. I DID NOT KNOW IT WAS YOU WHEN I STRUCK. I--
I THOUGHT YOU WERE DEAD, CERE!
I THOUGHT *YOU* WERE.
HOW WONDERFUL. REMEMBER WHEN YOU LEFT THE CARAVAN THE DAY OF THE ATTACK? WE NOTICED THE FORCE ENERGY IN THIS PLACE IS SO STRONG THAT IT OVERWHELMED US.
IT MUST HAVE BLINDED US IN OUR SEARCH FOR EACH OTHER.
MAKES ME WONDER WHAT OTHER MYSTERIES THIS PLANET HAS IN STORE.
YES, WONDERFUL. BUT HOW *ARE* YOU ALIVE?
THAT'S WHERE I COME IN, IF I MAY. AFTER THE ATTACK ON MY EXPEDITION, MASTER CORDOVA WAS BADLY INJURED.
YOU WERE THOUGHT DEAD. MY MEN BROUGHT HIM BACK HERE TO RECOVER IN MY PERSONAL BACTA TANKS.
I DEMANDED MY PEOPLE KEEP HIS SURVIVAL A SECRET FOR FEAR THAT WHOEVER ATTACKED YOU WOULD COME BACK TO FINISH WHAT THEY STARTED.

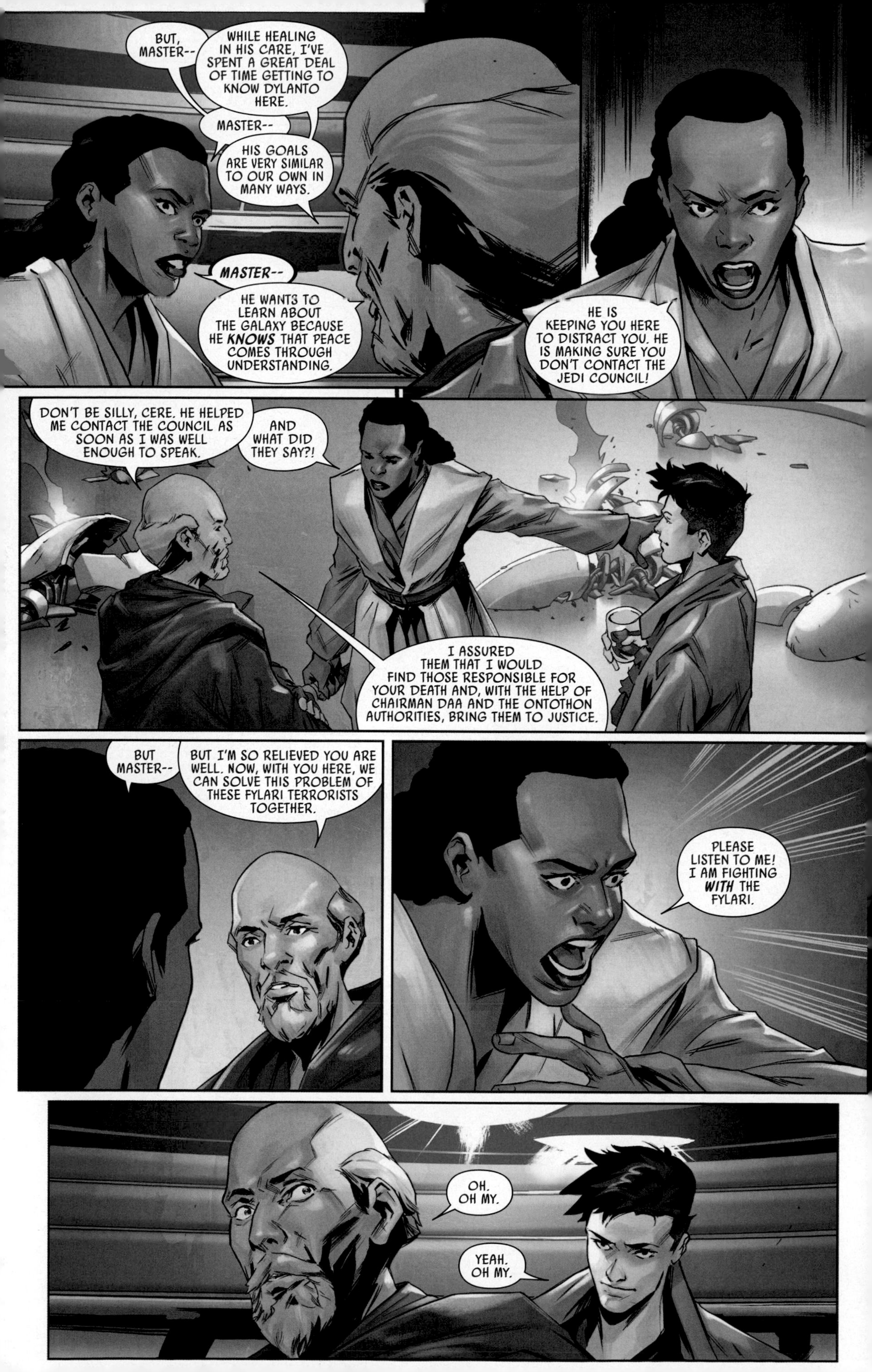
BUT, MASTER--
WHILE HEALING IN HIS CARE, I'VE SPENT A GREAT DEAL OF TIME GETTING TO KNOW DYLANTO HERE.
MASTER--
HIS GOALS ARE VERY SIMILAR TO OUR OWN IN MANY WAYS.
MASTER--
HE WANTS TO LEARN ABOUT THE GALAXY BECAUSE HE KNOWS THAT PEACE COMES THROUGH UNDERSTANDING.
HE IS KEEPING YOU HERE TO DISTRACT YOU. HE IS MAKING SURE YOU DON'T CONTACT THE JEDI COUNCIL!
DON'T BE SILLY, CERE. HE HELPED ME CONTACT THE COUNCIL AS SOON AS I WAS WELL ENOUGH TO SPEAK.
AND WHAT DID THEY SAY?!
I ASSURED THEM THAT I WOULD FIND THOSE RESPONSIBLE FOR YOUR DEATH AND, WITH THE HELP OF CHAIRMAN DAA AND THE ONTOTHON AUTHORITIES, BRING THEM TO JUSTICE.
BUT MASTER--
BUT I'M SO RELIEVED YOU ARE WELL. NOW, WITH YOU HERE, WE CAN SOLVE THIS PROBLEM OF THESE FYLARI TERRORISTS TOGETHER.
PLEASE LISTEN TO ME! I AM FIGHTING WITH THE FYLARI.
OH. OH MY.
YEAH. OH MY.

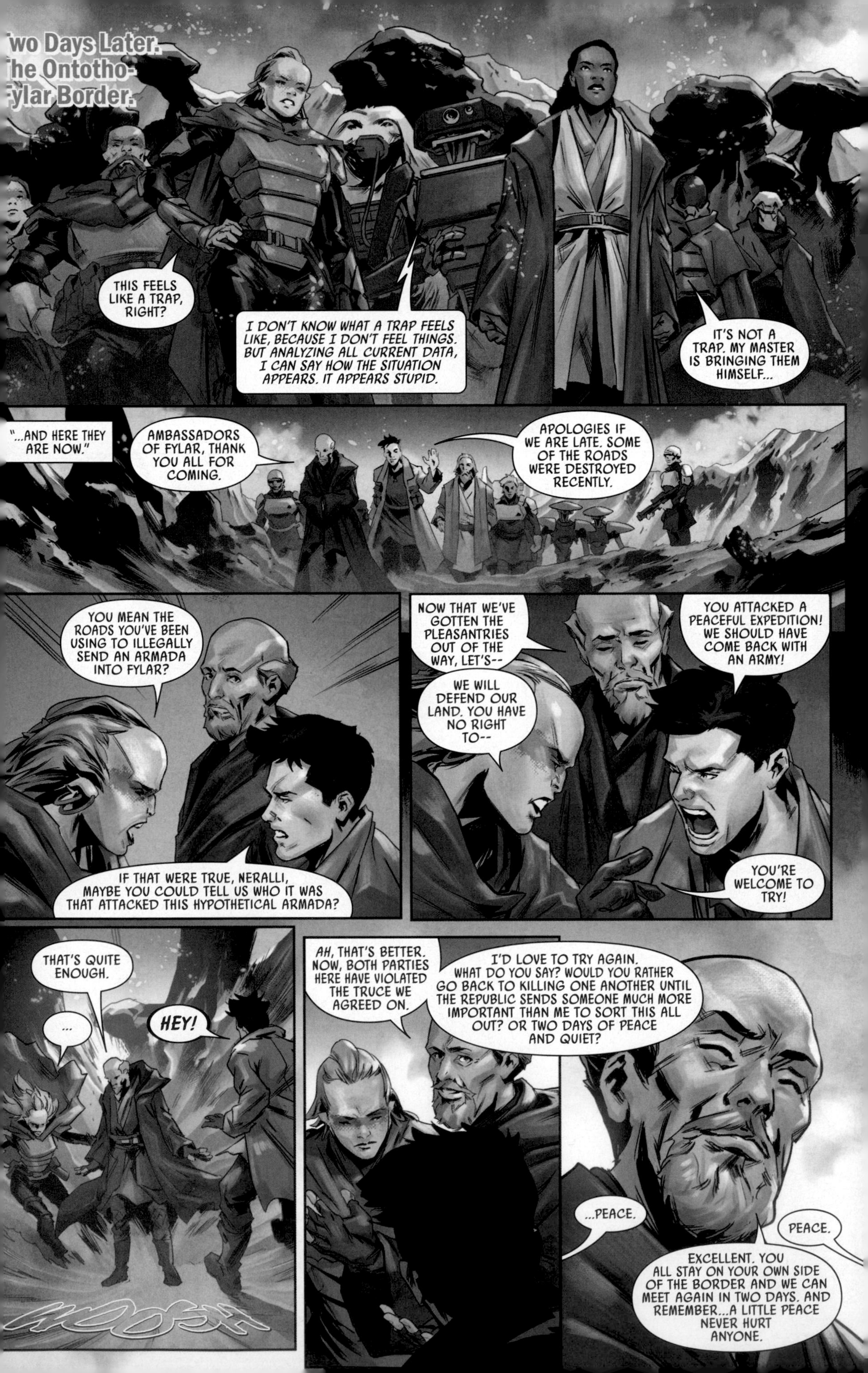
wo Days Later.
he Ontotho-
ylar Border.
THIS FEELS LIKE A TRAP, RIGHT?
I DON'T KNOW WHAT A TRAP FEELS LIKE, BECAUSE I DON'T FEEL THINGS. BUT ANALYZING ALL CURRENT DATA, I CAN SAY HOW THE SITUATION APPEARS. IT APPEARS STUPID.
IT'S NOT A TRAP. MY MASTER IS BRINGING THEM HIMSELF...
"...AND HERE THEY ARE NOW."
AMBASSADORS OF FYLAR, THANK YOU ALL FOR COMING.
APOLOGIES IF WE ARE LATE. SOME OF THE ROADS WERE DESTROYED RECENTLY.
YOU MEAN THE ROADS YOU'VE BEEN USING TO ILLEGALLY SEND AN ARMADA INTO FYLAR?
IF THAT WERE TRUE, NERALLI, MAYBE YOU COULD TELL US WHO IT WAS THAT ATTACKED THIS HYPOTHETICAL ARMADA?
NOW THAT WE'VE GOTTEN THE PLEASANTRIES OUT OF THE WAY, LET'S--
YOU ATTACKED A PEACEFUL EXPEDITION! WE SHOULD HAVE COME BACK WITH AN ARMY!
WE WILL DEFEND OUR LAND. YOU HAVE NO RIGHT TO--
YOU'RE WELCOME TO TRY!
THAT'S QUITE ENOUGH.
...
HEY!
AH, THAT'S BETTER. NOW, BOTH PARTIES HERE HAVE VIOLATED THE TRUCE WE AGREED ON.
I'D LOVE TO TRY AGAIN. WHAT DO YOU SAY? WOULD YOU RATHER GO BACK TO KILLING ONE ANOTHER UNTIL THE REPUBLIC SENDS SOMEONE MUCH MORE IMPORTANT THAN ME TO SORT THIS ALL OUT? OR TWO DAYS OF PEACE AND QUIET?
...PEACE.
PEACE.
EXCELLENT. YOU ALL STAY ON YOUR OWN SIDE OF THE BORDER AND WE CAN MEET AGAIN IN TWO DAYS. AND REMEMBER...A LITTLE PEACE NEVER HURT ANYONE.

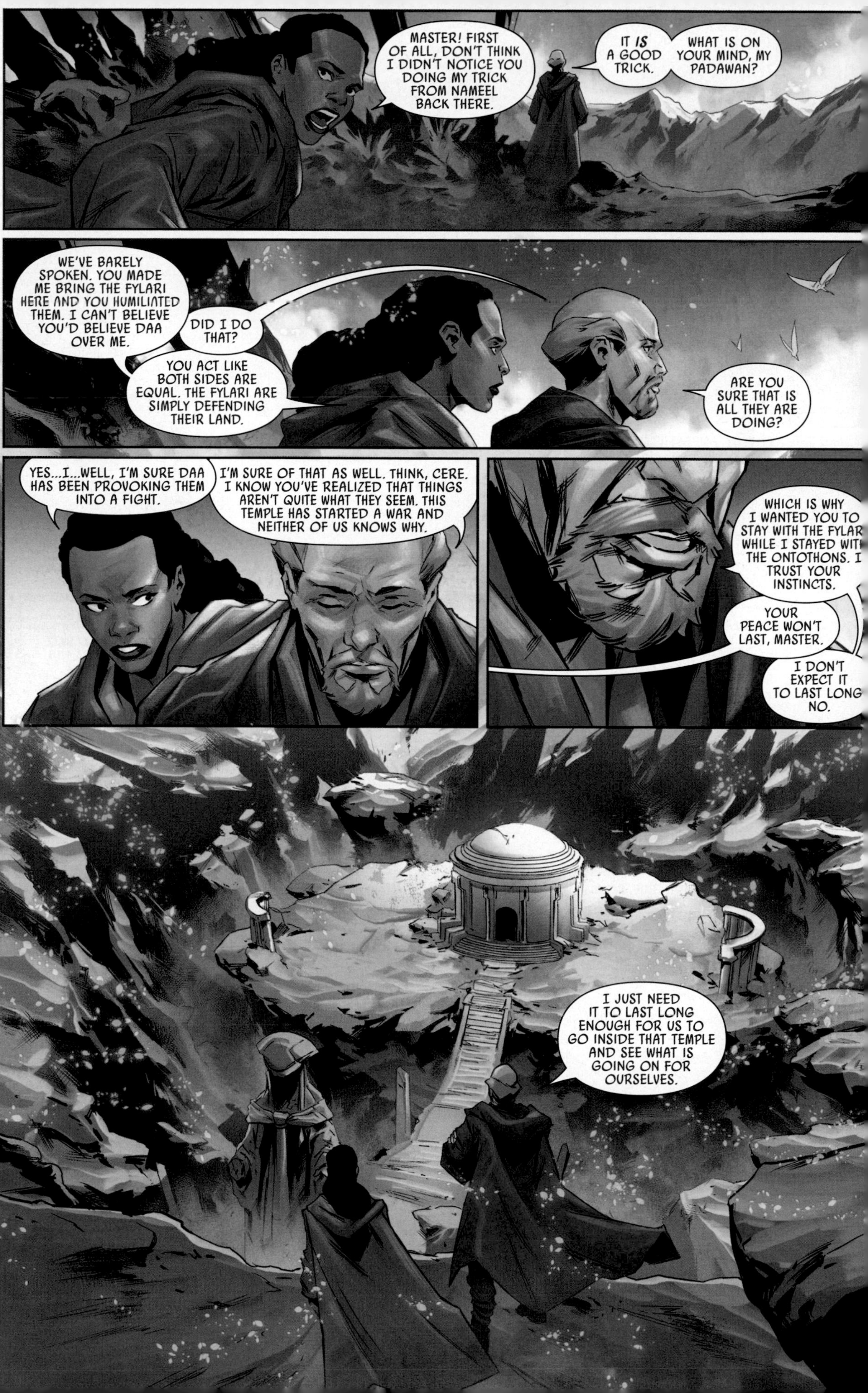
MASTER! FIRST OF ALL, DON'T THINK I DIDN'T NOTICE YOU DOING MY TRICK FROM NAMEEL BACK THERE.
IT *IS* A GOOD TRICK.
WHAT IS ON YOUR MIND, MY PADAWAN?
WE'VE BARELY SPOKEN. YOU MADE ME BRING THE FYLARI HERE AND YOU HUMILIATED THEM. I CAN'T BELIEVE YOU'D BELIEVE DAA OVER ME.
DID I DO THAT?
YOU ACT LIKE BOTH SIDES ARE EQUAL. THE FYLARI ARE SIMPLY DEFENDING THEIR LAND.
ARE YOU SURE THAT IS ALL THEY ARE DOING?
YES...I...WELL, I'M SURE DAA HAS BEEN PROVOKING THEM INTO A FIGHT.
I'M SURE OF THAT AS WELL. THINK, CERE. I KNOW YOU'VE REALIZED THAT THINGS AREN'T QUITE WHAT THEY SEEM. THIS TEMPLE HAS STARTED A WAR AND NEITHER OF US KNOWS WHY.
WHICH IS WHY I WANTED YOU TO STAY WITH THE FYLARI WHILE I STAYED WITH THE ONTOTHONS. I TRUST YOUR INSTINCTS.
YOUR PEACE WON'T LAST, MASTER.
I DON'T EXPECT IT TO LAST LONG NO.
I JUST NEED IT TO LAST LONG ENOUGH FOR US TO GO INSIDE THAT TEMPLE AND SEE WHAT IS GOING ON FOR OURSELVES.

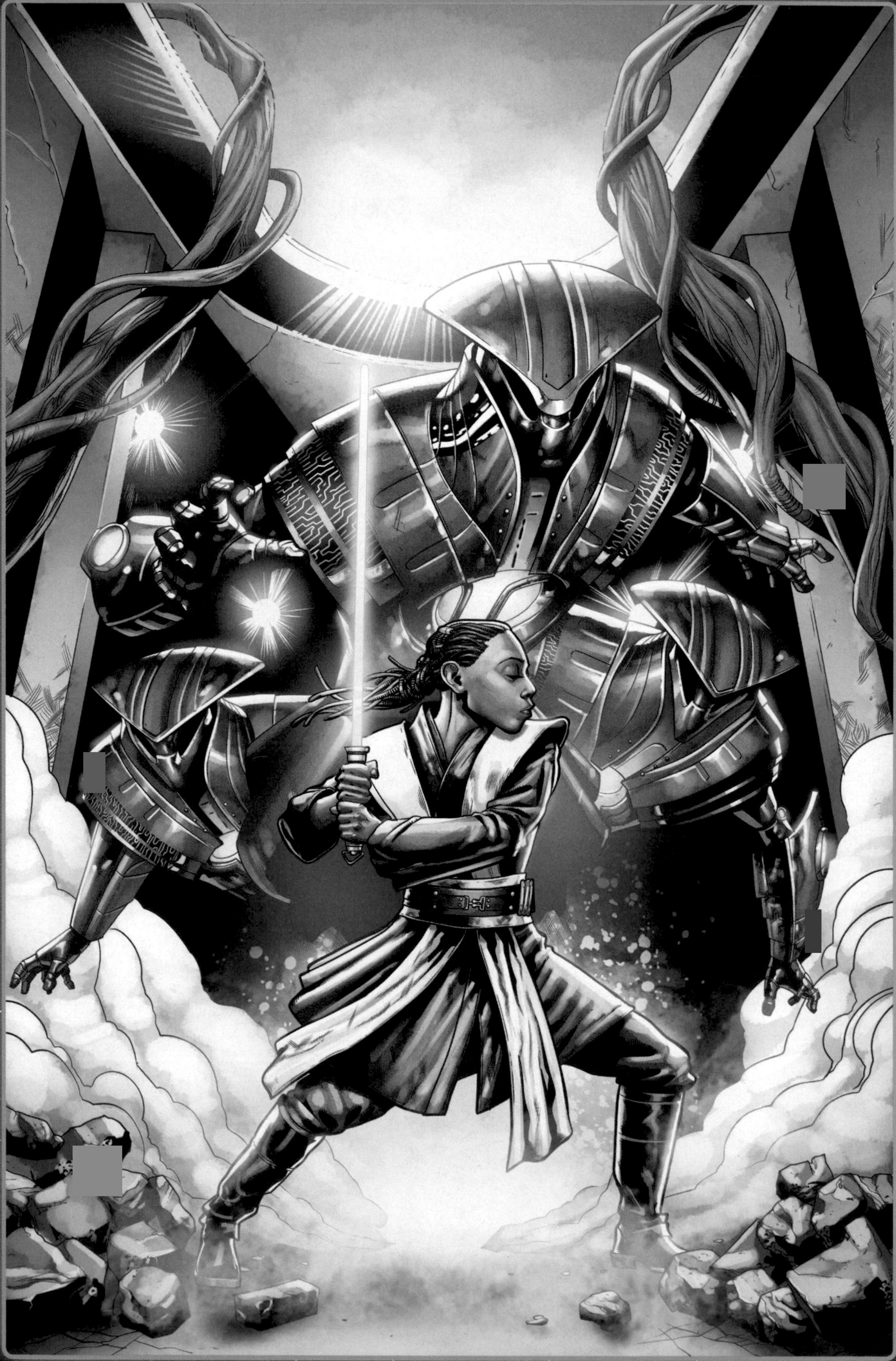

4 – A TRUCE, A TRAP AND A TRAITOR

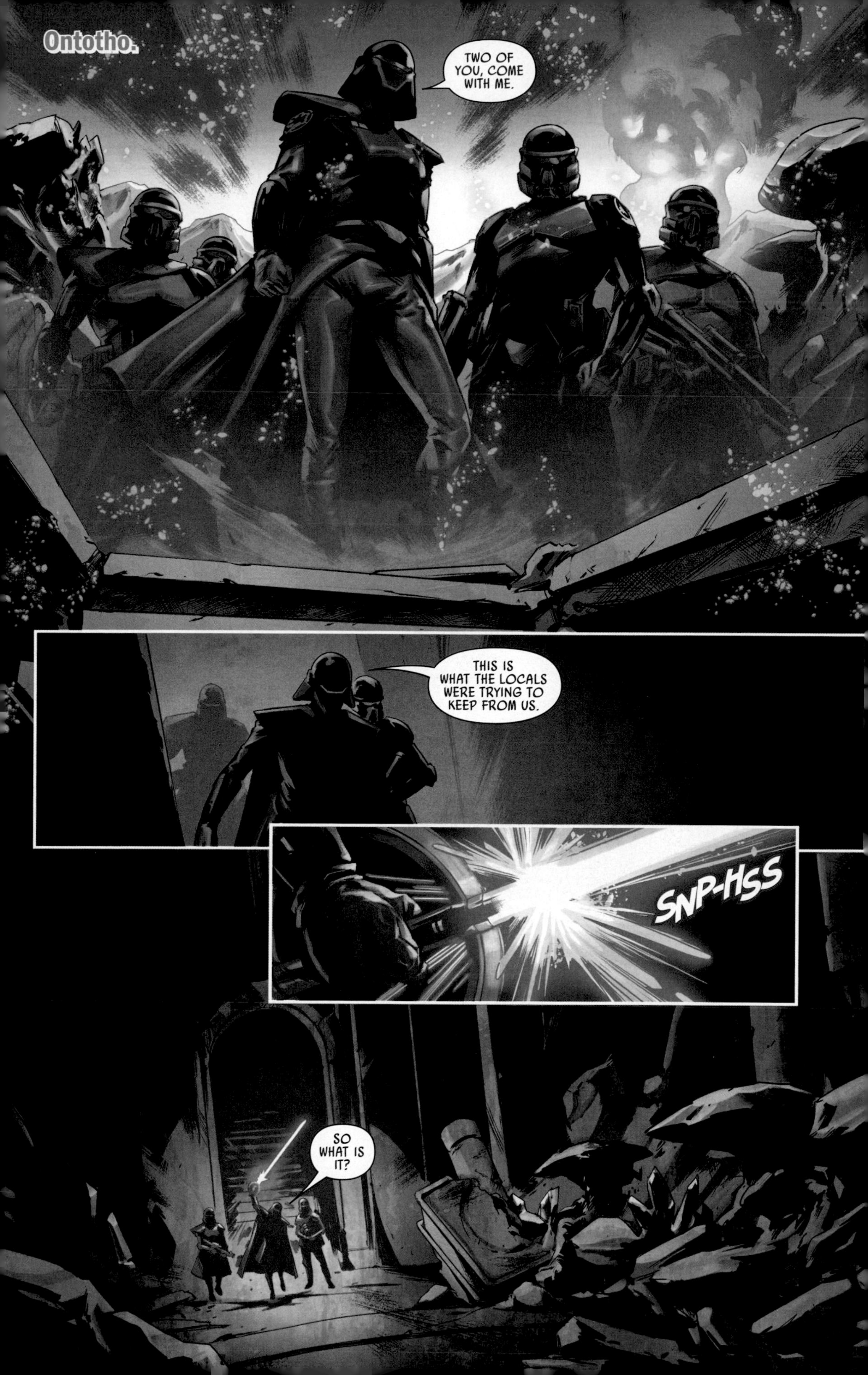
Ontotho.
TWO OF YOU, COME WITH ME.
THIS IS WHAT THE LOCALS WERE TRYING TO KEEP FROM US.
SNP-HSS
SO WHAT IS IT?

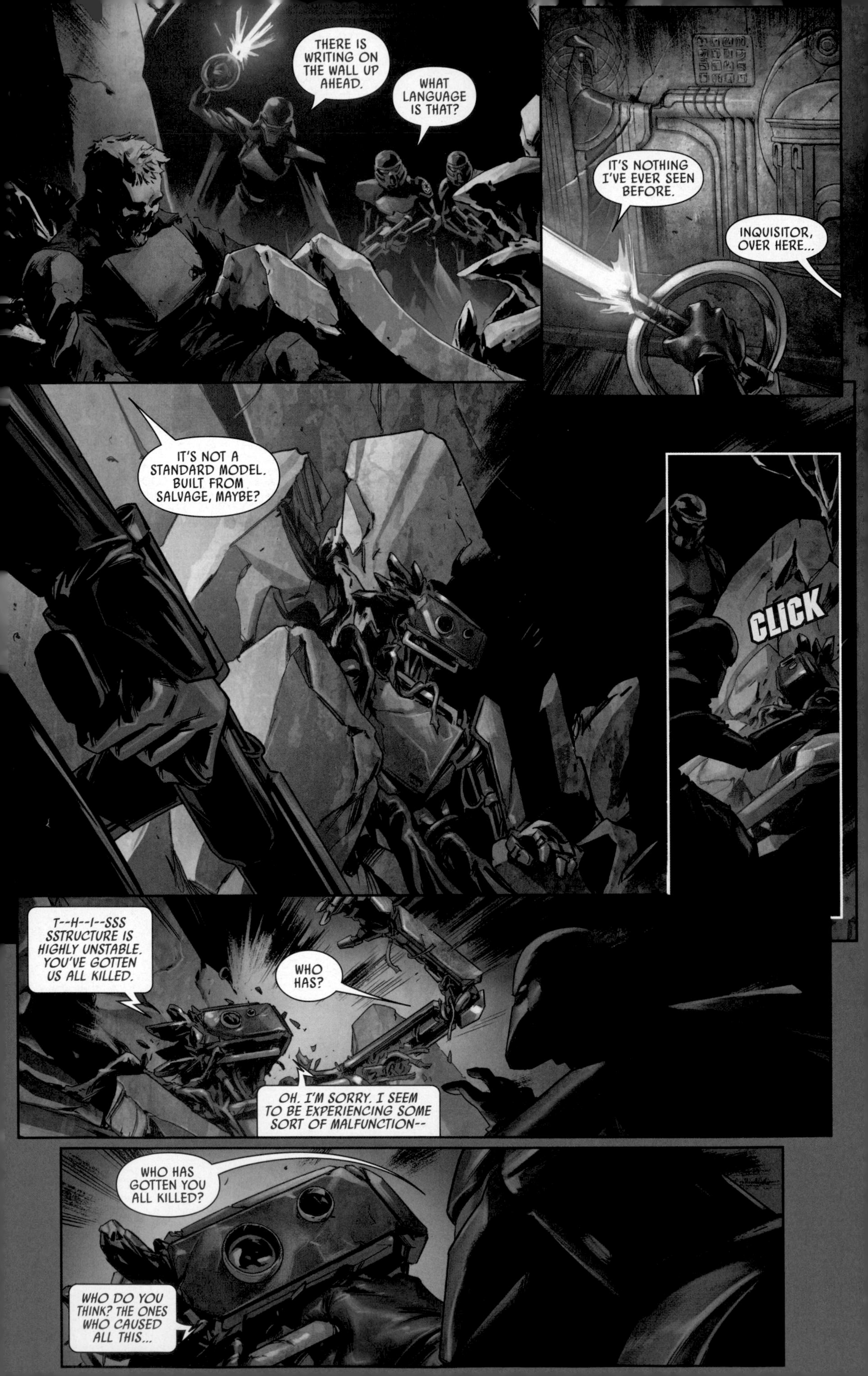

THERE IS WRITING ON THE WALL UP AHEAD.
WHAT LANGUAGE IS THAT?
IT'S NOTHING I'VE EVER SEEN BEFORE.
INQUISITOR, OVER HERE...
IT'S NOT A STANDARD MODEL. BUILT FROM SALVAGE, MAYBE?
CLICK
T--H--I--SSS SSTRUCTURE IS HIGHLY UNSTABLE. YOU'VE GOTTEN US ALL KILLED.
WHO HAS?
OH. I'M SORRY. I SEEM TO BE EXPERIENCING SOME SORT OF MALFUNCTION--
WHO HAS GOTTEN YOU ALL KILLED?
WHO DO YOU THINK? THE ONES WHO CAUSED ALL THIS...

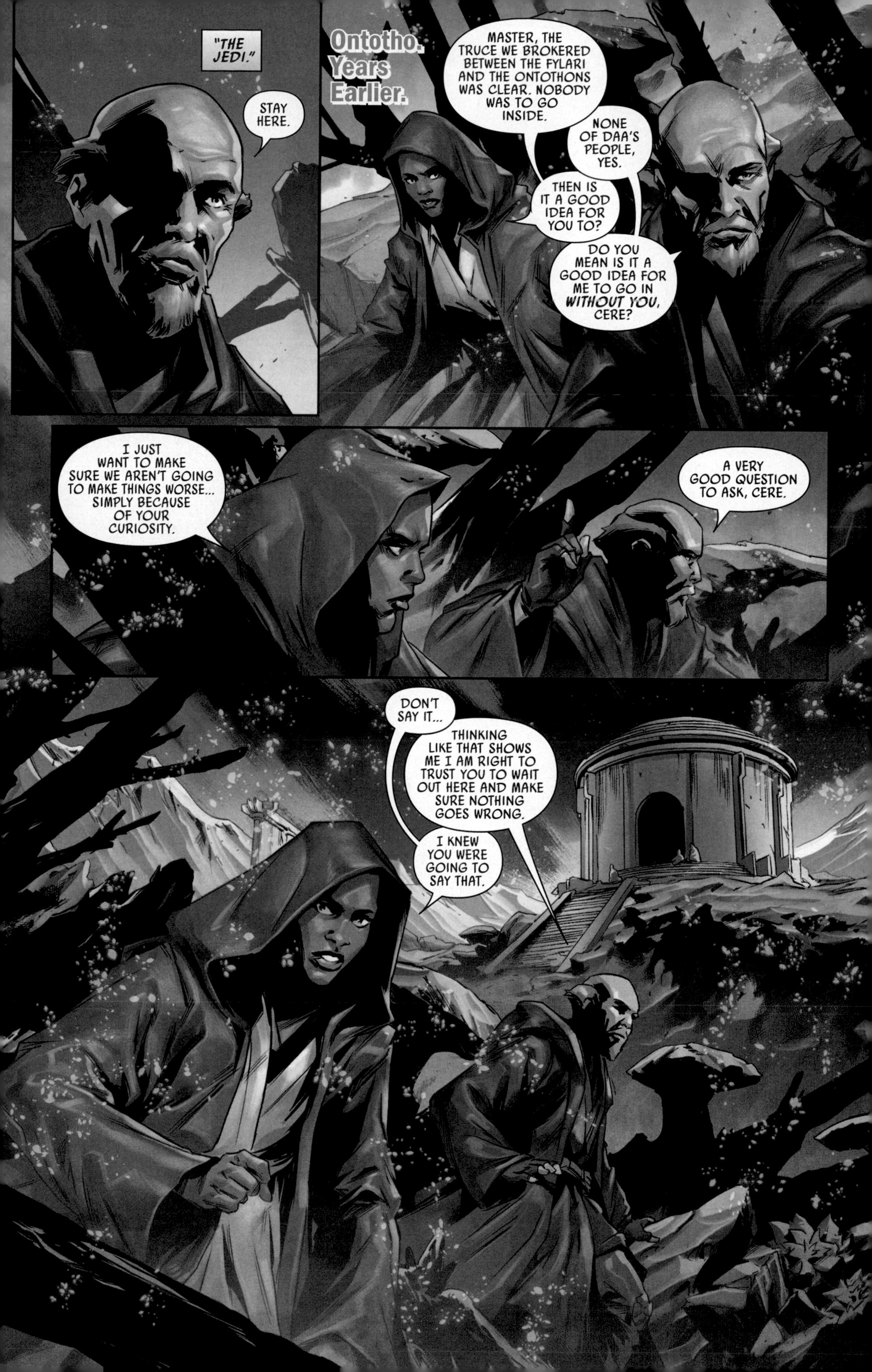
"THE JEDI."
STAY HERE.
Ontotho. Years Earlier.
MASTER, THE TRUCE WE BROKERED BETWEEN THE FYLARI AND THE ONTOTHONS WAS CLEAR. NOBODY WAS TO GO INSIDE.
NONE OF DAA'S PEOPLE, YES.
THEN IS IT A GOOD IDEA FOR YOU TO?
DO YOU MEAN IS IT A GOOD IDEA FOR ME TO GO IN WITHOUT YOU, CERE?
I JUST WANT TO MAKE SURE WE AREN'T GOING TO MAKE THINGS WORSE... SIMPLY BECAUSE OF YOUR CURIOSITY.
A VERY GOOD QUESTION TO ASK, CERE.
DON'T SAY IT...
THINKING LIKE THAT SHOWS ME I AM RIGHT TO TRUST YOU TO WAIT OUT HERE AND MAKE SURE NOTHING GOES WRONG.
I KNEW YOU WERE GOING TO SAY THAT.

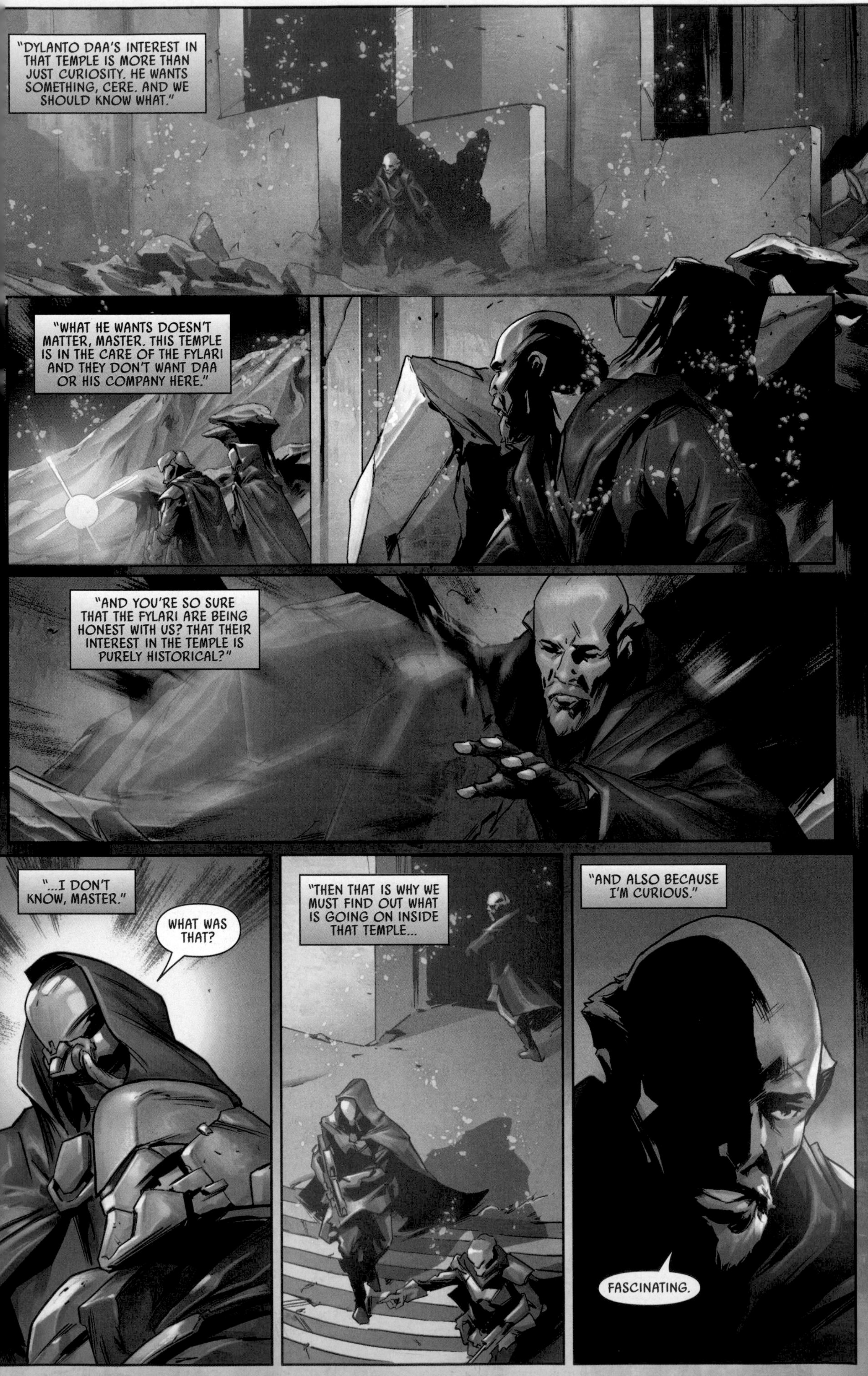
"DYLANTO DAA'S INTEREST IN THAT TEMPLE IS MORE THAN JUST CURIOSITY. HE WANTS SOMETHING, CERE. AND WE SHOULD KNOW WHAT."
"WHAT HE WANTS DOESN'T MATTER, MASTER. THIS TEMPLE IS IN THE CARE OF THE FYLARI AND THEY DON'T WANT DAA OR HIS COMPANY HERE."
"AND YOU'RE SO SURE THAT THE FYLARI ARE BEING HONEST WITH US? THAT THEIR INTEREST IN THE TEMPLE IS PURELY HISTORICAL?"
"...I DON'T KNOW, MASTER."
WHAT WAS THAT?
"THEN THAT IS WHY WE MUST FIND OUT WHAT IS GOING ON INSIDE THAT TEMPLE...
"AND ALSO BECAUSE I'M CURIOUS."
FASCINATING.

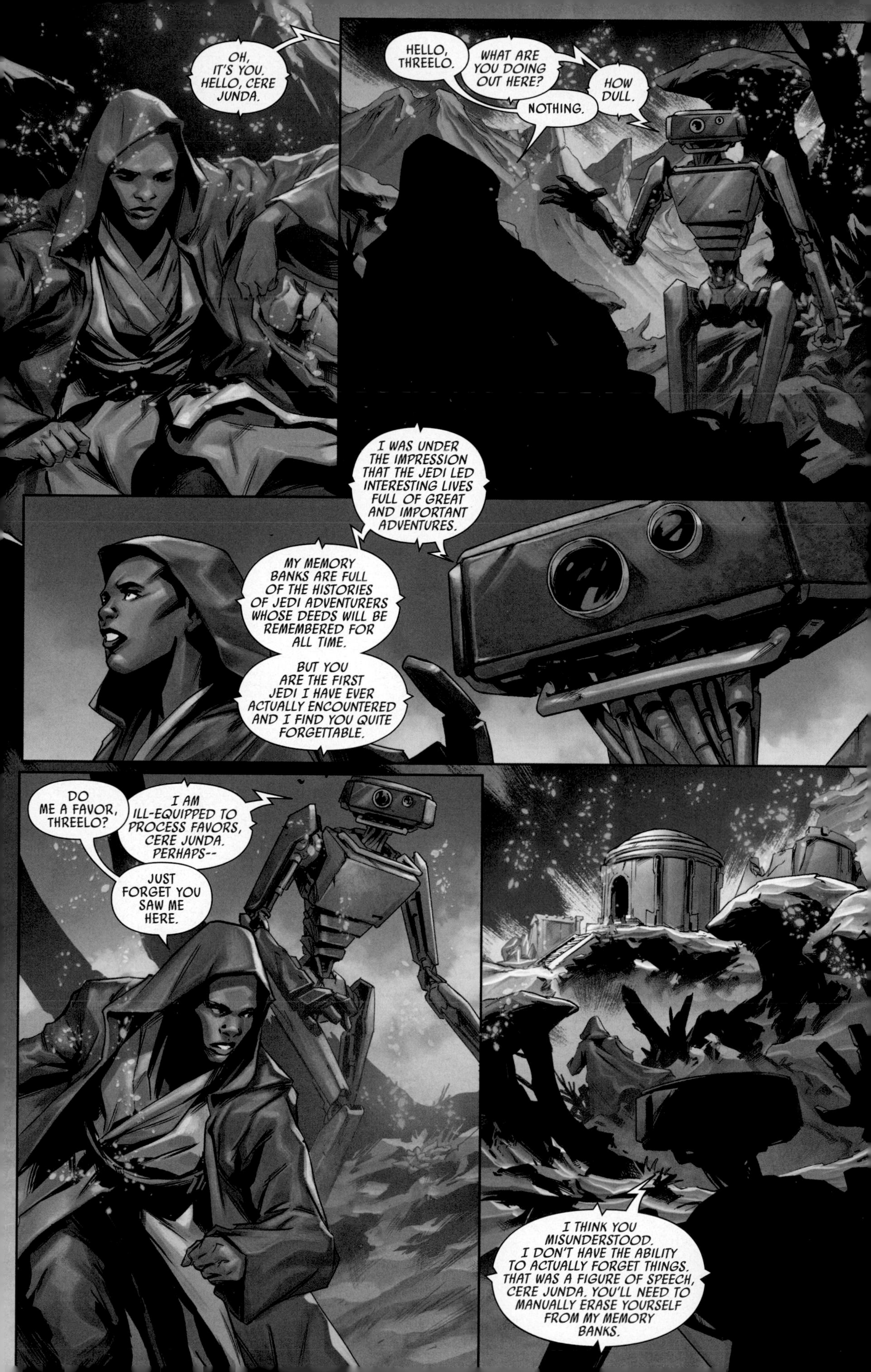
OH, IT'S YOU. HELLO, CERE JUNDA.
HELLO, THREELO.
WHAT ARE YOU DOING OUT HERE?
NOTHING.
HOW DULL.
I WAS UNDER THE IMPRESSION THAT THE JEDI LED INTERESTING LIVES FULL OF GREAT AND IMPORTANT ADVENTURES.
MY MEMORY BANKS ARE FULL OF THE HISTORIES OF JEDI ADVENTURERS WHOSE DEEDS WILL BE REMEMBERED FOR ALL TIME.
BUT YOU ARE THE FIRST JEDI I HAVE EVER ACTUALLY ENCOUNTERED AND I FIND YOU QUITE FORGETTABLE.
DO ME A FAVOR, THREELO?
I AM ILL-EQUIPPED TO PROCESS FAVORS, CERE JUNDA. PERHAPS--
JUST FORGET YOU SAW ME HERE.
I THINK YOU MISUNDERSTOOD. I DON'T HAVE THE ABILITY TO ACTUALLY FORGET THINGS. THAT WAS A FIGURE OF SPEECH, CERE JUNDA. YOU'LL NEED TO MANUALLY ERASE YOURSELF FROM MY MEMORY BANKS.

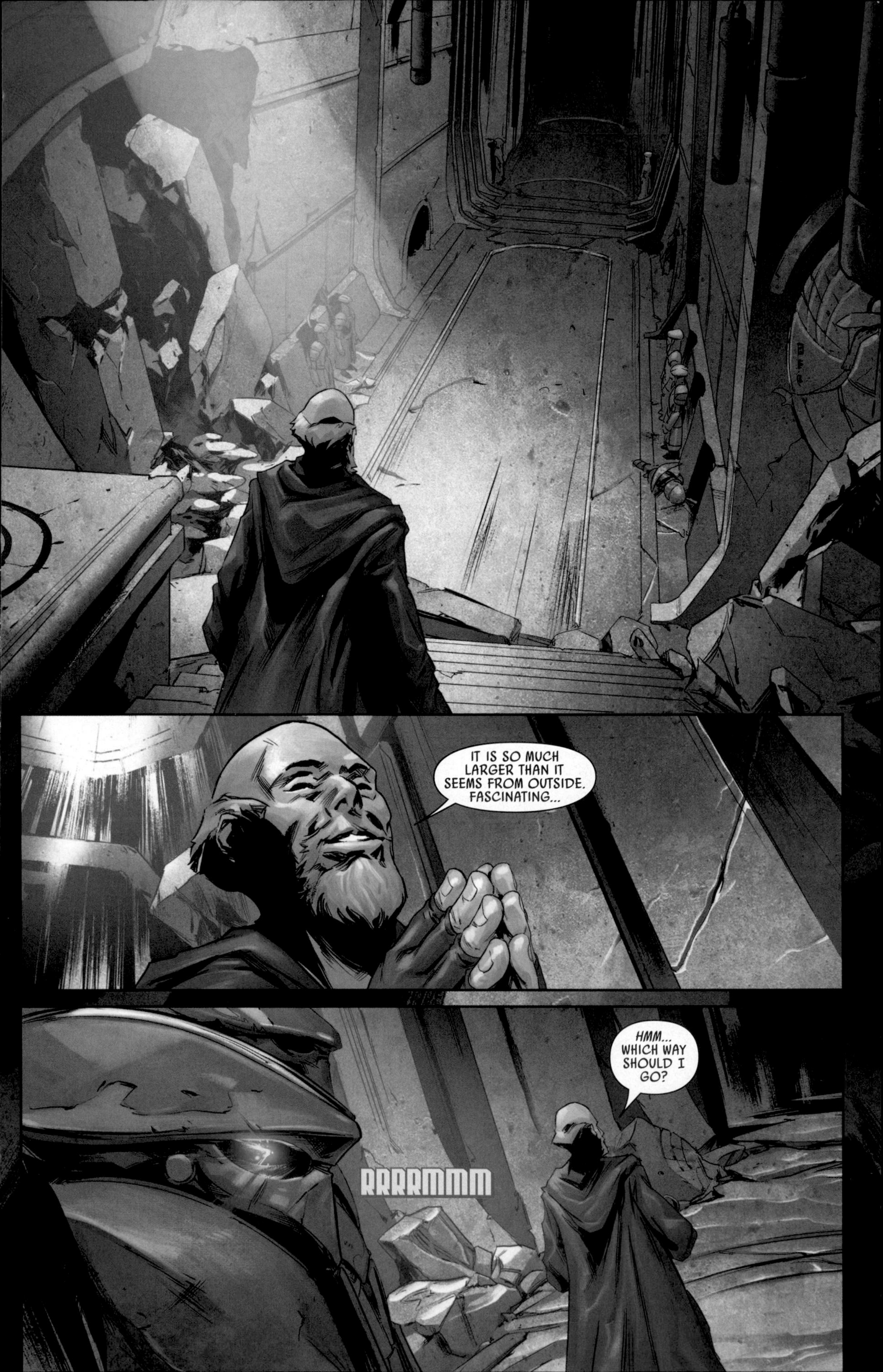
IT IS SO MUCH LARGER THAN IT SEEMS FROM OUTSIDE. FASCINATING...
HMM... WHICH WAY SHOULD I GO?
RRRRMMM

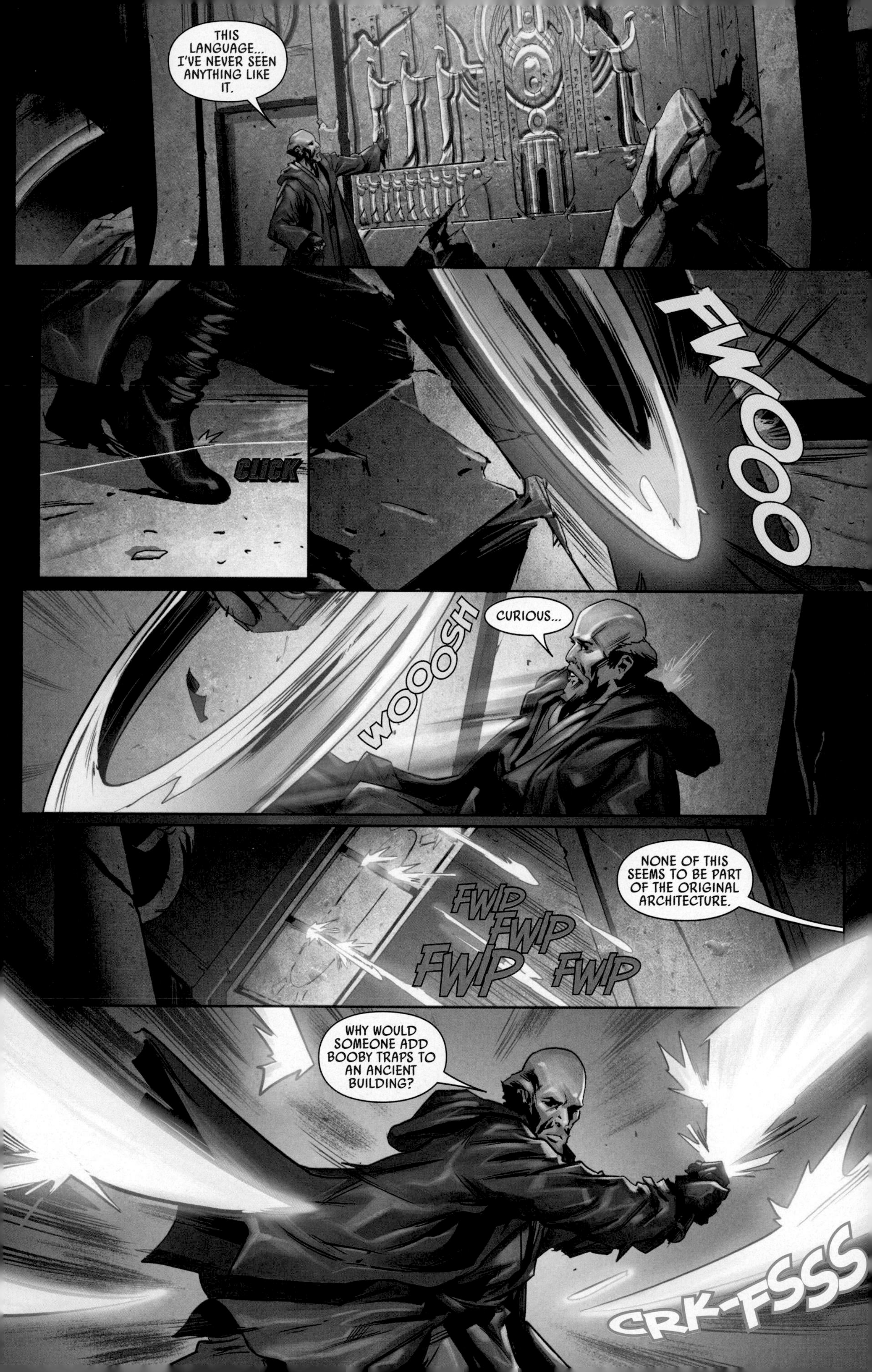
THIS LANGUAGE... I'VE NEVER SEEN ANYTHING LIKE IT.
CLICK
FWOOO
CURIOUS...
WOOOSH
NONE OF THIS SEEMS TO BE PART OF THE ORIGINAL ARCHITECTURE.
FWIP FWIP FWIP FWIP
WHY WOULD SOMEONE ADD BOOBY TRAPS TO AN ANCIENT BUILDING?
CRK-FSSS

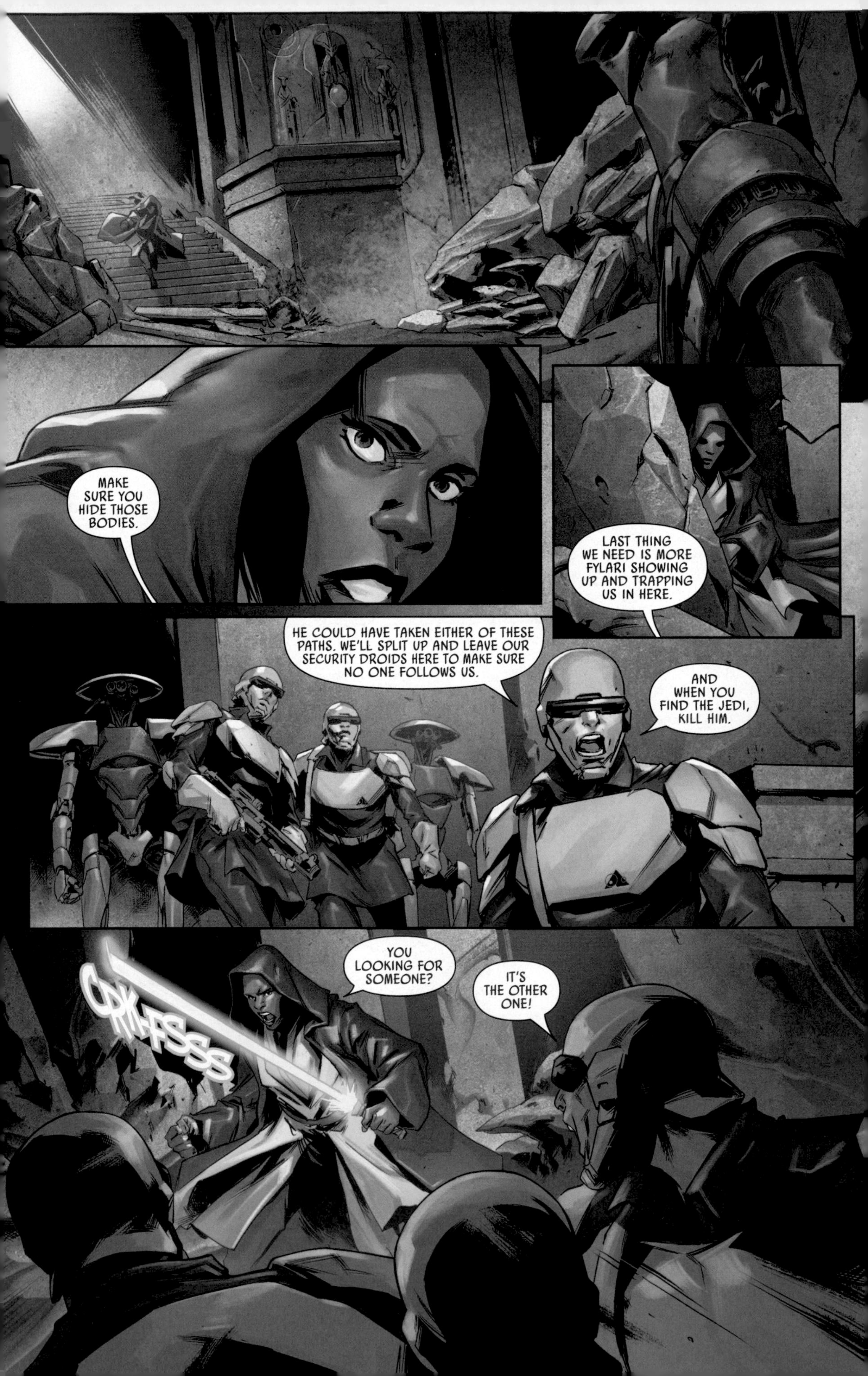
MAKE SURE YOU HIDE THOSE BODIES.
LAST THING WE NEED IS MORE FYLARI SHOWING UP AND TRAPPING US IN HERE.
HE COULD HAVE TAKEN EITHER OF THESE PATHS. WE'LL SPLIT UP AND LEAVE OUR SECURITY DROIDS HERE TO MAKE SURE NO ONE FOLLOWS US.
AND WHEN YOU FIND THE JEDI, KILL HIM.
CRK-FSSSS
YOU LOOKING FOR SOMEONE?
IT'S THE OTHER ONE!

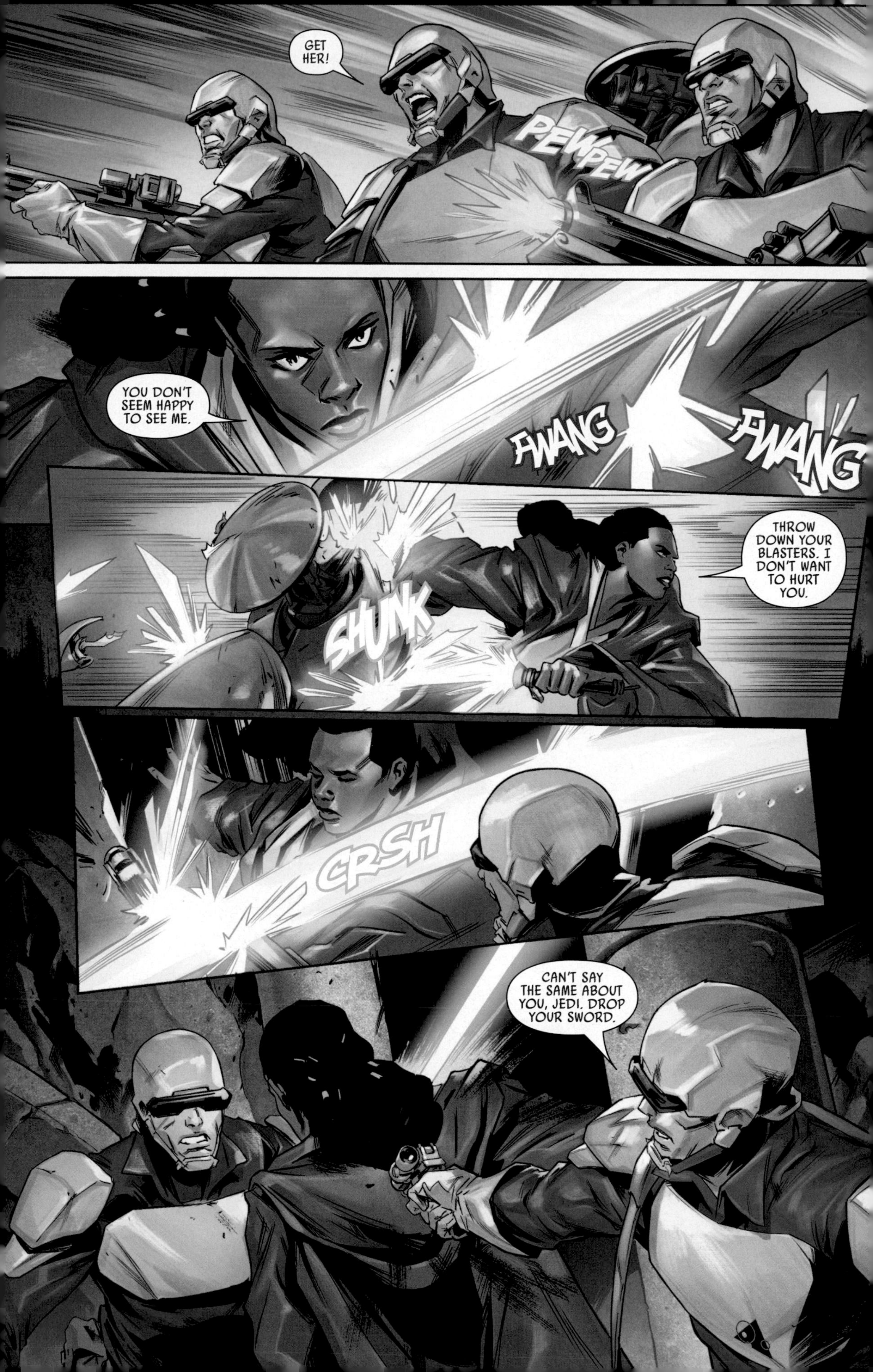
GET HER!
PEWPEW
YOU DON'T SEEM HAPPY TO SEE ME.
FWANG
FWANG
THROW DOWN YOUR BLASTERS. I DON'T WANT TO HURT YOU.
SHUNK
CRSH
CAN'T SAY THE SAME ABOUT YOU, JEDI. DROP YOUR SWORD.

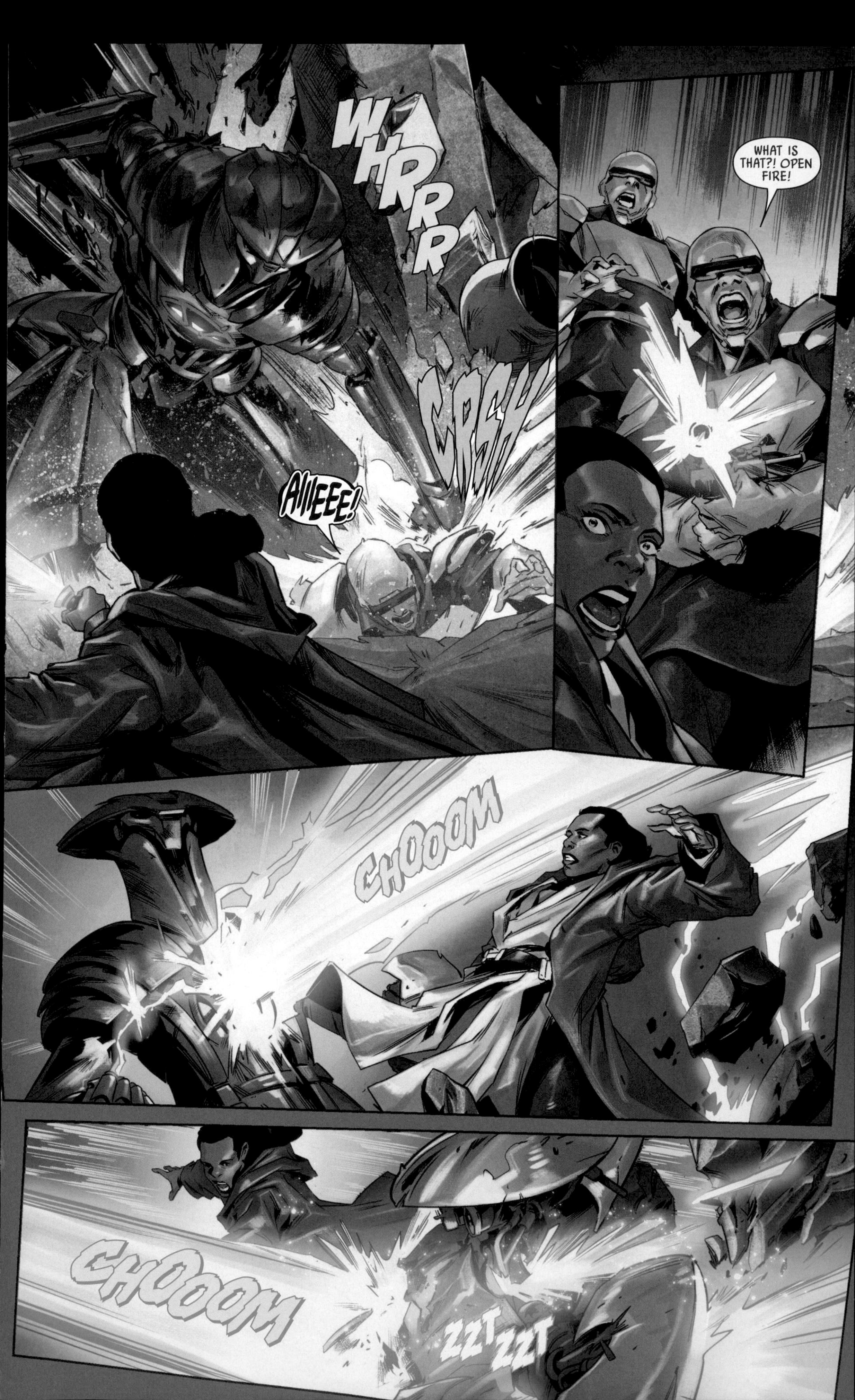
WHRRR
CRSH
AIIEEE!
WHAT IS THAT?! OPEN FIRE!
CHOOOM
CHOOOM
ZZT ZZT

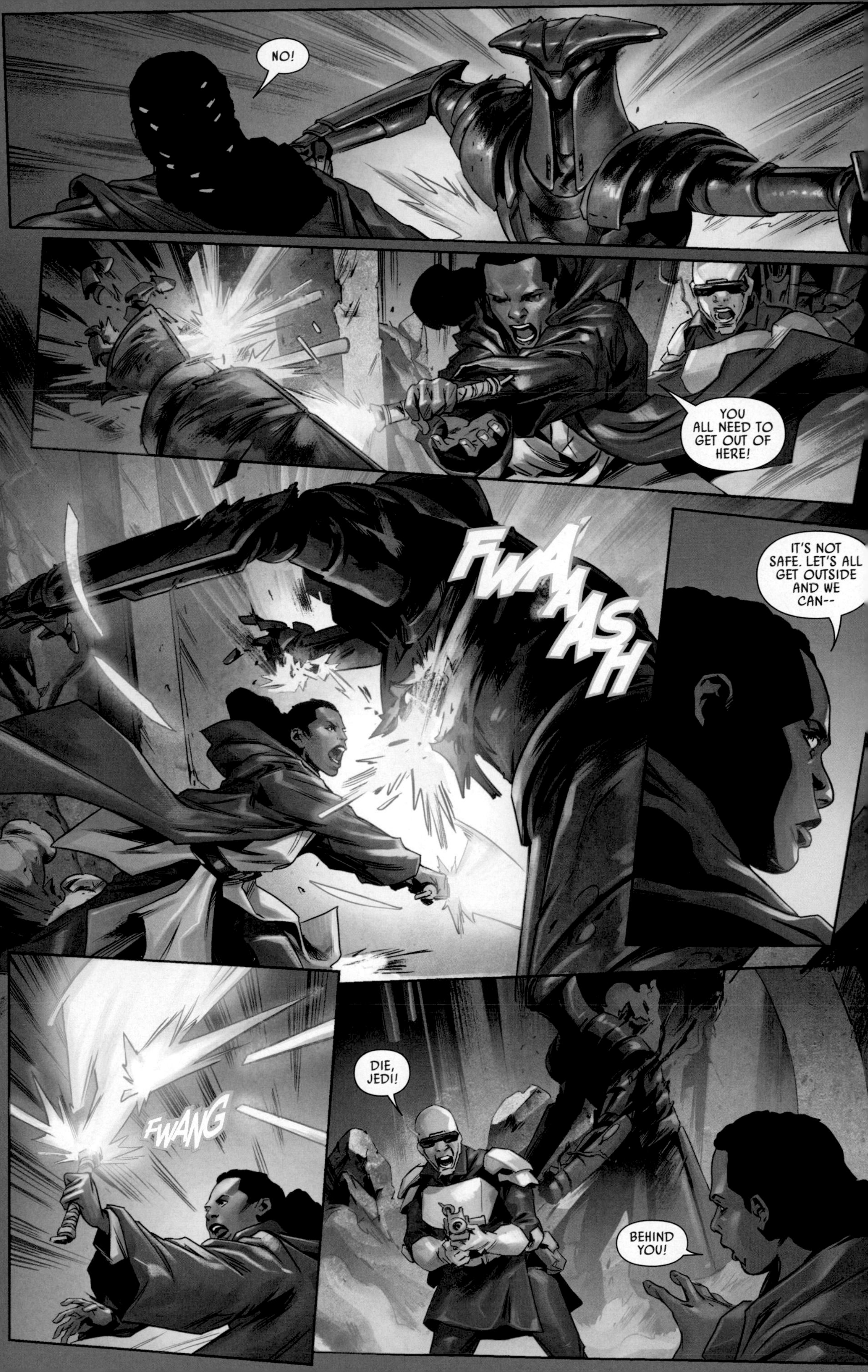
NO!
YOU ALL NEED TO GET OUT OF HERE!
FWAAAASH
IT'S NOT SAFE. LET'S ALL GET OUTSIDE AND WE CAN--
FWANG
DIE, JEDI!
BEHIND YOU!

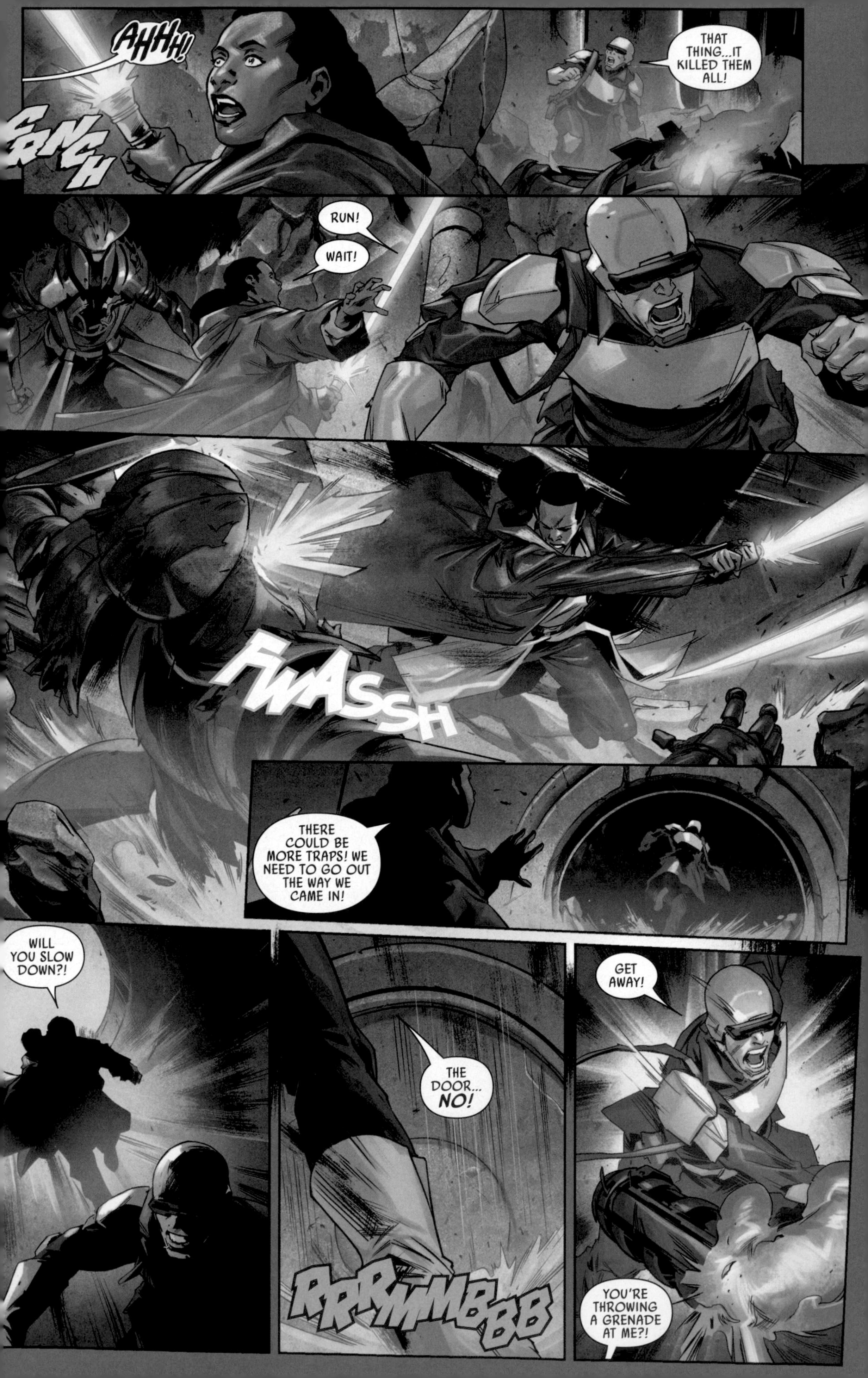
AHHH!
CRNCH
THAT THING...IT KILLED THEM ALL!
RUN!
WAIT!
FWASSH
THERE COULD BE MORE TRAPS! WE NEED TO GO OUT THE WAY WE CAME IN!
WILL YOU SLOW DOWN?!
THE DOOR... NO!
RRRMMBBB
GET AWAY!
YOU'RE THROWING A GRENADE AT ME?!

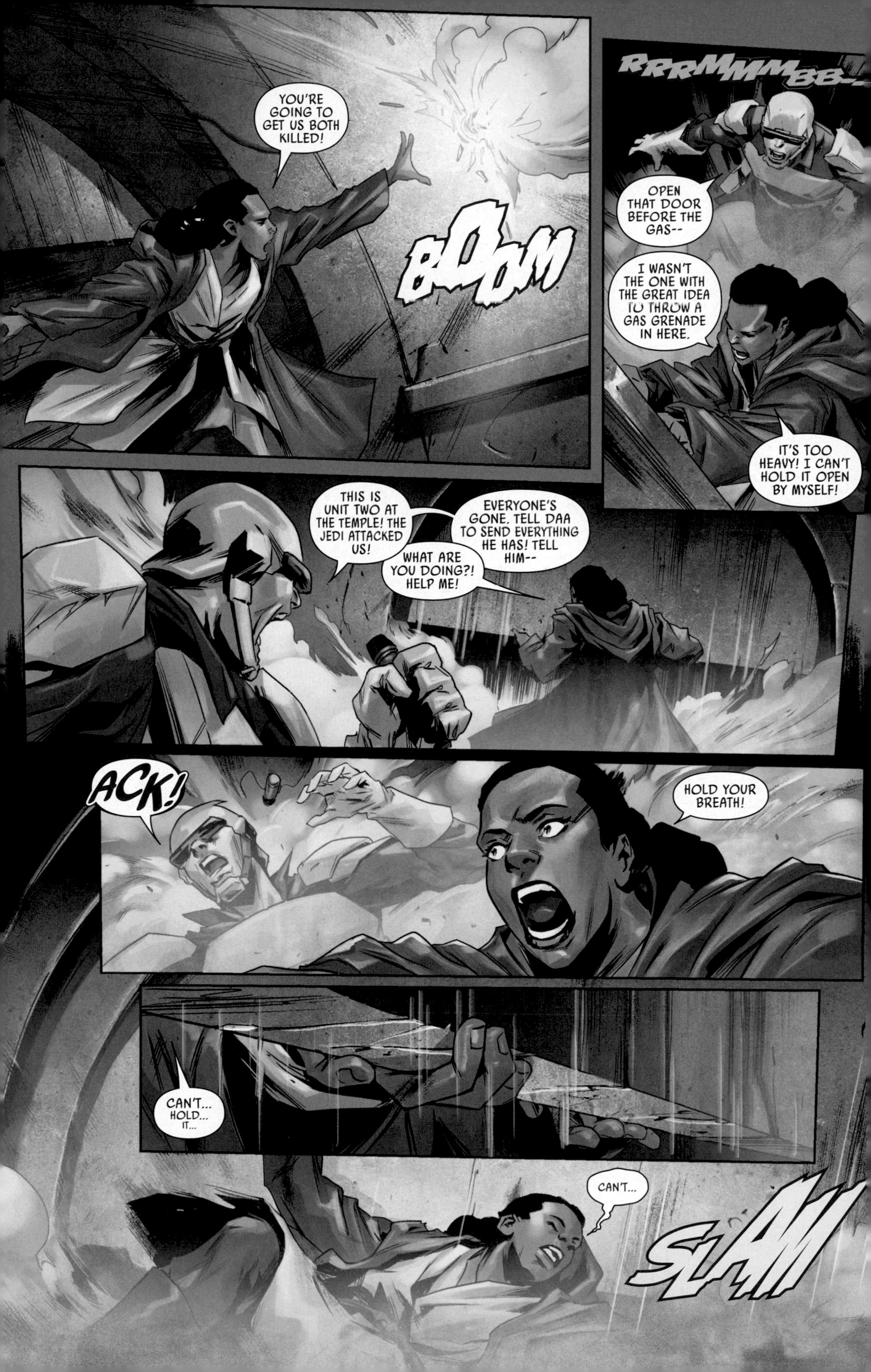
YOU'RE GOING TO GET US BOTH KILLED!
BOOM
RRRMMMMBB--
OPEN THAT DOOR BEFORE THE GAS--
I WASN'T THE ONE WITH THE GREAT IDEA TO THROW A GAS GRENADE IN HERE.
IT'S TOO HEAVY! I CAN'T HOLD IT OPEN BY MYSELF!
THIS IS UNIT TWO AT THE TEMPLE! THE JEDI ATTACKED US!
EVERYONE'S GONE. TELL DAA TO SEND EVERYTHING HE HAS! TELL HIM--
WHAT ARE YOU DOING?! HELP ME!
ACK!
HOLD YOUR BREATH!
CAN'T... HOLD... IT...
CAN'T...
SLAM

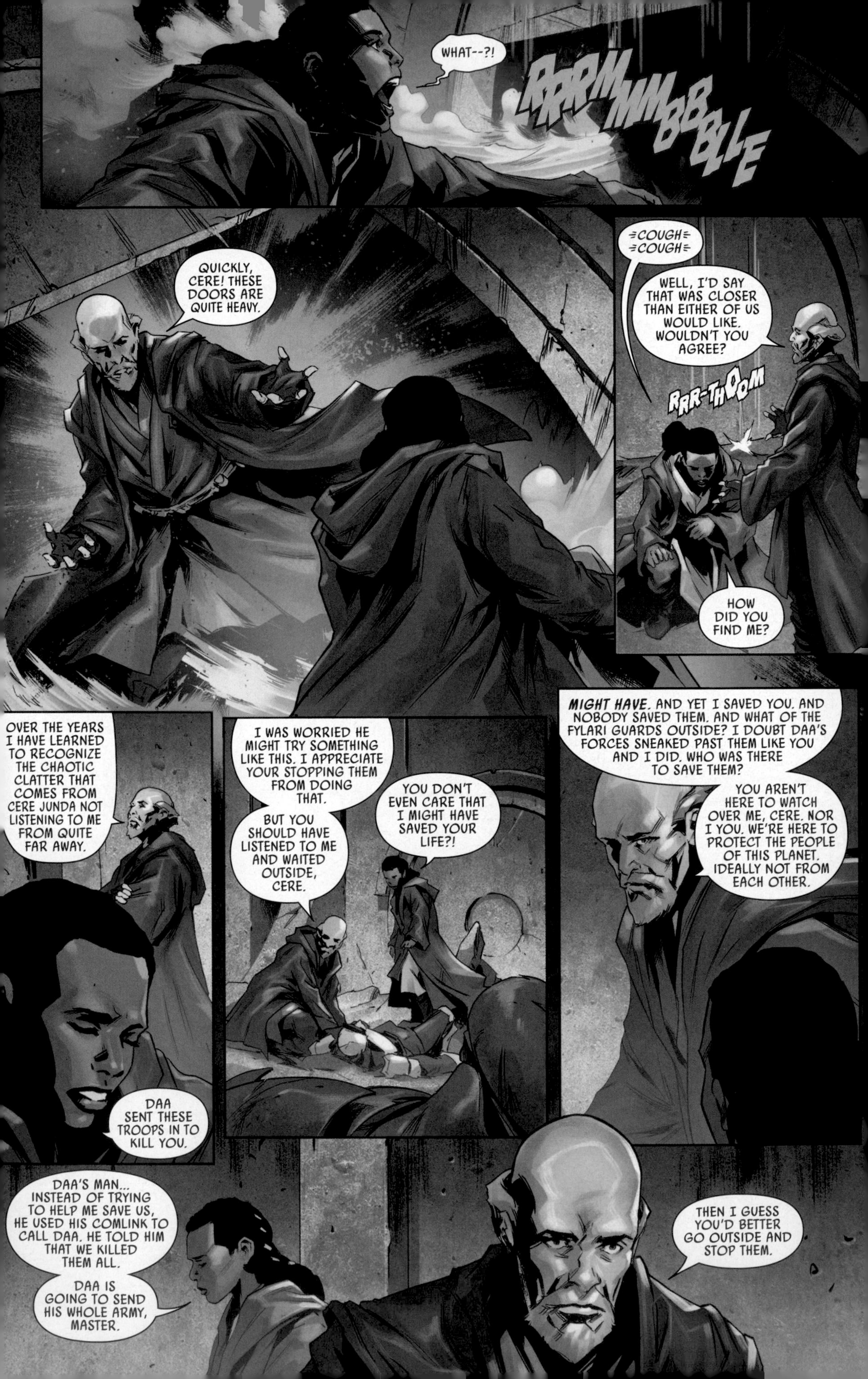
WHAT--?!
RRRMMMBBLLE
QUICKLY, CERE! THESE DOORS ARE QUITE HEAVY.
COUGH COUGH
WELL, I'D SAY THAT WAS CLOSER THAN EITHER OF US WOULD LIKE. WOULDN'T YOU AGREE?
RRR-THOOM
HOW DID YOU FIND ME?
OVER THE YEARS I HAVE LEARNED TO RECOGNIZE THE CHAOTIC CLATTER THAT COMES FROM CERE JUNDA NOT LISTENING TO ME FROM QUITE FAR AWAY.
DAA SENT THESE TROOPS IN TO KILL YOU.
I WAS WORRIED HE MIGHT TRY SOMETHING LIKE THIS. I APPRECIATE YOUR STOPPING THEM FROM DOING THAT.
BUT YOU SHOULD HAVE LISTENED TO ME AND WAITED OUTSIDE, CERE.
YOU DON'T EVEN CARE THAT I MIGHT HAVE SAVED YOUR LIFE?!
MIGHT HAVE. AND YET I SAVED YOU. AND NOBODY SAVED THEM. AND WHAT OF THE FYLARI GUARDS OUTSIDE? I DOUBT DAA'S FORCES SNEAKED PAST THEM LIKE YOU AND I DID. WHO WAS THERE TO SAVE THEM?
YOU AREN'T HERE TO WATCH OVER ME, CERE. NOR I YOU. WE'RE HERE TO PROTECT THE PEOPLE OF THIS PLANET. IDEALLY NOT FROM EACH OTHER.
DAA'S MAN... INSTEAD OF TRYING TO HELP ME SAVE US, HE USED HIS COMLINK TO CALL DAA. HE TOLD HIM THAT WE KILLED THEM ALL.
DAA IS GOING TO SEND HIS WHOLE ARMY, MASTER.
THEN I GUESS YOU'D BETTER GO OUTSIDE AND STOP THEM.

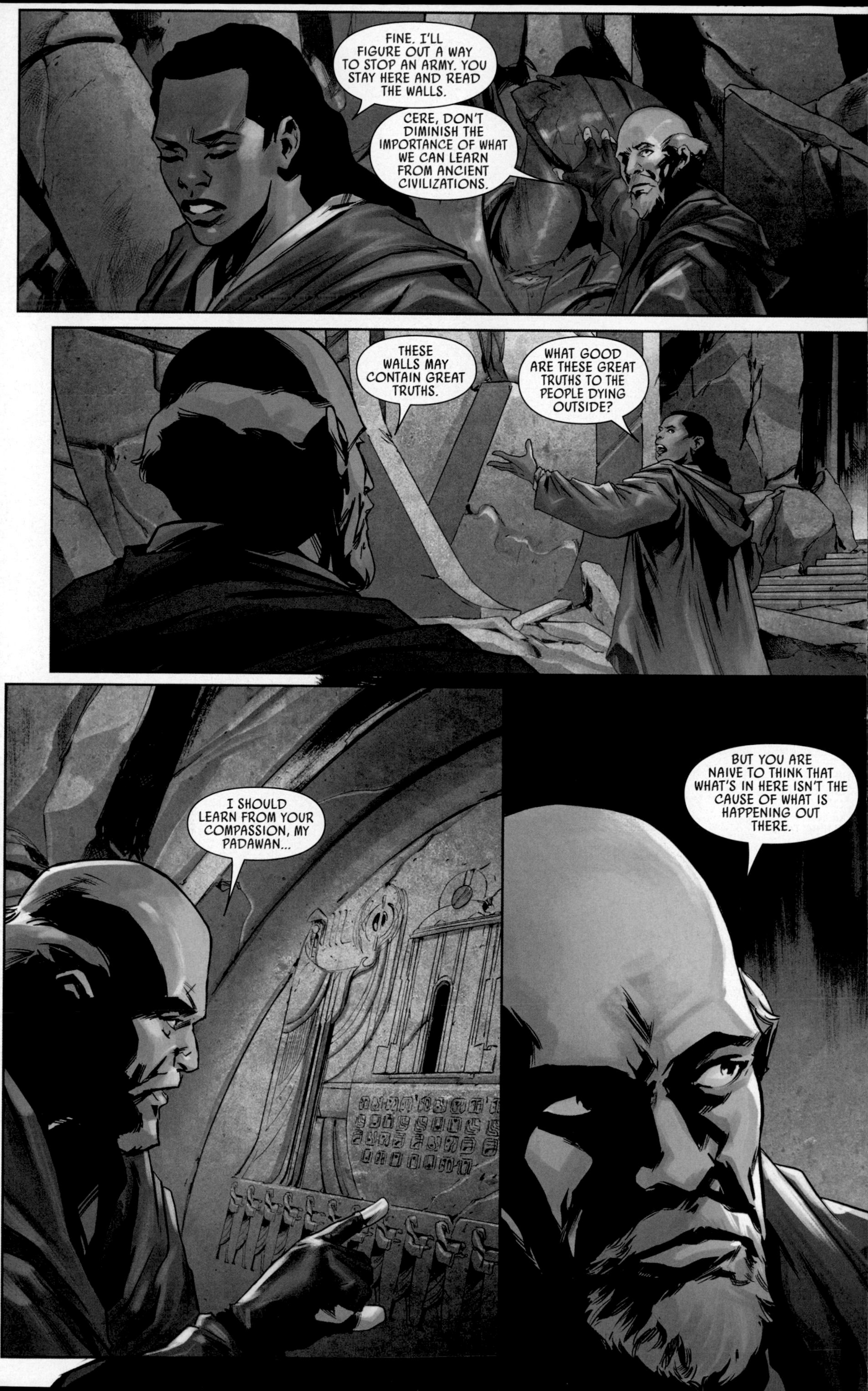
FINE. I'LL FIGURE OUT A WAY TO STOP AN ARMY. YOU STAY HERE AND READ THE WALLS.
CERE, DON'T DIMINISH THE IMPORTANCE OF WHAT WE CAN LEARN FROM ANCIENT CIVILIZATIONS.
THESE WALLS MAY CONTAIN GREAT TRUTHS.
WHAT GOOD ARE THESE GREAT TRUTHS TO THE PEOPLE DYING OUTSIDE?
I SHOULD LEARN FROM YOUR COMPASSION, MY PADAWAN...
BUT YOU ARE NAIVE TO THINK THAT WHAT'S IN HERE ISN'T THE CAUSE OF WHAT IS HAPPENING OUT THERE.

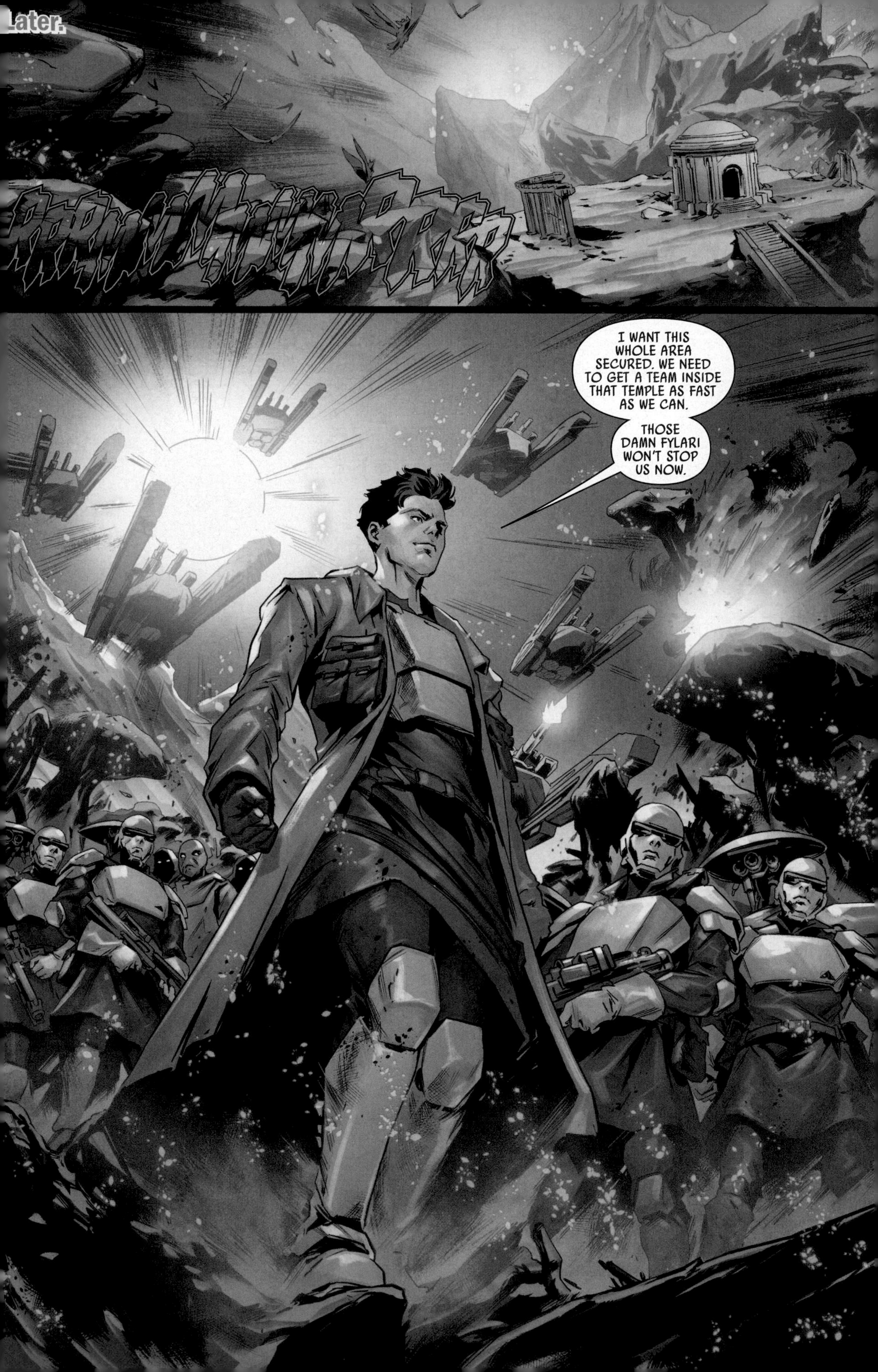
Later.
I WANT THIS WHOLE AREA SECURED. WE NEED TO GET A TEAM INSIDE THAT TEMPLE AS FAST AS WE CAN.
THOSE DAMN FYLARI WON'T STOP US NOW.

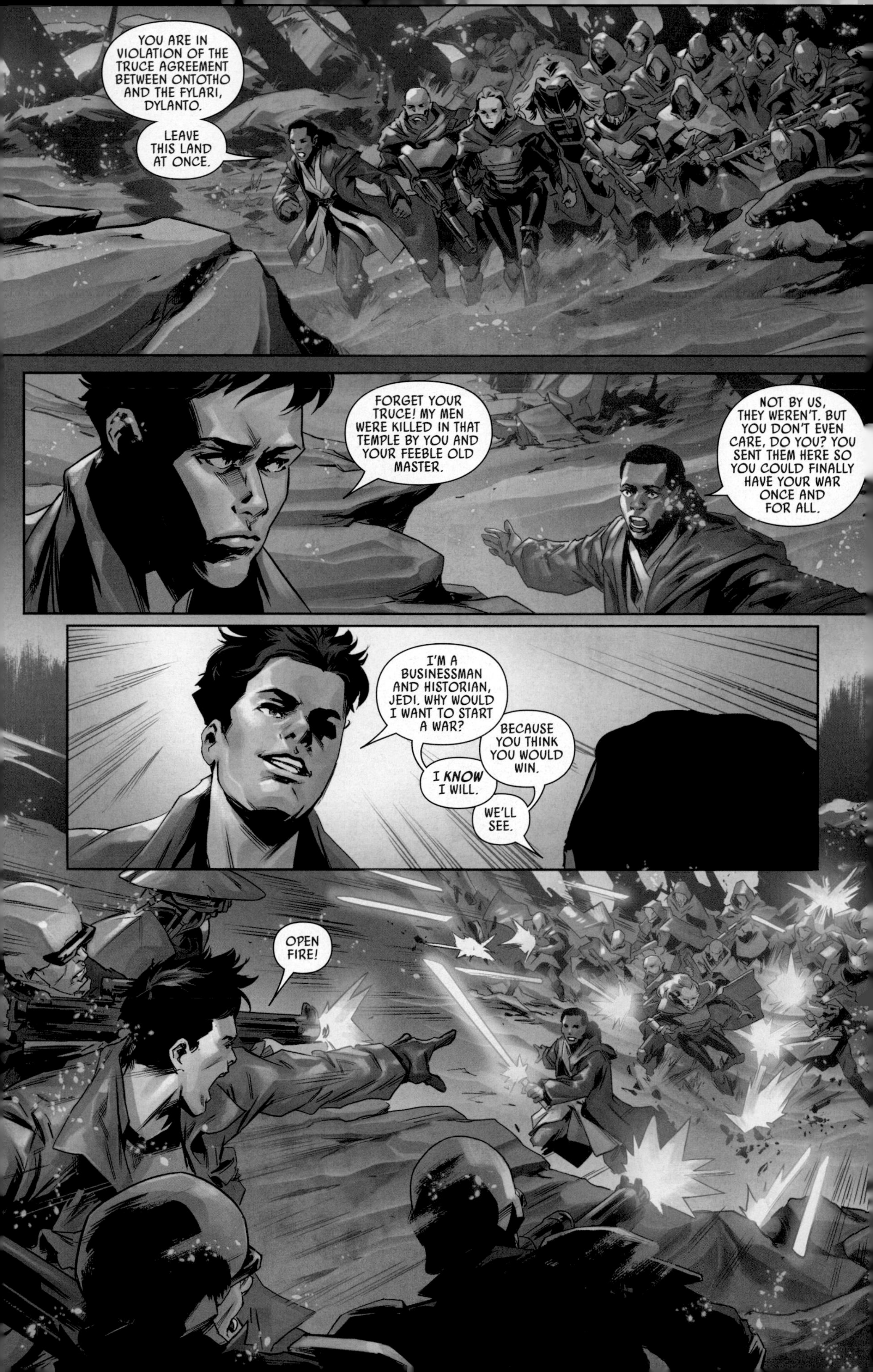
YOU ARE IN VIOLATION OF THE TRUCE AGREEMENT BETWEEN ONTOTHO AND THE FYLARI, DYLANTO.
LEAVE THIS LAND AT ONCE.
FORGET YOUR TRUCE! MY MEN WERE KILLED IN THAT TEMPLE BY YOU AND YOUR FEEBLE OLD MASTER.
NOT BY US, THEY WEREN'T. BUT YOU DON'T EVEN CARE, DO YOU? YOU SENT THEM HERE SO YOU COULD FINALLY HAVE YOUR WAR ONCE AND FOR ALL.
I'M A BUSINESSMAN AND HISTORIAN, JEDI. WHY WOULD I WANT TO START A WAR?
BECAUSE YOU THINK YOU WOULD WIN.
I ***KNOW*** I WILL.
WE'LL SEE.
OPEN FIRE!

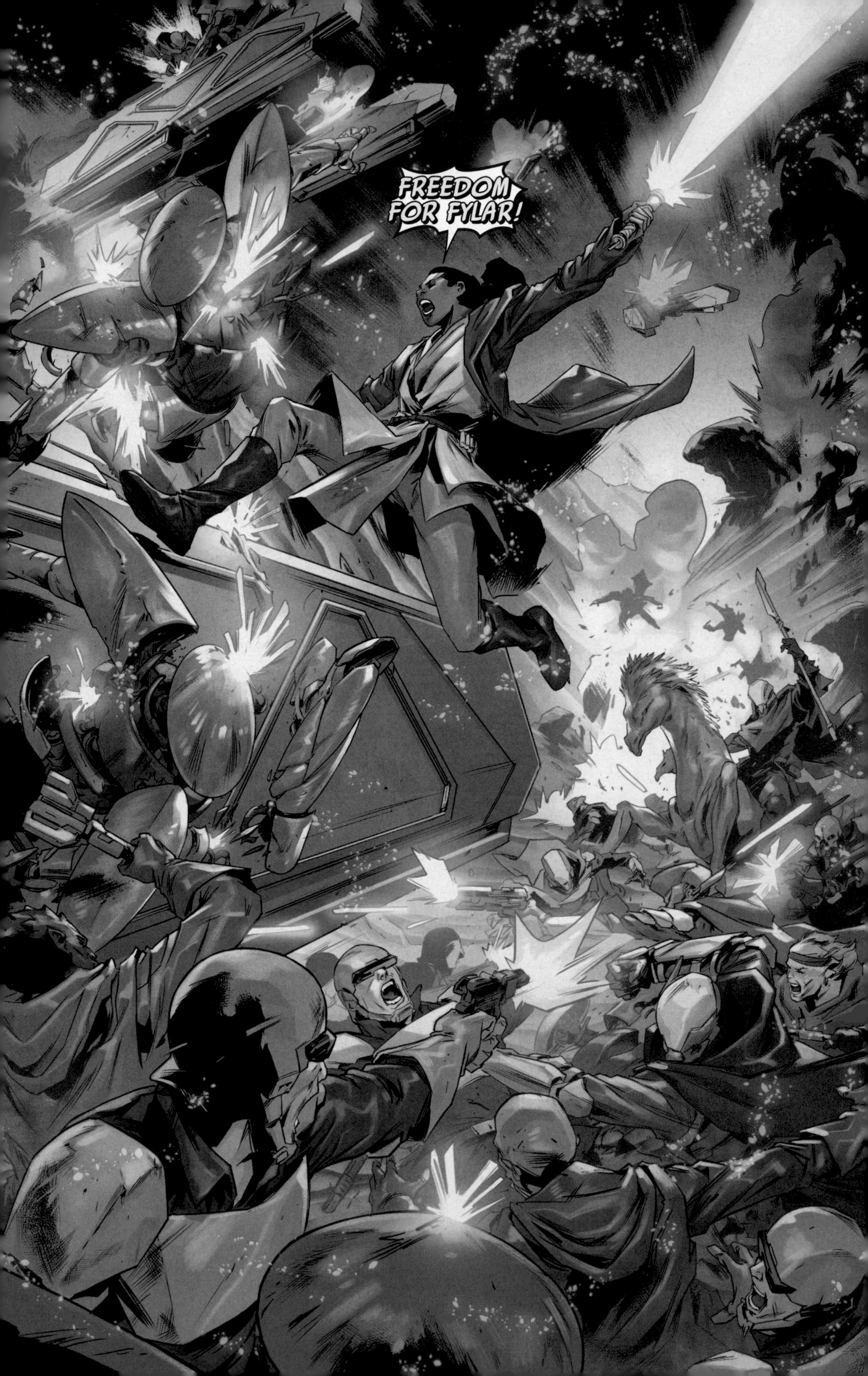
FREEDOM FOR FYLAR!

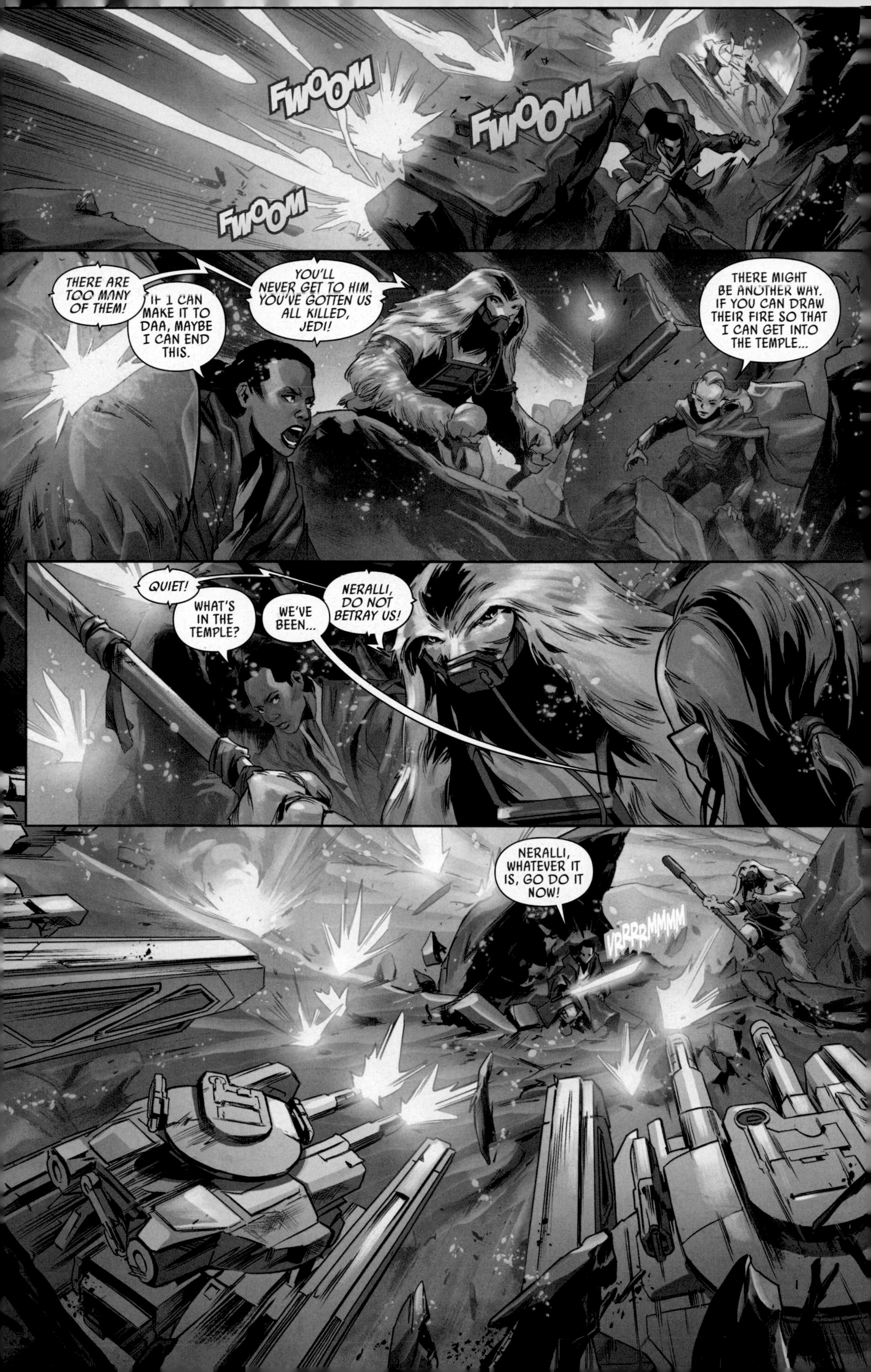
FWOOM
FWOOM
FWOOM
THERE ARE TOO MANY OF THEM!
IF I CAN MAKE IT TO DAA, MAYBE I CAN END THIS.
YOU'LL NEVER GET TO HIM. YOU'VE GOTTEN US ALL KILLED, JEDI!
THERE MIGHT BE ANOTHER WAY. IF YOU CAN DRAW THEIR FIRE SO THAT I CAN GET INTO THE TEMPLE...
QUIET!
WHAT'S IN THE TEMPLE?
WE'VE BEEN...
NERALLI, DO NOT BETRAY US!
NERALLI, WHATEVER IT IS, GO DO IT NOW!
VRRRRMMMM

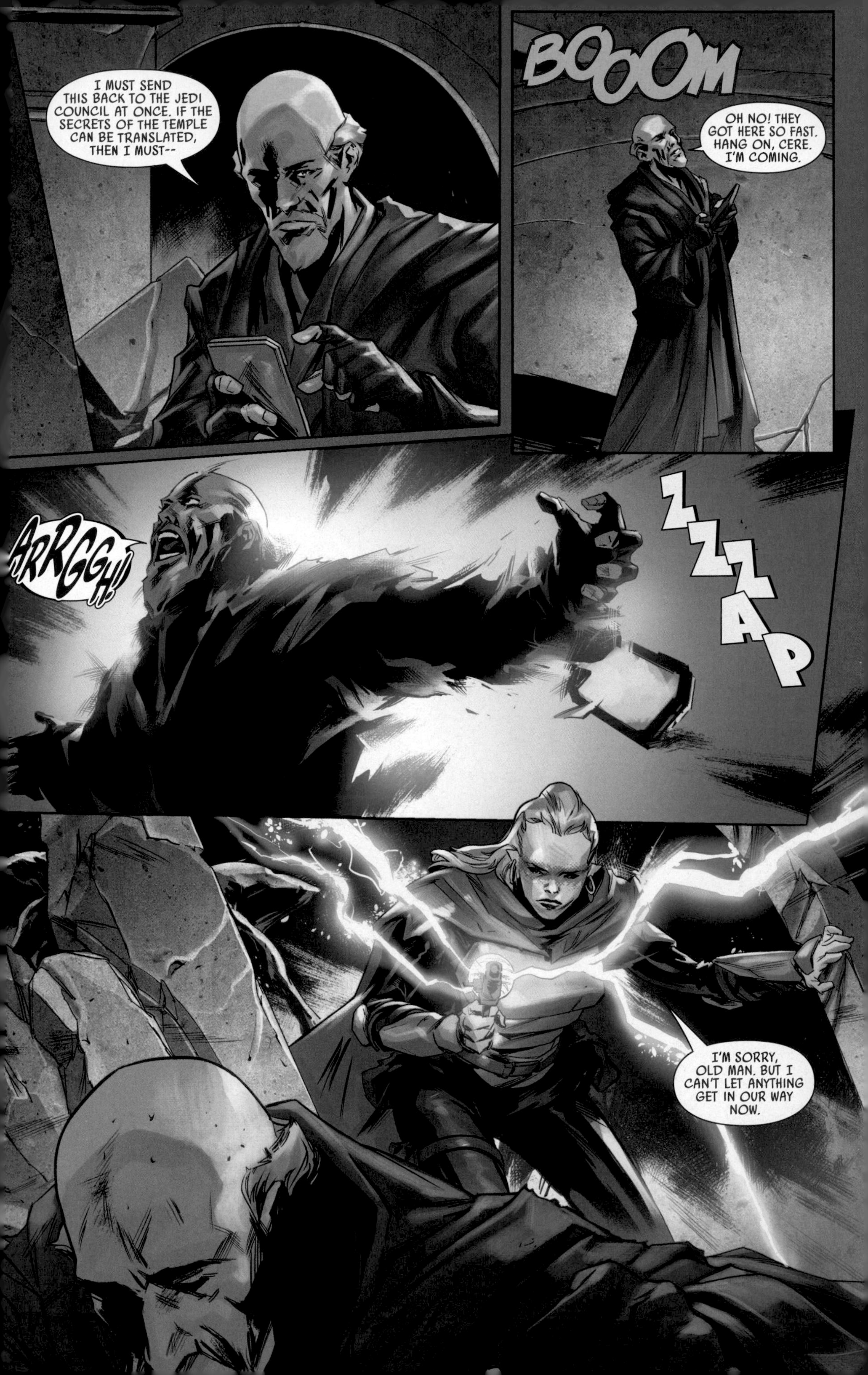
I MUST SEND THIS BACK TO THE JEDI COUNCIL AT ONCE. IF THE SECRETS OF THE TEMPLE CAN BE TRANSLATED, THEN I MUST--
BOOOOM
OH NO! THEY GOT HERE SO FAST. HANG ON, CERE. I'M COMING.
ARRGGH!
ZZZZAP
I'M SORRY, OLD MAN. BUT I CAN'T LET ANYTHING GET IN OUR WAY NOW.

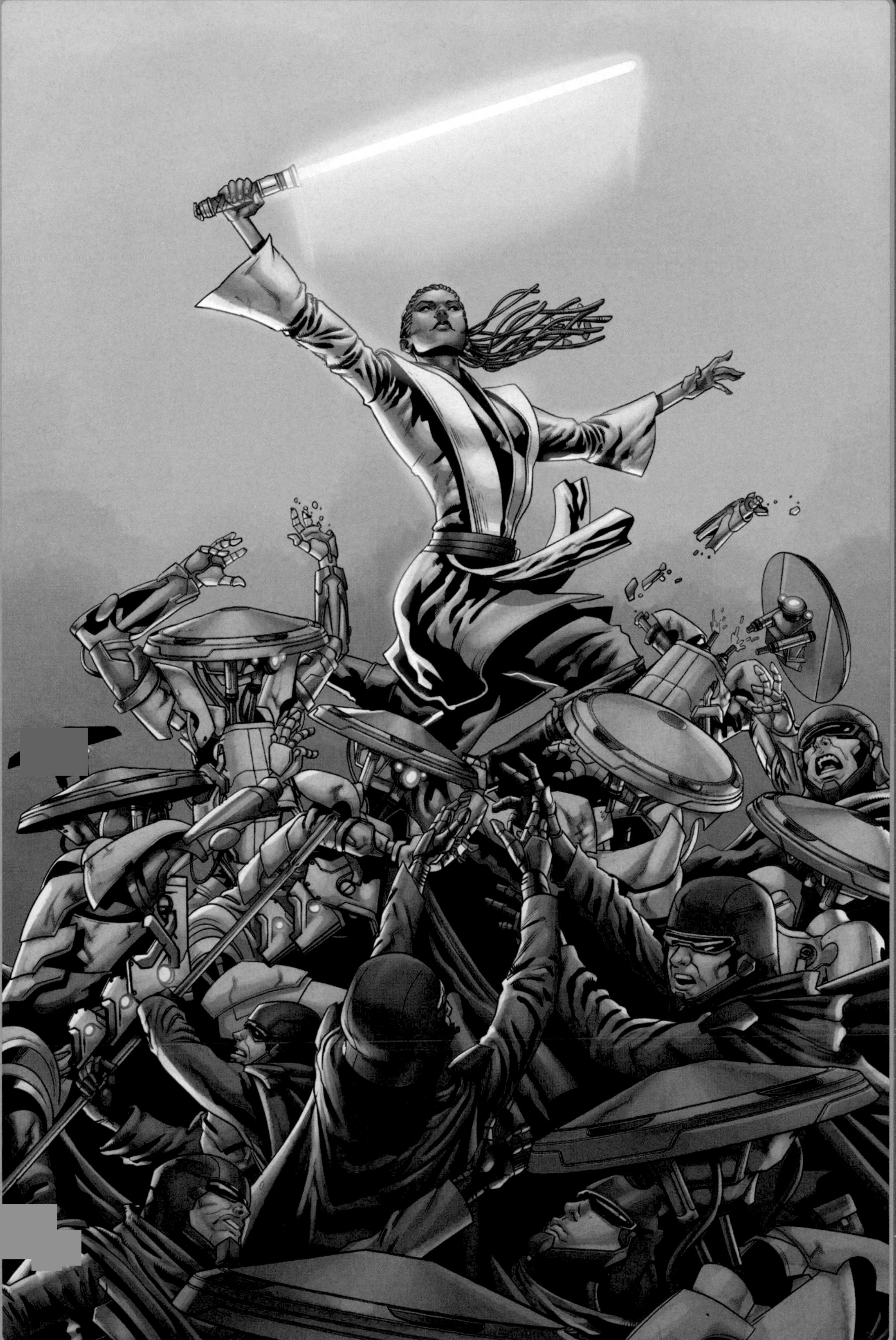

5 – THE COLLAPSE OF ALL THINGS

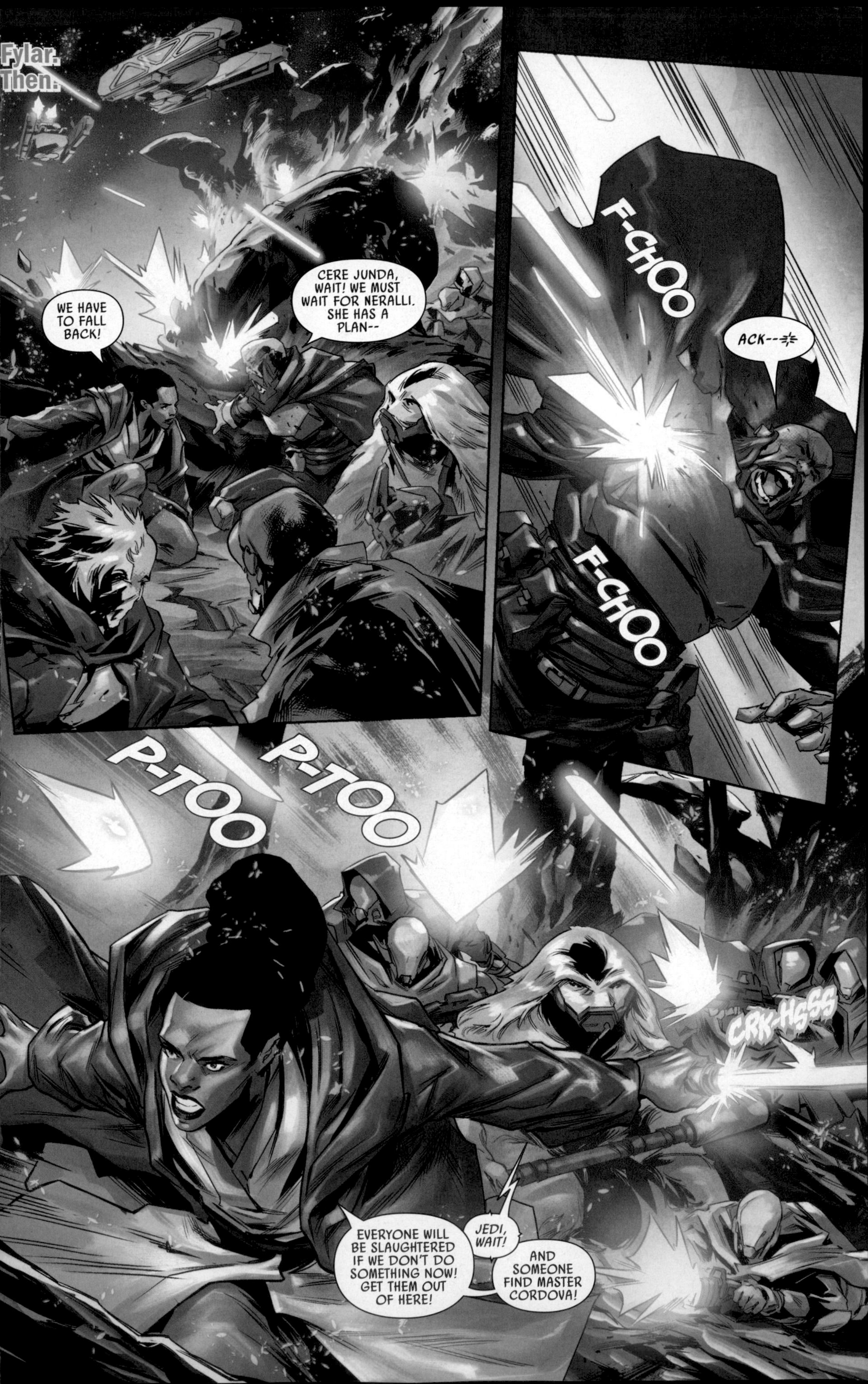
Fylar.
Then.
WE HAVE TO FALL BACK!
CERE JUNDA, WAIT! WE MUST WAIT FOR NERALLI. SHE HAS A PLAN--
F-CHOO
ACK--
F-CHOO
P-TOO
P-TOO
CRK-HSSS
EVERYONE WILL BE SLAUGHTERED IF WE DON'T DO SOMETHING NOW! GET THEM OUT OF HERE!
JEDI, WAIT!
AND SOMEONE FIND MASTER CORDOVA!

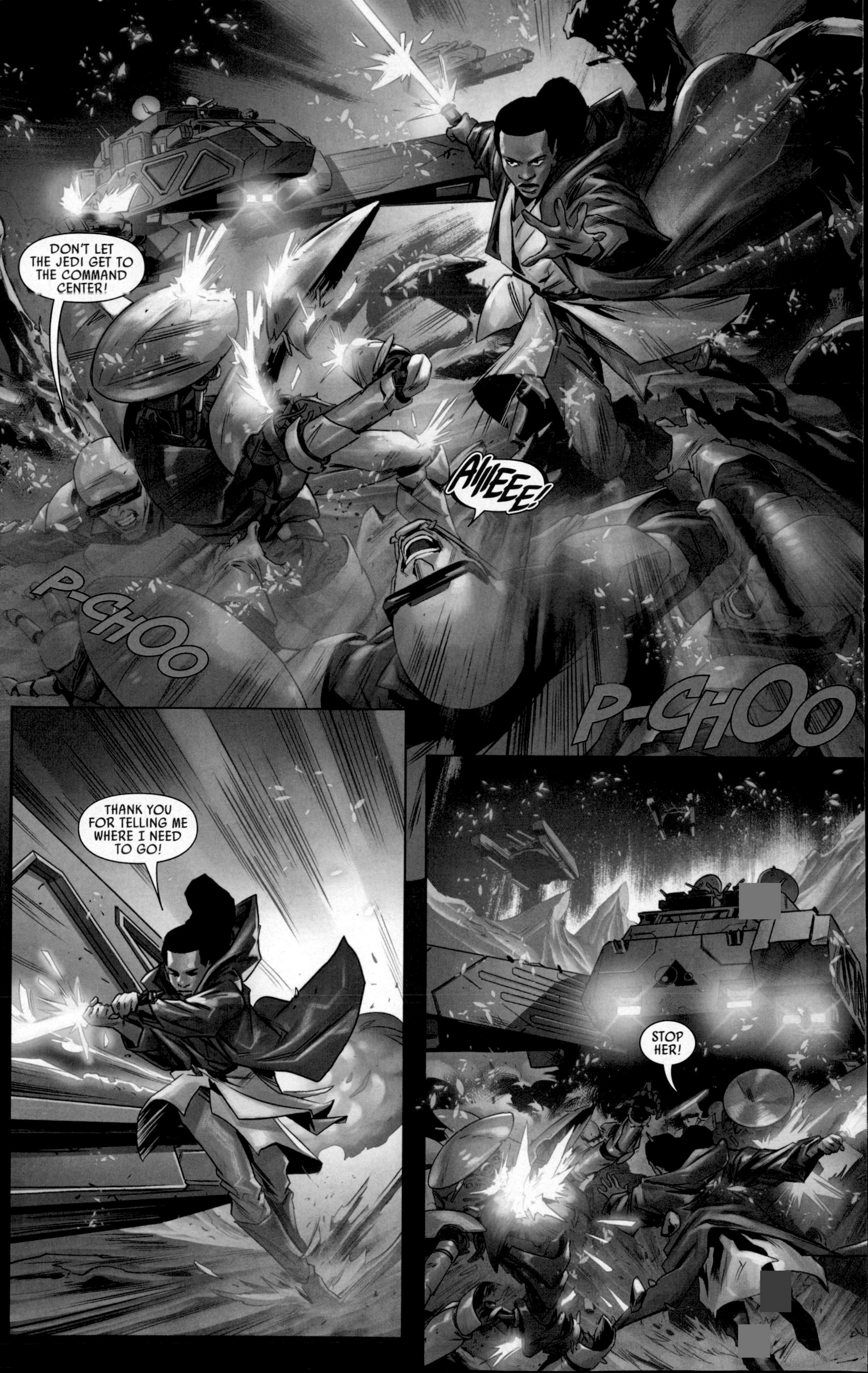
DON'T LET THE JEDI GET TO THE COMMAND CENTER!
AIIEEE!
P-CHOO
P-CHOO
THANK YOU FOR TELLING ME WHERE I NEED TO GO!
STOP HER!

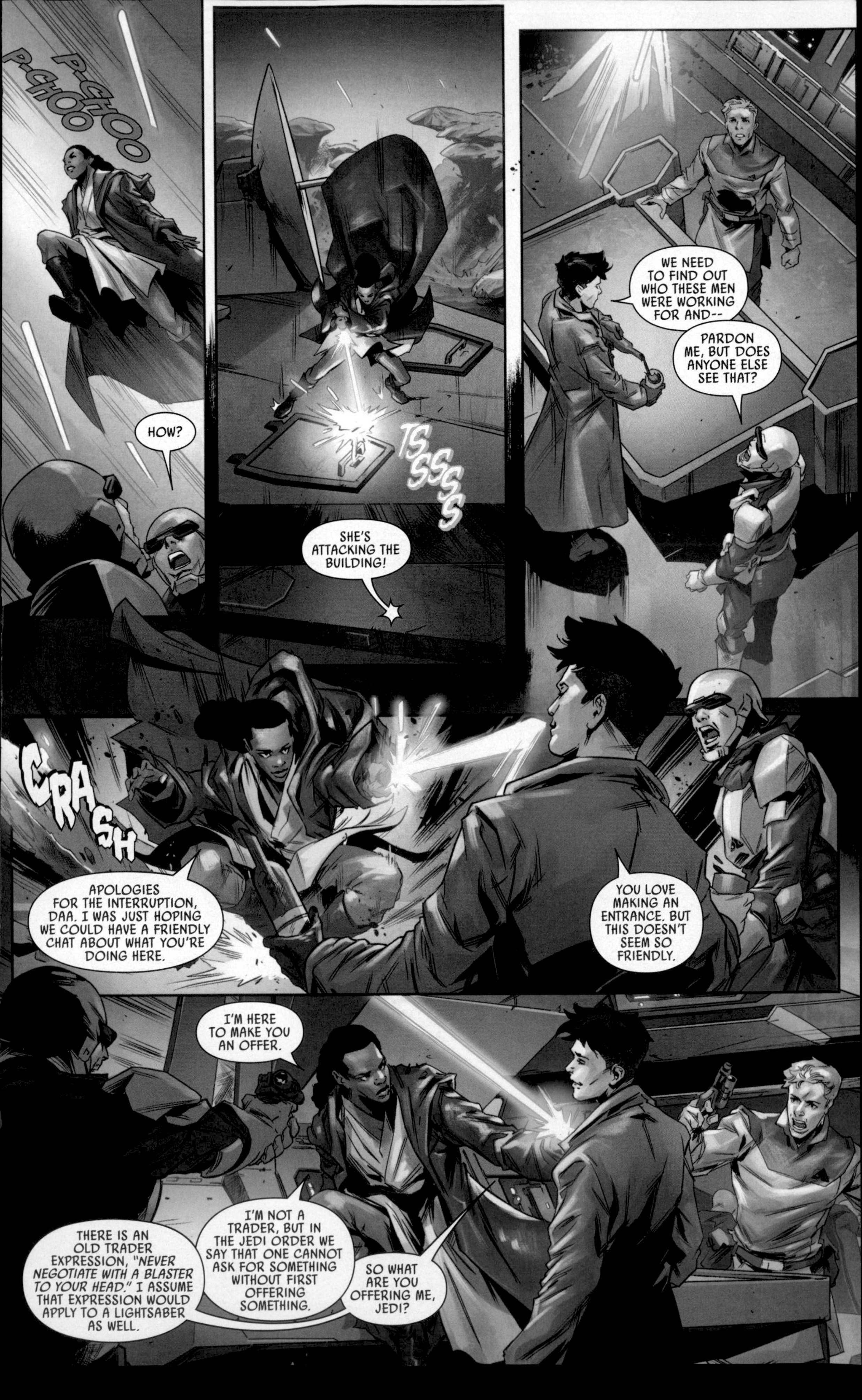
P-CHOO P-CHOO
HOW?
TSSSSS
SHE'S ATTACKING THE BUILDING!
WE NEED TO FIND OUT WHO THESE MEN WERE WORKING FOR AND--
PARDON ME, BUT DOES ANYONE ELSE SEE THAT?
CRASH
APOLOGIES FOR THE INTERRUPTION, DAA. I WAS JUST HOPING WE COULD HAVE A FRIENDLY CHAT ABOUT WHAT YOU'RE DOING HERE.
YOU LOVE MAKING AN ENTRANCE. BUT THIS DOESN'T SEEM SO FRIENDLY.
I'M HERE TO MAKE YOU AN OFFER.
SO WHAT ARE YOU OFFERING ME, JEDI?
I'M NOT A TRADER, BUT IN THE JEDI ORDER WE SAY THAT ONE CANNOT ASK FOR SOMETHING WITHOUT FIRST OFFERING SOMETHING.
THERE IS AN OLD TRADER EXPRESSION, "NEVER NEGOTIATE WITH A BLASTER TO YOUR HEAD." I ASSUME THAT EXPRESSION WOULD APPLY TO A LIGHTSABER AS WELL.

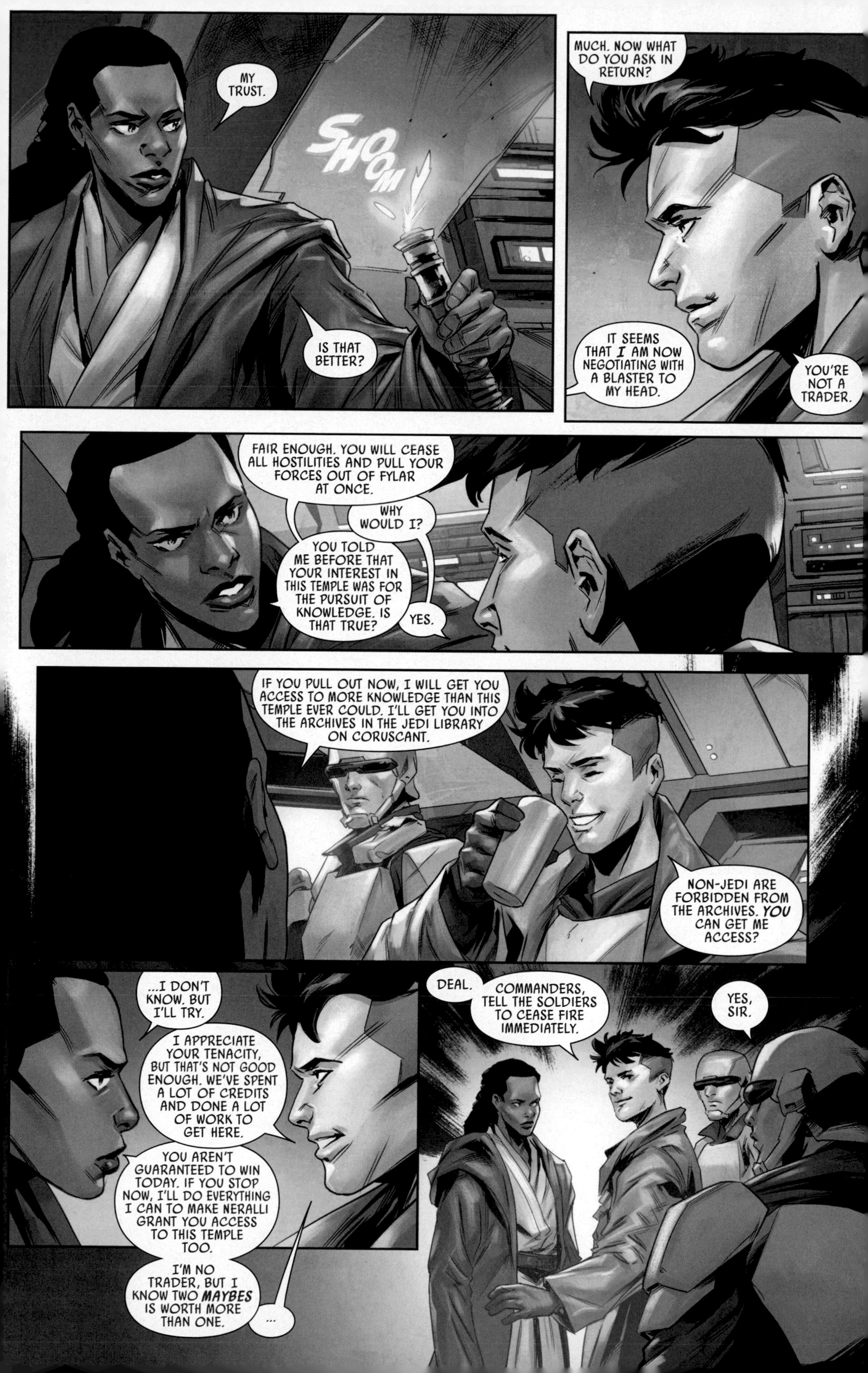
MY TRUST.
SHOOM
IS THAT BETTER?
MUCH. NOW WHAT DO YOU ASK IN RETURN?
IT SEEMS THAT *I* AM NOW NEGOTIATING WITH A BLASTER TO MY HEAD.
YOU'RE NOT A TRADER.
FAIR ENOUGH. YOU WILL CEASE ALL HOSTILITIES AND PULL YOUR FORCES OUT OF FYLAR AT ONCE.
WHY WOULD I?
YOU TOLD ME BEFORE THAT YOUR INTEREST IN THIS TEMPLE WAS FOR THE PURSUIT OF KNOWLEDGE. IS THAT TRUE?
YES.
IF YOU PULL OUT NOW, I WILL GET YOU ACCESS TO MORE KNOWLEDGE THAN THIS TEMPLE EVER COULD. I'LL GET YOU INTO THE ARCHIVES IN THE JEDI LIBRARY ON CORUSCANT.
NON-JEDI ARE FORBIDDEN FROM THE ARCHIVES. *YOU* CAN GET ME ACCESS?
...I DON'T KNOW. BUT I'LL TRY.
I APPRECIATE YOUR TENACITY, BUT THAT'S NOT GOOD ENOUGH. WE'VE SPENT A LOT OF CREDITS AND DONE A LOT OF WORK TO GET HERE.
YOU AREN'T GUARANTEED TO WIN TODAY. IF YOU STOP NOW, I'LL DO EVERYTHING I CAN TO MAKE NERALLI GRANT YOU ACCESS TO THIS TEMPLE TOO.
I'M NO TRADER, BUT I KNOW TWO ***MAYBES*** IS WORTH MORE THAN ONE.
...
DEAL.
COMMANDERS, TELL THE SOLDIERS TO CEASE FIRE IMMEDIATELY.
YES, SIR.

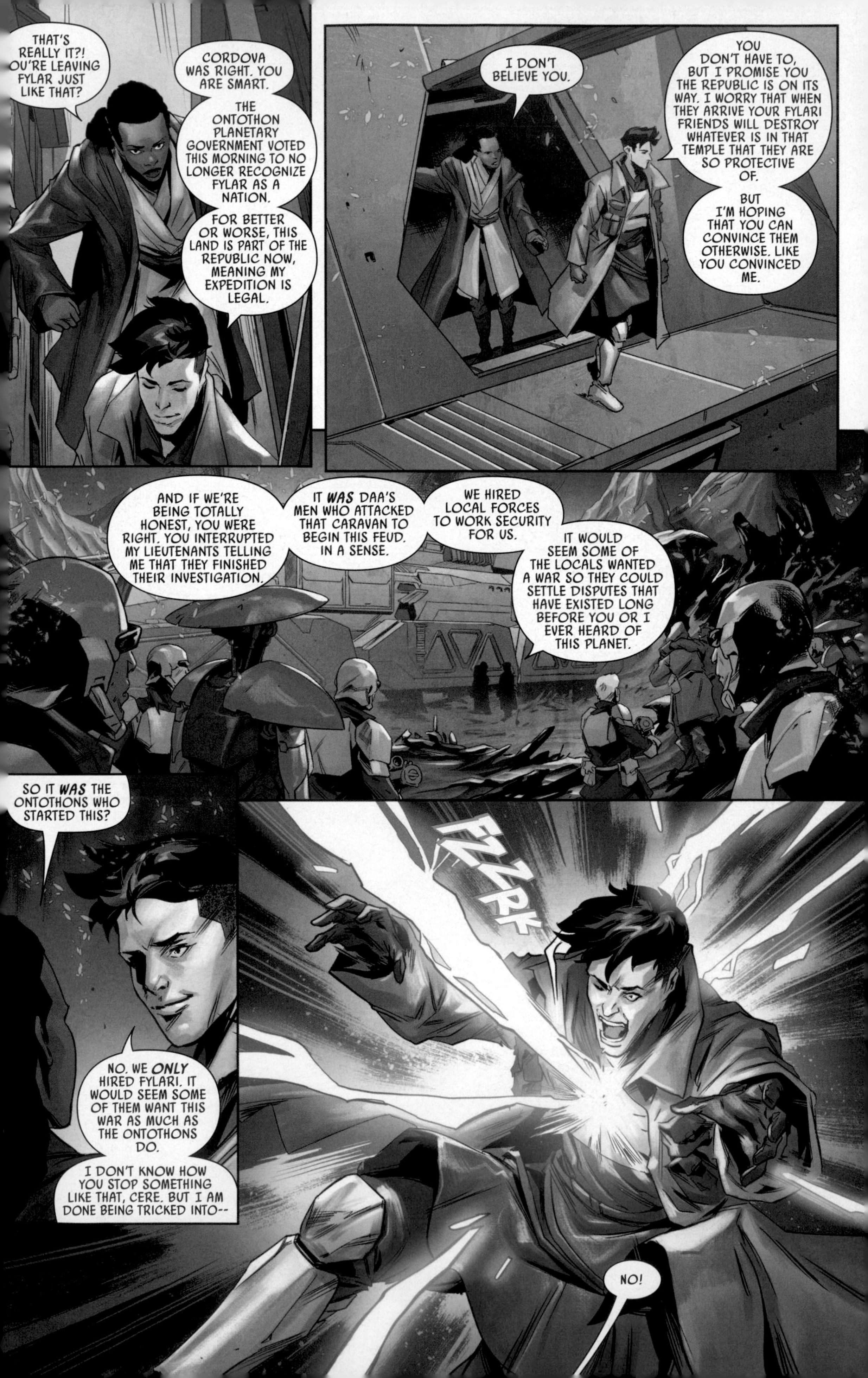
THAT'S REALLY IT?! OU'RE LEAVING FYLAR JUST LIKE THAT?
CORDOVA WAS RIGHT. YOU ARE SMART.
THE ONTOTHON PLANETARY GOVERNMENT VOTED THIS MORNING TO NO LONGER RECOGNIZE FYLAR AS A NATION.
FOR BETTER OR WORSE, THIS LAND IS PART OF THE REPUBLIC NOW, MEANING MY EXPEDITION IS LEGAL.
I DON'T BELIEVE YOU.
YOU DON'T HAVE TO, BUT I PROMISE YOU THE REPUBLIC IS ON ITS WAY. I WORRY THAT WHEN THEY ARRIVE YOUR FYLARI FRIENDS WILL DESTROY WHATEVER IS IN THAT TEMPLE THAT THEY ARE SO PROTECTIVE OF.
BUT I'M HOPING THAT YOU CAN CONVINCE THEM OTHERWISE. LIKE YOU CONVINCED ME.
AND IF WE'RE BEING TOTALLY HONEST, YOU WERE RIGHT. YOU INTERRUPTED MY LIEUTENANTS TELLING ME THAT THEY FINISHED THEIR INVESTIGATION.
IT WAS DAA'S MEN WHO ATTACKED THAT CARAVAN TO BEGIN THIS FEUD. IN A SENSE.
WE HIRED LOCAL FORCES TO WORK SECURITY FOR US.
IT WOULD SEEM SOME OF THE LOCALS WANTED A WAR SO THEY COULD SETTLE DISPUTES THAT HAVE EXISTED LONG BEFORE YOU OR I EVER HEARD OF THIS PLANET.
SO IT WAS THE ONTOTHONS WHO STARTED THIS?
NO. WE ONLY HIRED FYLARI. IT WOULD SEEM SOME OF THEM WANT THIS WAR AS MUCH AS THE ONTOTHONS DO.
I DON'T KNOW HOW YOU STOP SOMETHING LIKE THAT, CERE. BUT I AM DONE BEING TRICKED INTO--
FZZRK
NO!

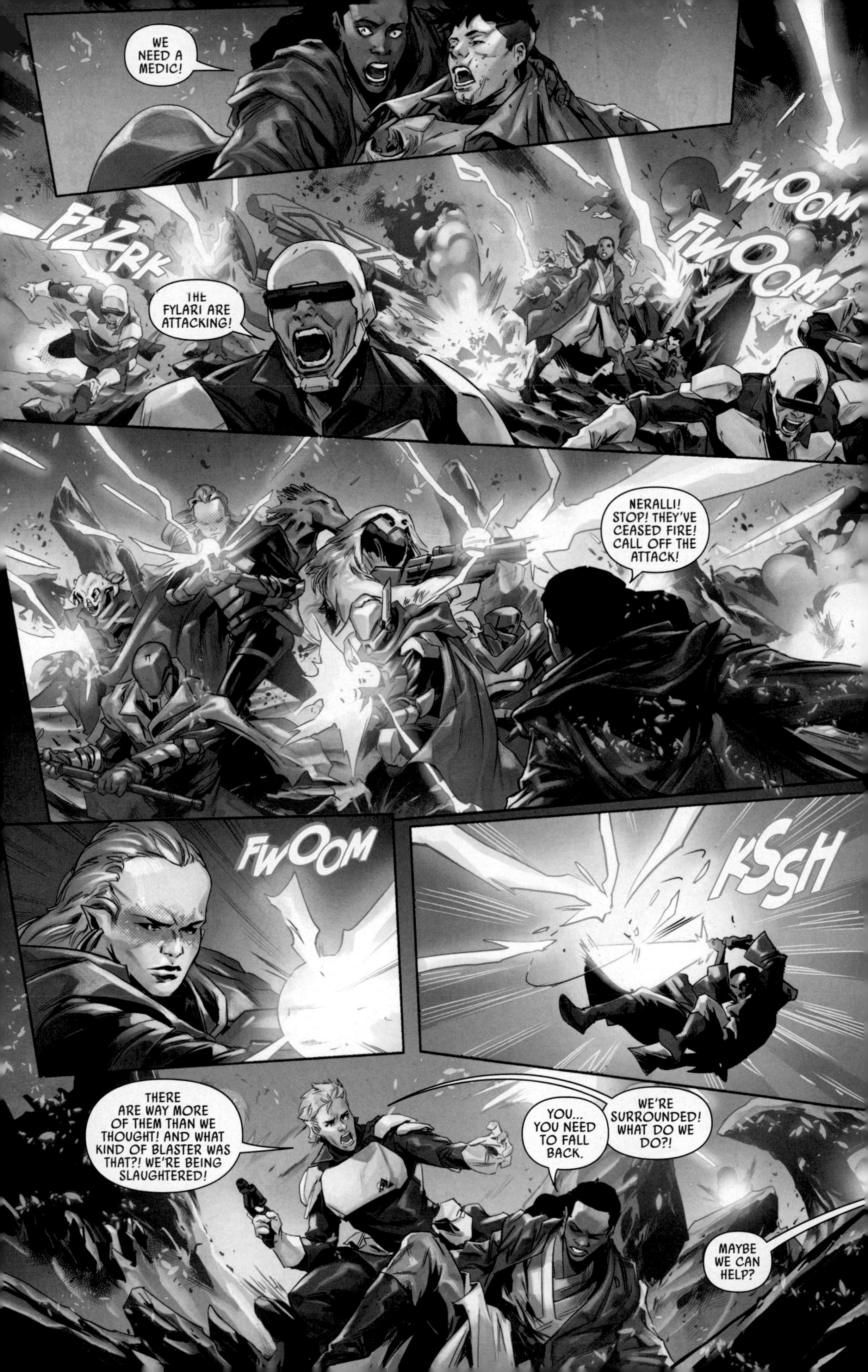

WE NEED A MEDIC!
FWOOM
FWOOM
FZZRK
THE FYLARI ARE ATTACKING!
NERALLI! STOP! THEY'VE CEASED FIRE! CALL OFF THE ATTACK!
FWOOM
KSSH
THERE ARE WAY MORE OF THEM THAN WE THOUGHT! AND WHAT KIND OF BLASTER WAS THAT?! WE'RE BEING SLAUGHTERED!
WE'RE SURROUNDED! WHAT DO WE DO?!
YOU... YOU NEED TO FALL BACK.
MAYBE WE CAN HELP?

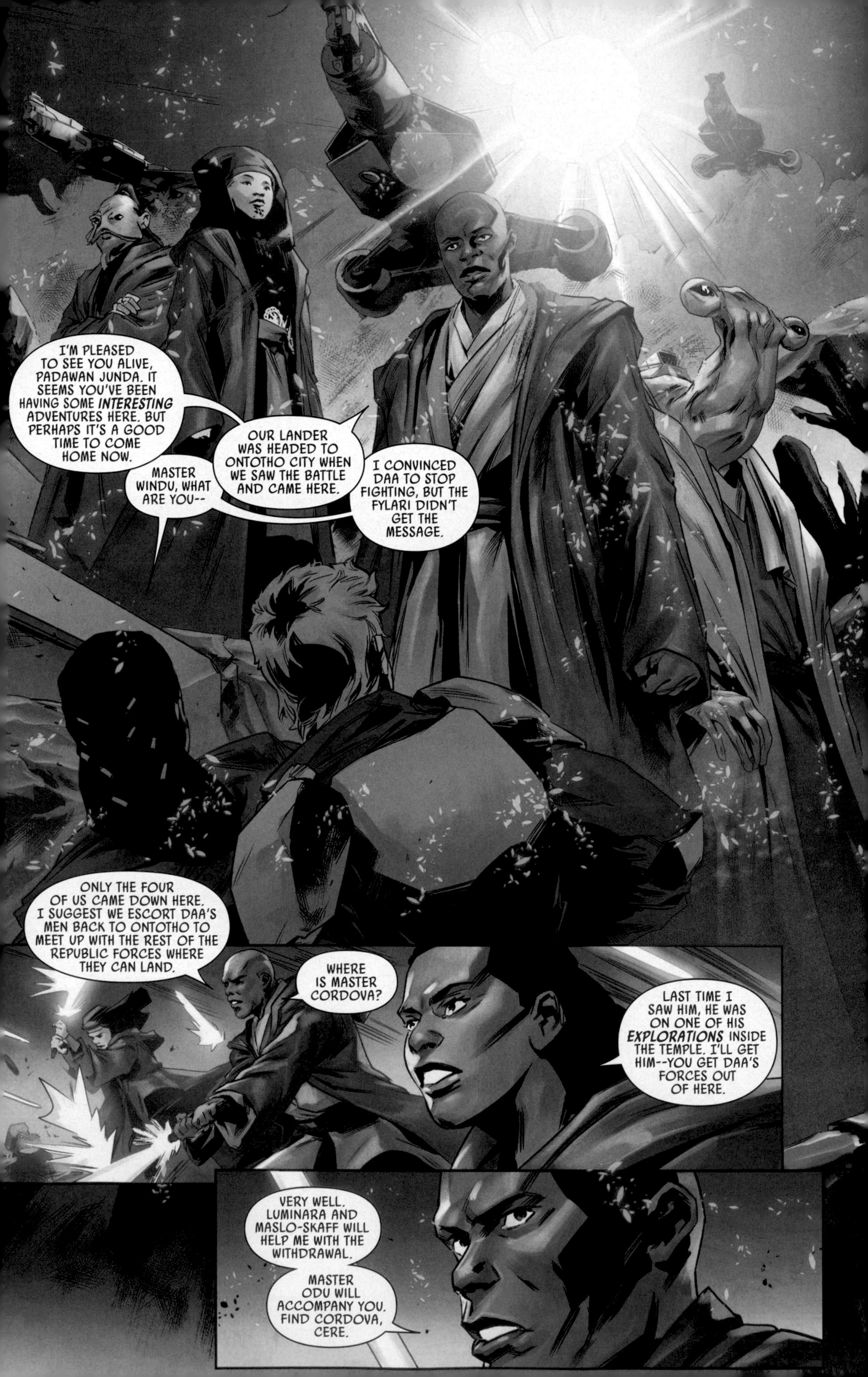
I'M PLEASED TO SEE YOU ALIVE, PADAWAN JUNDA. IT SEEMS YOU'VE BEEN HAVING SOME *INTERESTING* ADVENTURES HERE. BUT PERHAPS IT'S A GOOD TIME TO COME HOME NOW.
MASTER WINDU, WHAT ARE YOU--
OUR LANDER WAS HEADED TO ONTOTHO CITY WHEN WE SAW THE BATTLE AND CAME HERE.
I CONVINCED DAA TO STOP FIGHTING, BUT THE FYLARI DIDN'T GET THE MESSAGE.
ONLY THE FOUR OF US CAME DOWN HERE. I SUGGEST WE ESCORT DAA'S MEN BACK TO ONTOTHO TO MEET UP WITH THE REST OF THE REPUBLIC FORCES WHERE THEY CAN LAND.
WHERE IS MASTER CORDOVA?
LAST TIME I SAW HIM, HE WAS ON ONE OF HIS *EXPLORATIONS* INSIDE THE TEMPLE. I'LL GET HIM--YOU GET DAA'S FORCES OUT OF HERE.
VERY WELL. LUMINARA AND MASLO-SKAFF WILL HELP ME WITH THE WITHDRAWAL.
MASTER ODU WILL ACCOMPANY YOU. FIND CORDOVA, CERE.

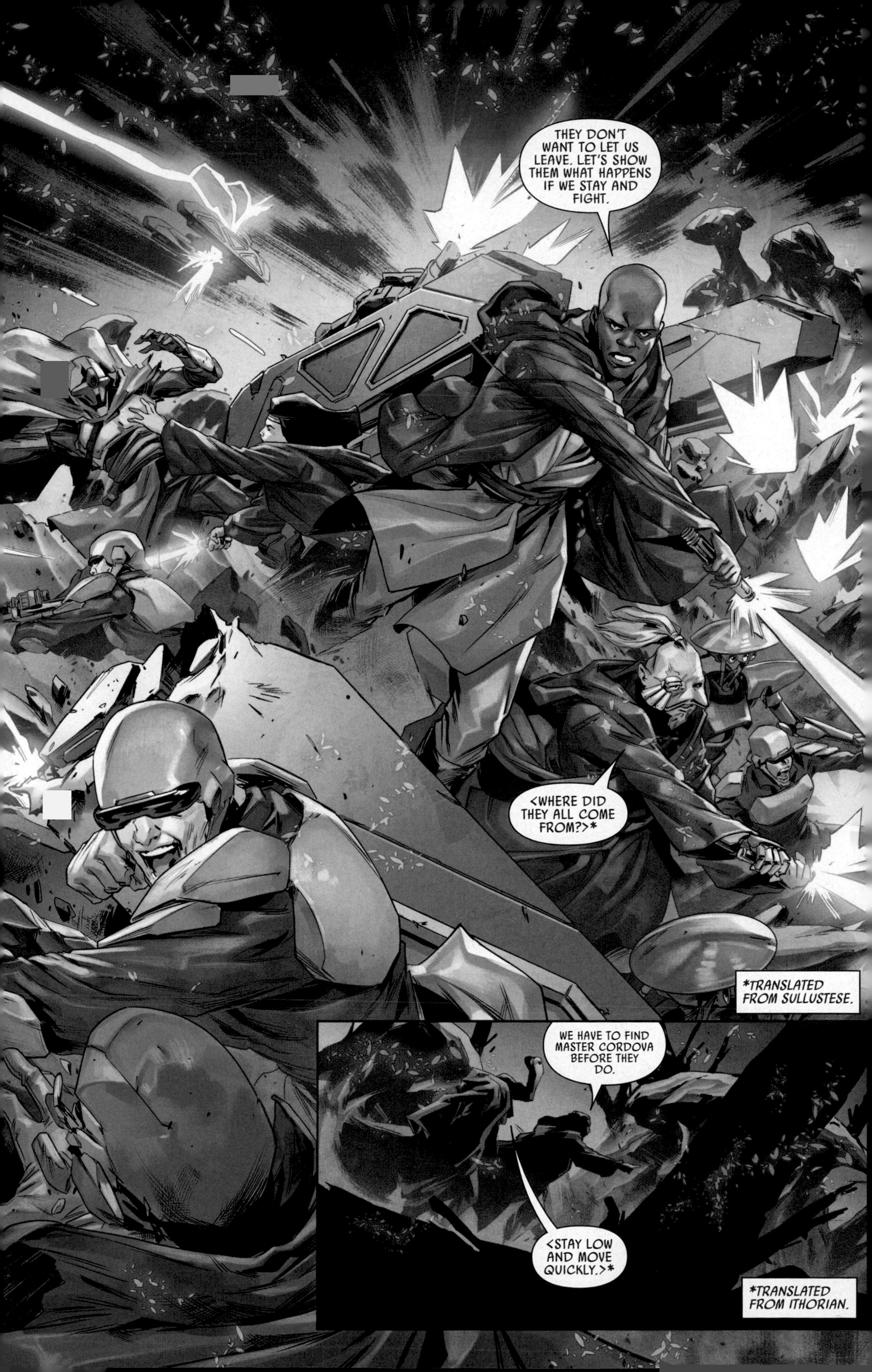
THEY DON'T WANT TO LET US LEAVE. LET'S SHOW THEM WHAT HAPPENS IF WE STAY AND FIGHT.
<WHERE DID THEY ALL COME FROM?>*
*TRANSLATED FROM SULLUSTESE.
WE HAVE TO FIND MASTER CORDOVA BEFORE THEY DO.
<STAY LOW AND MOVE QUICKLY.>*
*TRANSLATED FROM ITHORIAN.

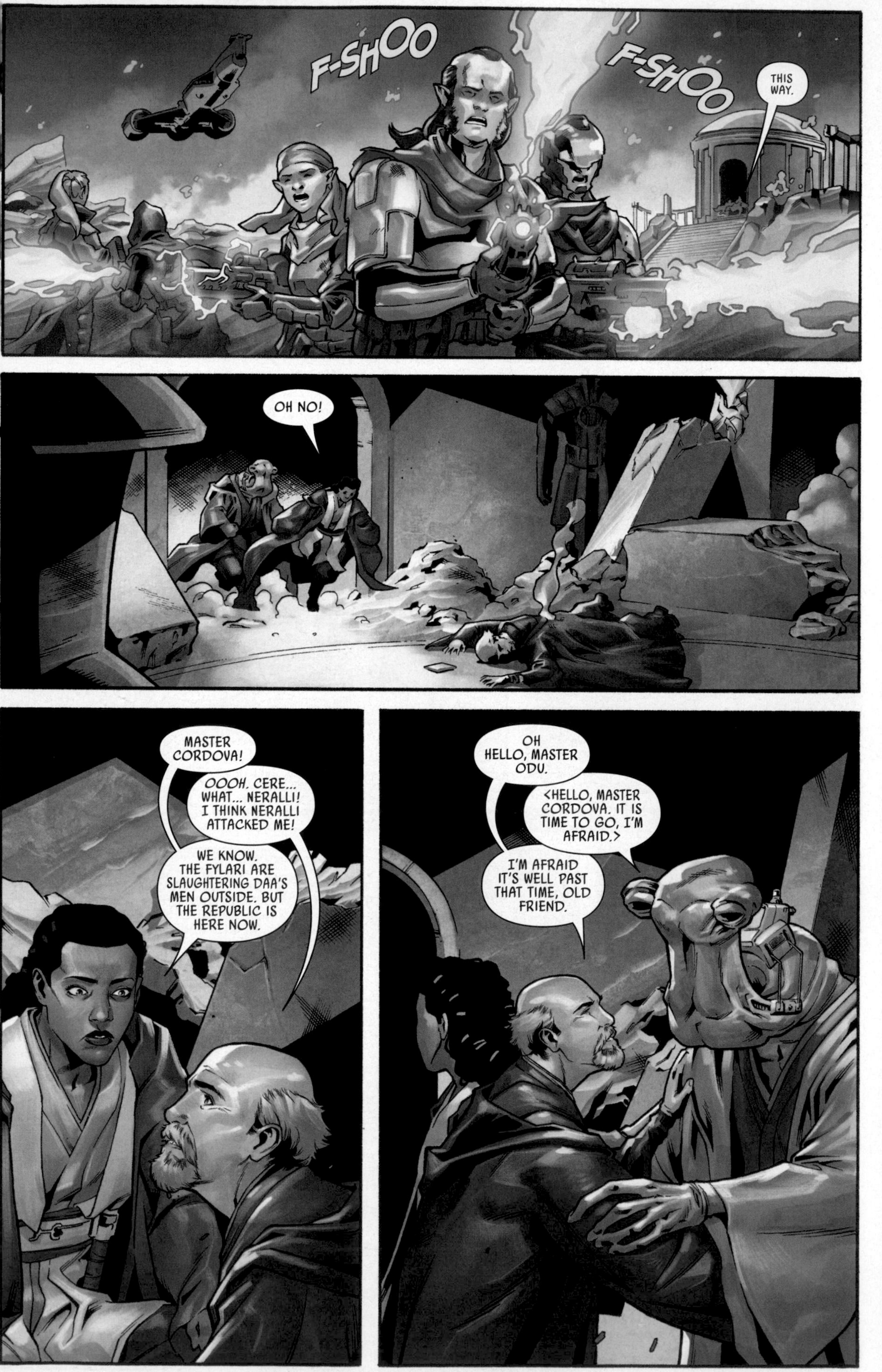
F-SHOO
F-SHOO
THIS WAY.
OH NO!
MASTER CORDOVA!
OOOH. CERE... WHAT... NERALLI! I THINK NERALLI ATTACKED ME!
WE KNOW. THE FYLARI ARE SLAUGHTERING DAA'S MEN OUTSIDE. BUT THE REPUBLIC IS HERE NOW.
OH HELLO, MASTER ODU.
<HELLO, MASTER CORDOVA. IT IS TIME TO GO, I'M AFRAID.>
I'M AFRAID IT'S WELL PAST THAT TIME, OLD FRIEND.

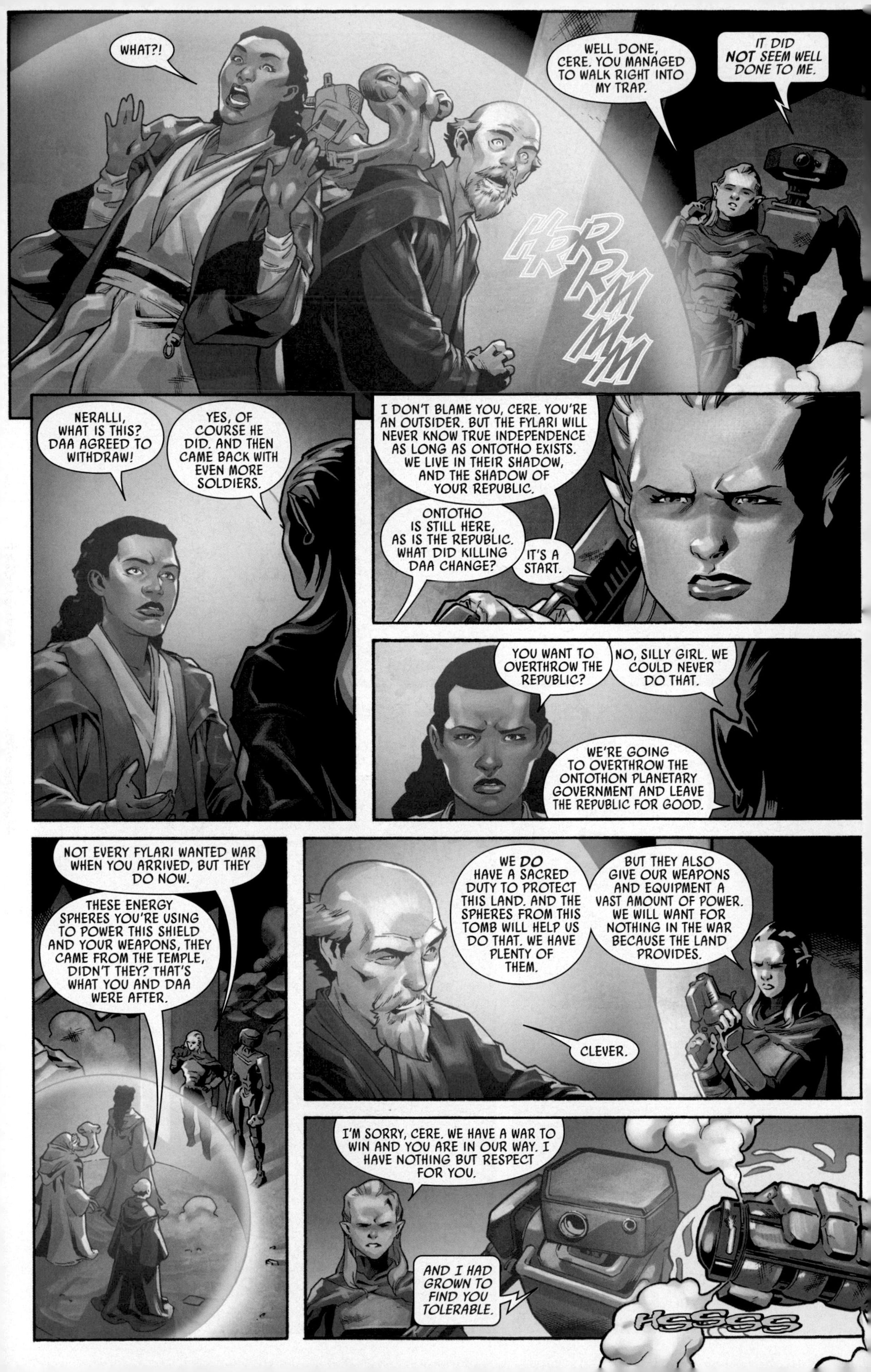
WHAT?!
WELL DONE, CERE. YOU MANAGED TO WALK RIGHT INTO MY TRAP.
IT DID NOT SEEM WELL DONE TO ME.
HDRRMMM
NERALLI, WHAT IS THIS? DAA AGREED TO WITHDRAW!
YES, OF COURSE HE DID. AND THEN CAME BACK WITH EVEN MORE SOLDIERS.
I DON'T BLAME YOU, CERE. YOU'RE AN OUTSIDER. BUT THE FYLARI WILL NEVER KNOW TRUE INDEPENDENCE AS LONG AS ONTOTHO EXISTS. WE LIVE IN THEIR SHADOW, AND THE SHADOW OF YOUR REPUBLIC.
ONTOTHO IS STILL HERE, AS IS THE REPUBLIC. WHAT DID KILLING DAA CHANGE?
IT'S A START.
YOU WANT TO OVERTHROW THE REPUBLIC?
NO, SILLY GIRL. WE COULD NEVER DO THAT.
WE'RE GOING TO OVERTHROW THE ONTOTHON PLANETARY GOVERNMENT AND LEAVE THE REPUBLIC FOR GOOD.
NOT EVERY FYLARI WANTED WAR WHEN YOU ARRIVED, BUT THEY DO NOW.
THESE ENERGY SPHERES YOU'RE USING TO POWER THIS SHIELD AND YOUR WEAPONS, THEY CAME FROM THE TEMPLE, DIDN'T THEY? THAT'S WHAT YOU AND DAA WERE AFTER.
WE DO HAVE A SACRED DUTY TO PROTECT THIS LAND. AND THE SPHERES FROM THIS TOMB WILL HELP US DO THAT. WE HAVE PLENTY OF THEM.
BUT THEY ALSO GIVE OUR WEAPONS AND EQUIPMENT A VAST AMOUNT OF POWER. WE WILL WANT FOR NOTHING IN THE WAR BECAUSE THE LAND PROVIDES.
CLEVER.
I'M SORRY, CERE. WE HAVE A WAR TO WIN AND YOU ARE IN OUR WAY. I HAVE NOTHING BUT RESPECT FOR YOU.
AND I HAD GROWN TO FIND YOU TOLERABLE.
HSSSSS

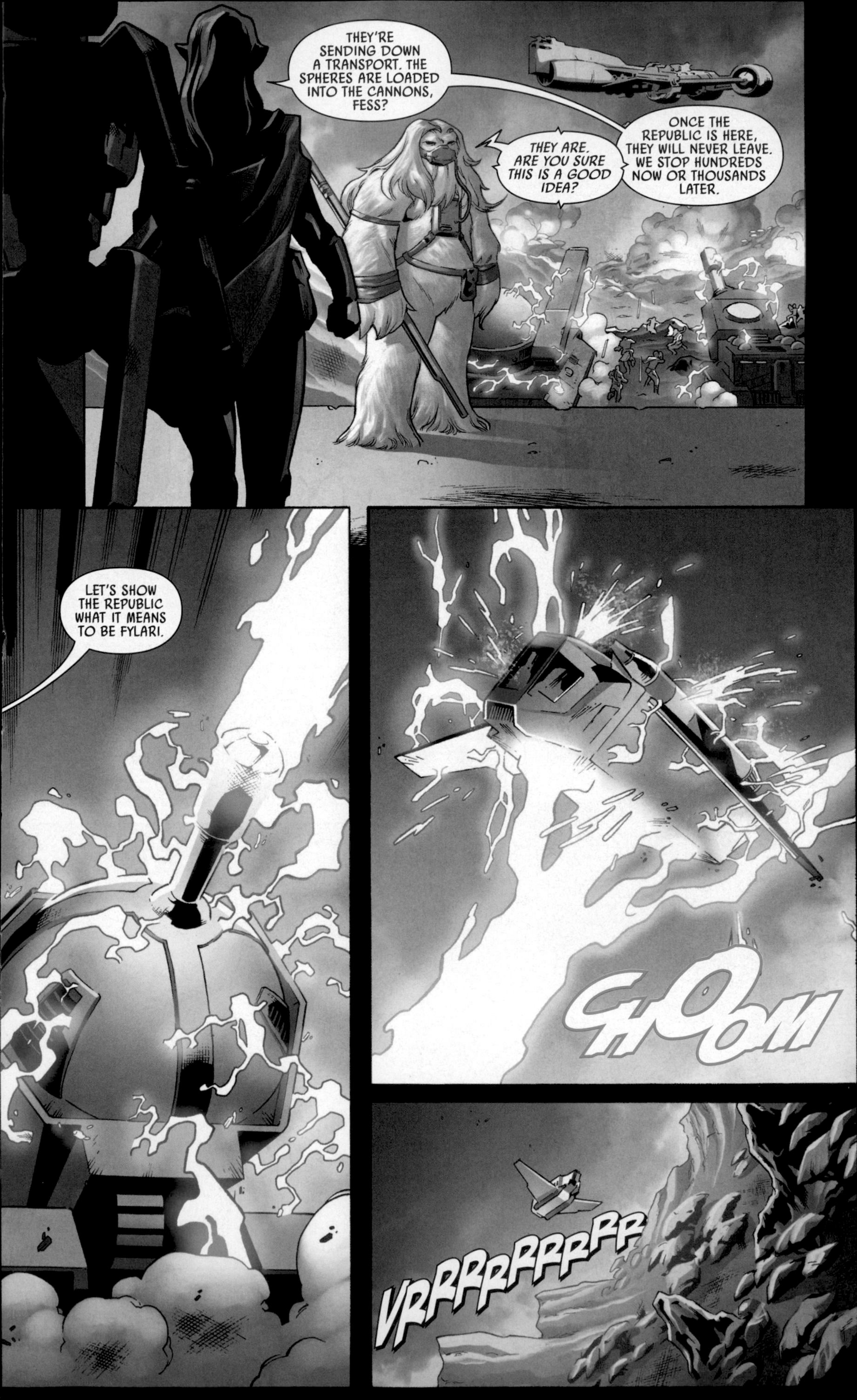
THEY'RE SENDING DOWN A TRANSPORT. THE SPHERES ARE LOADED INTO THE CANNONS, FESS?
THEY ARE. ARE YOU SURE THIS IS A GOOD IDEA?
ONCE THE REPUBLIC IS HERE, THEY WILL NEVER LEAVE. WE STOP HUNDREDS NOW OR THOUSANDS LATER.
LET'S SHOW THE REPUBLIC WHAT IT MEANS TO BE FYLARI.
CHOOM
VRRRRRRRRRR

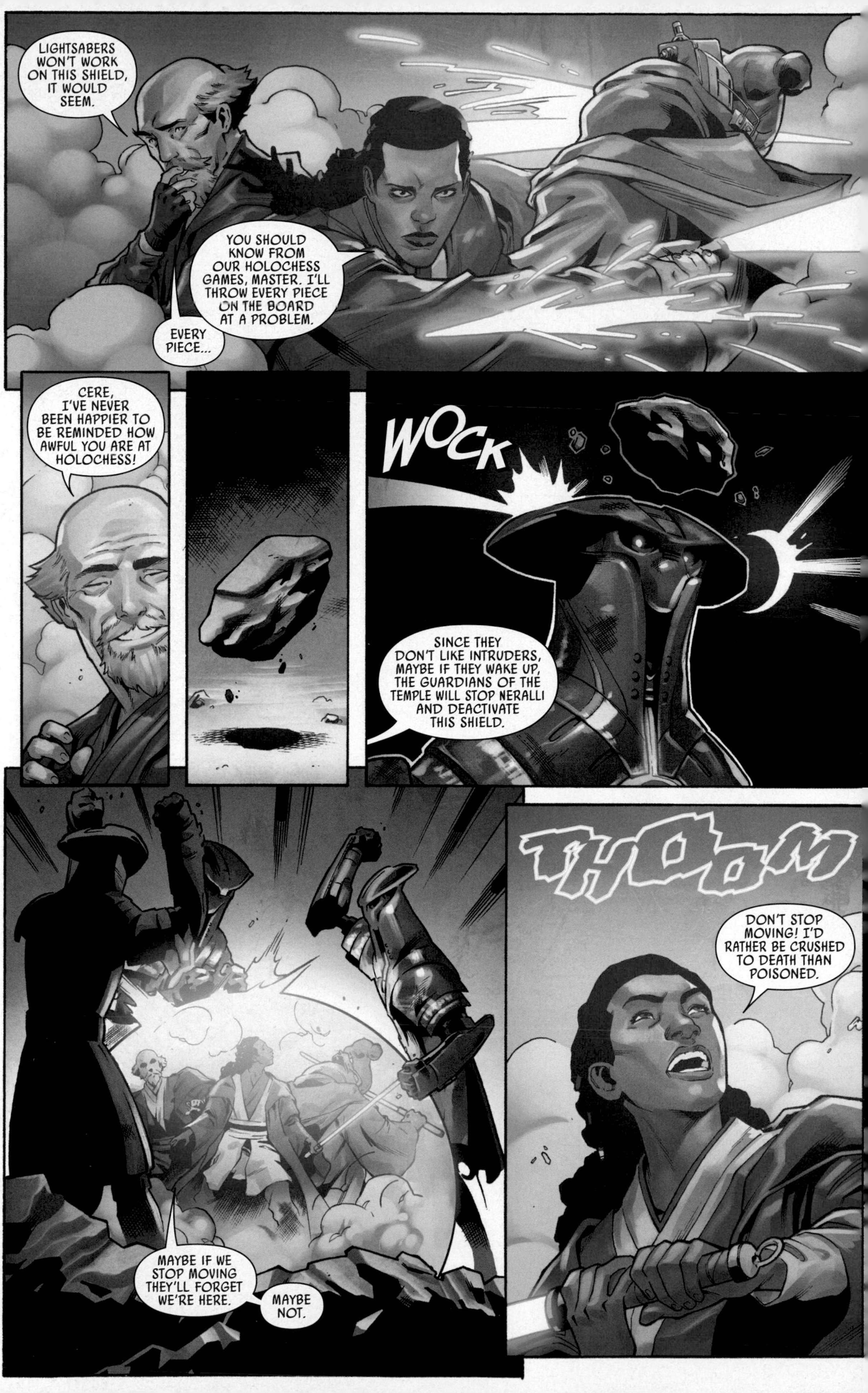
LIGHTSABERS WON'T WORK ON THIS SHIELD, IT WOULD SEEM.
YOU SHOULD KNOW FROM OUR HOLOCHESS GAMES, MASTER. I'LL THROW EVERY PIECE ON THE BOARD AT A PROBLEM.
EVERY PIECE...
CERE, I'VE NEVER BEEN HAPPIER TO BE REMINDED HOW AWFUL YOU ARE AT HOLOCHESS!
WOCK
SINCE THEY DON'T LIKE INTRUDERS, MAYBE IF THEY WAKE UP, THE GUARDIANS OF THE TEMPLE WILL STOP NERALLI AND DEACTIVATE THIS SHIELD.
MAYBE IF WE STOP MOVING THEY'LL FORGET WE'RE HERE.
MAYBE NOT.
THOOM
DON'T STOP MOVING! I'D RATHER BE CRUSHED TO DEATH THAN POISONED.

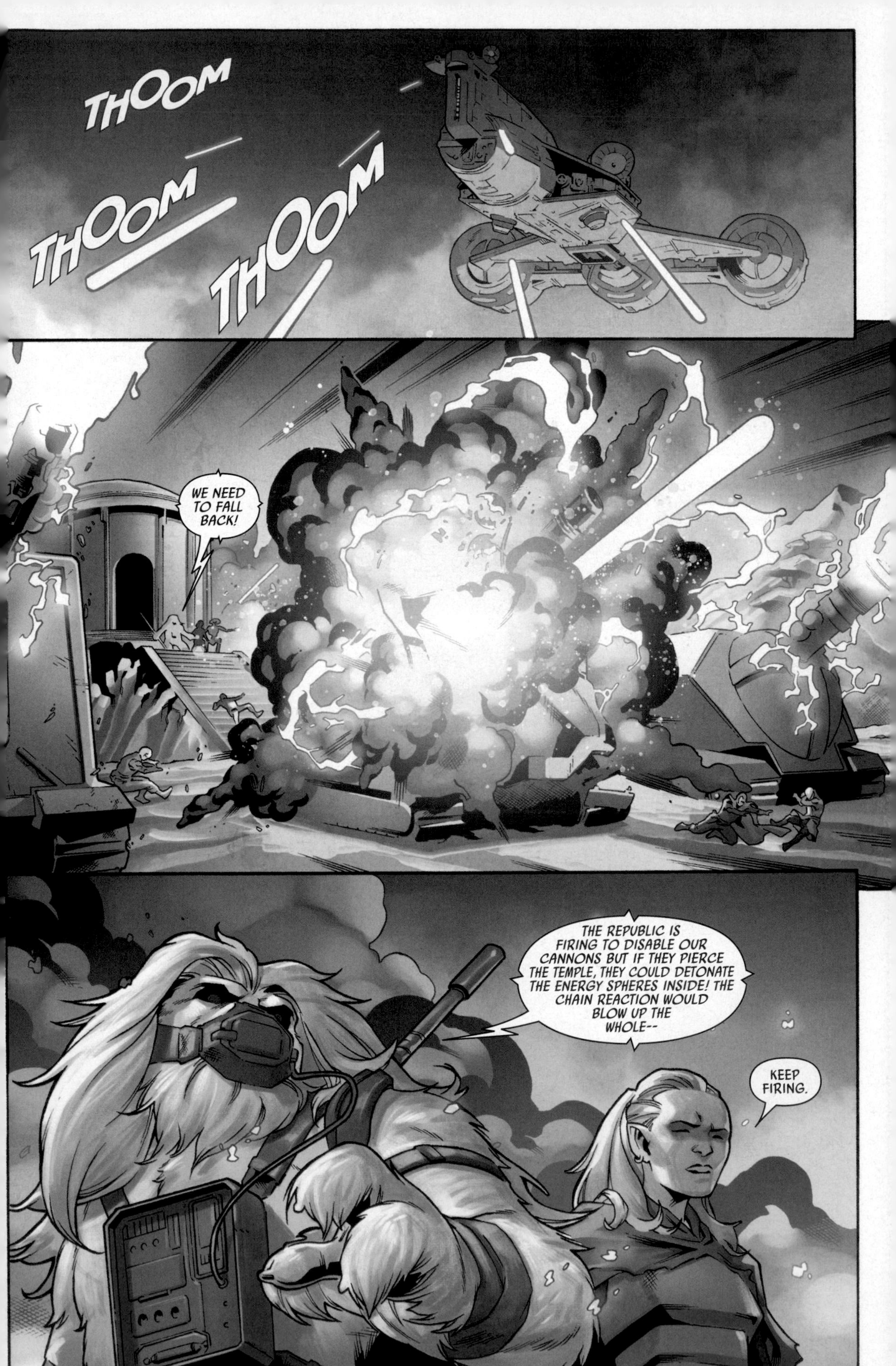
THOOM
THOOM
THOOM
WE NEED TO FALL BACK!
THE REPUBLIC IS FIRING TO DISABLE OUR CANNONS BUT IF THEY PIERCE THE TEMPLE, THEY COULD DETONATE THE ENERGY SPHERES INSIDE! THE CHAIN REACTION WOULD BLOW UP THE WHOLE--
KEEP FIRING.

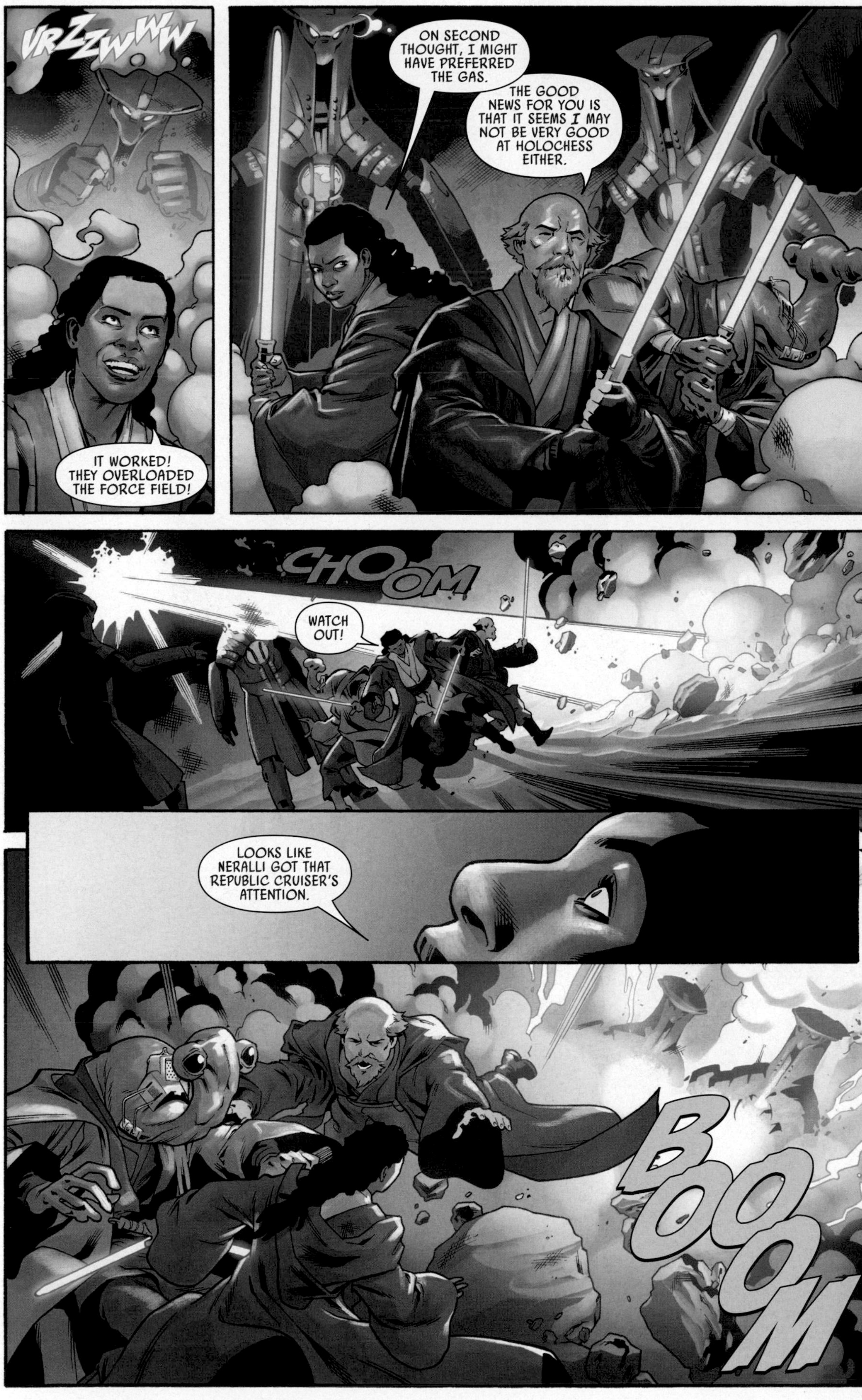
VRZZWWW
IT WORKED! THEY OVERLOADED THE FORCE FIELD!
ON SECOND THOUGHT, I MIGHT HAVE PREFERRED THE GAS.
THE GOOD NEWS FOR YOU IS THAT IT SEEMS I MAY NOT BE VERY GOOD AT HOLOCHESS EITHER.
CHOOM
WATCH OUT!
LOOKS LIKE NERALLI GOT THAT REPUBLIC CRUISER'S ATTENTION.
BOOOM

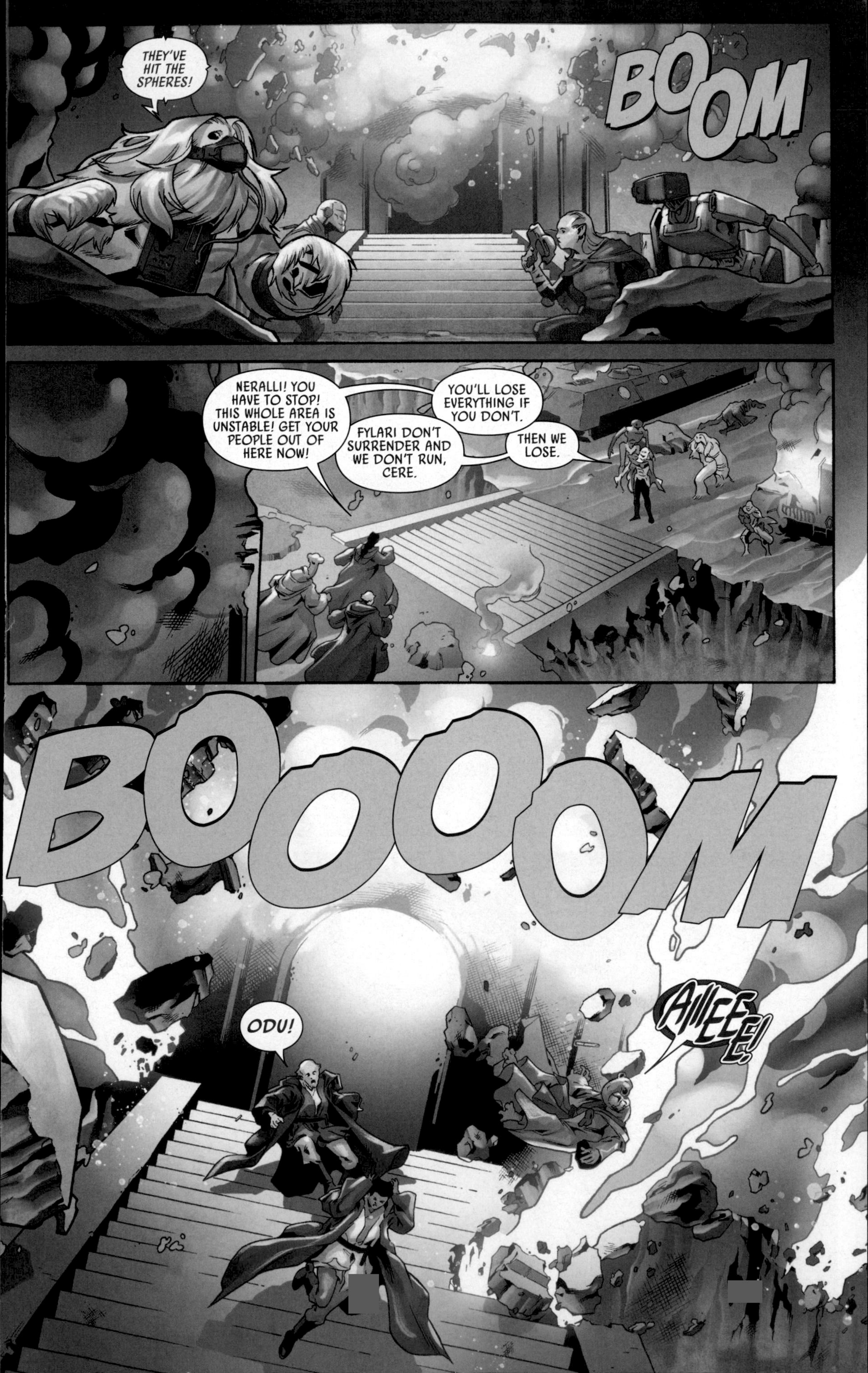
THEY'VE HIT THE SPHERES!
BOOM
NERALLI! YOU HAVE TO STOP! THIS WHOLE AREA IS UNSTABLE! GET YOUR PEOPLE OUT OF HERE NOW!
FYLARI DON'T SURRENDER AND WE DON'T RUN, CERE.
YOU'LL LOSE EVERYTHING IF YOU DON'T.
THEN WE LOSE.
BOOOOM
ODU!
AIIEEE!

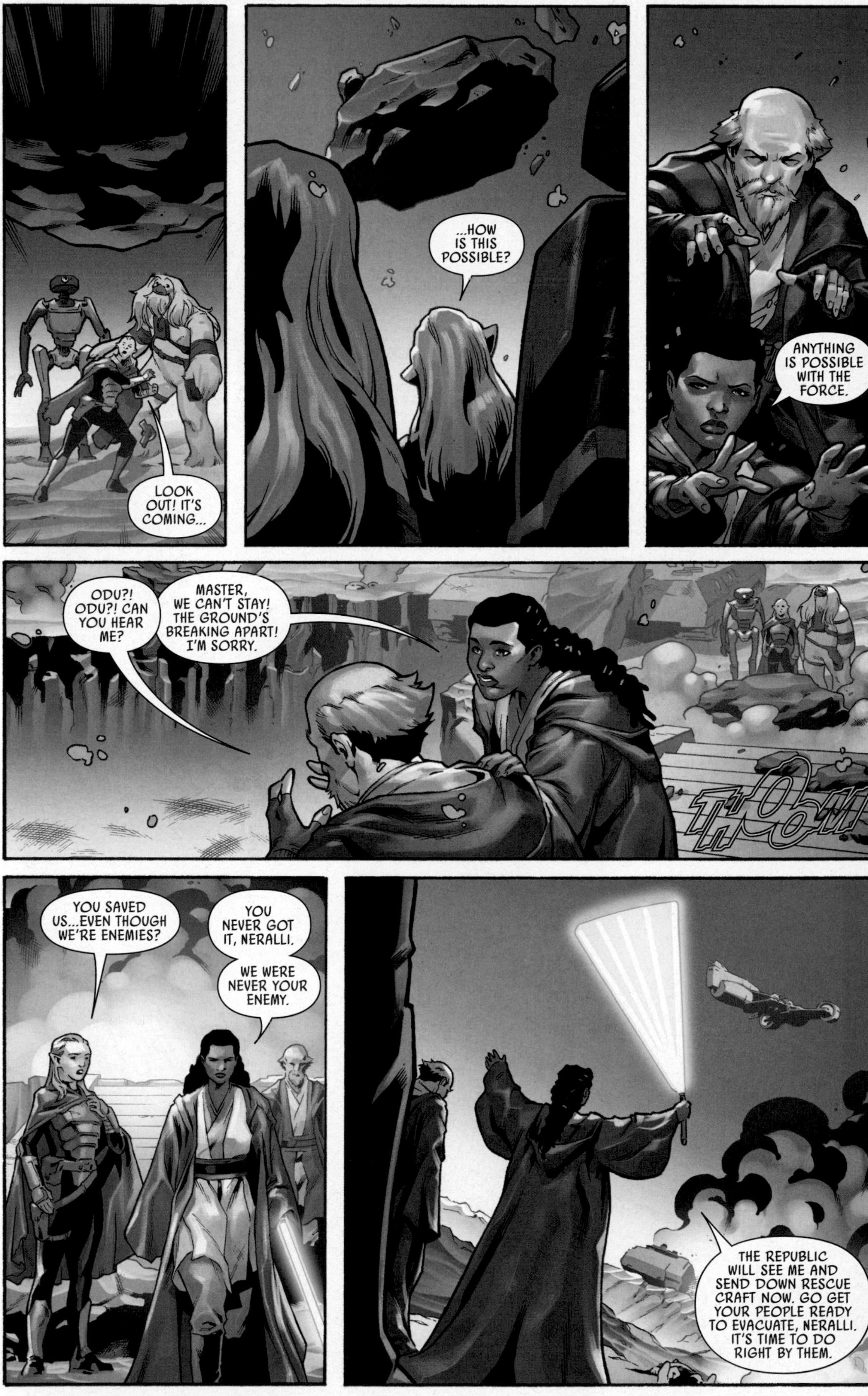

LOOK OUT! IT'S COMING...
...HOW IS THIS POSSIBLE?
ANYTHING IS POSSIBLE WITH THE FORCE.
ODU?! ODU?! CAN YOU HEAR ME?
MASTER, WE CAN'T STAY! THE GROUND'S BREAKING APART! I'M SORRY.
THOOM
YOU SAVED US...EVEN THOUGH WE'RE ENEMIES?
YOU NEVER GOT IT, NERALLI.
WE WERE NEVER YOUR ENEMY.
THE REPUBLIC WILL SEE ME AND SEND DOWN RESCUE CRAFT NOW. GO GET YOUR PEOPLE READY TO EVACUATE, NERALLI. IT'S TIME TO DO RIGHT BY THEM.

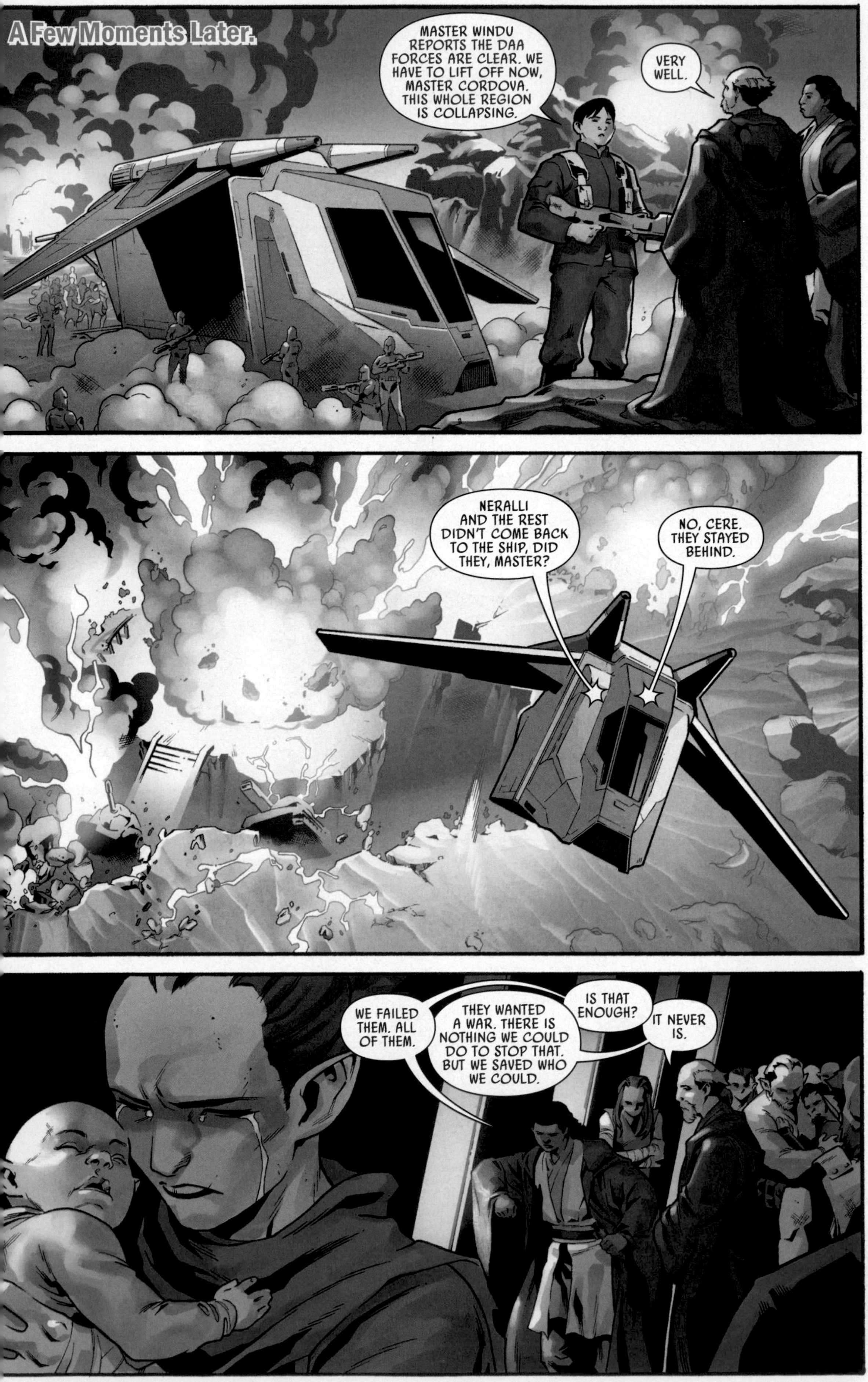
A Few Moments Later.
MASTER WINDU REPORTS THE DAA FORCES ARE CLEAR. WE HAVE TO LIFT OFF NOW, MASTER CORDOVA. THIS WHOLE REGION IS COLLAPSING.
VERY WELL.
NERALLI AND THE REST DIDN'T COME BACK TO THE SHIP, DID THEY, MASTER?
NO, CERE. THEY STAYED BEHIND.
WE FAILED THEM. ALL OF THEM.
THEY WANTED A WAR. THERE IS NOTHING WE COULD DO TO STOP THAT. BUT WE SAVED WHO WE COULD.
IS THAT ENOUGH?
IT NEVER IS.

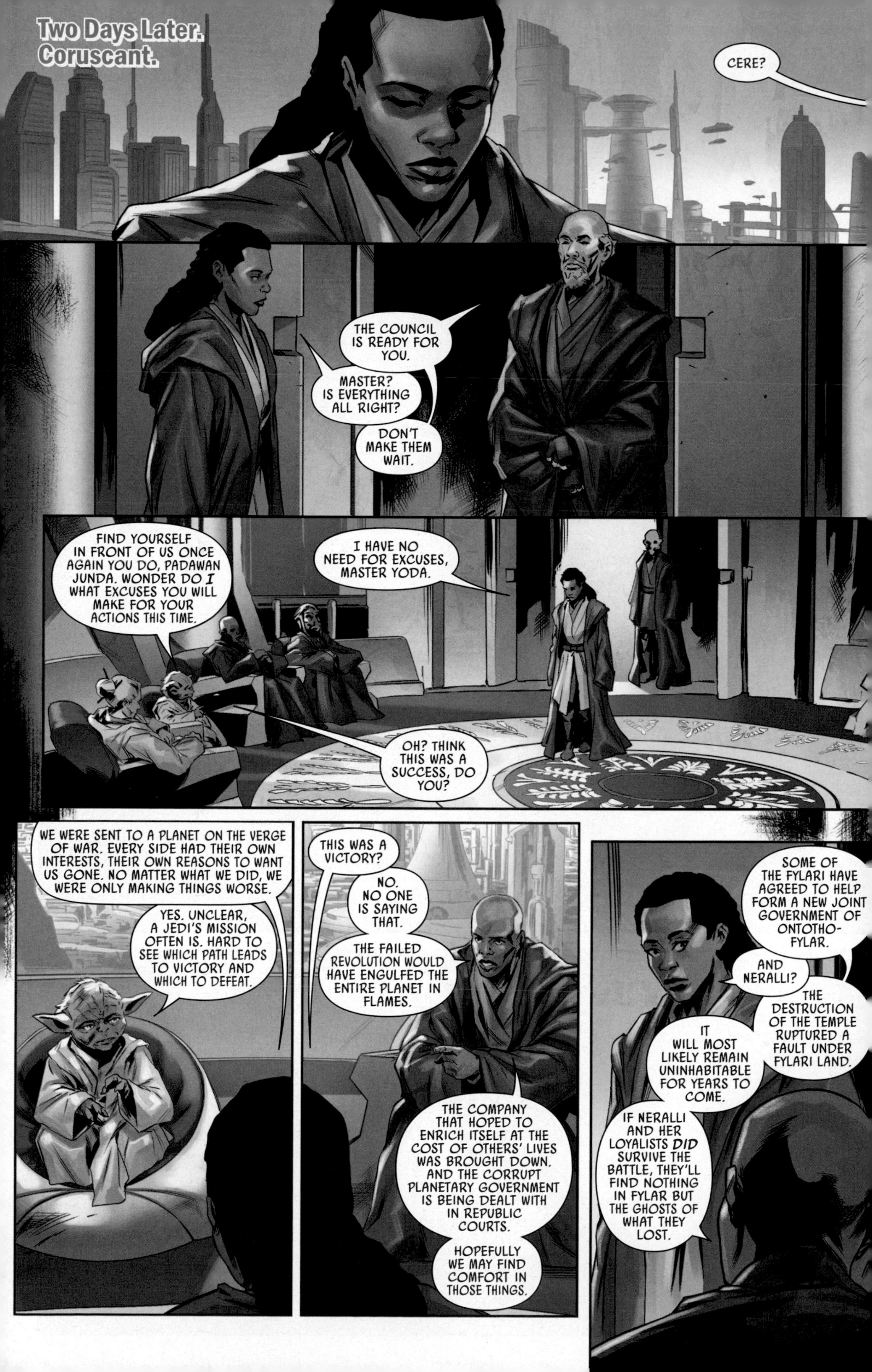
Two Days Later. Coruscant.
CERE?
THE COUNCIL IS READY FOR YOU.
MASTER? IS EVERYTHING ALL RIGHT?
DON'T MAKE THEM WAIT.
FIND YOURSELF IN FRONT OF US ONCE AGAIN YOU DO, PADAWAN JUNDA. WONDER DO *I* WHAT EXCUSES YOU WILL MAKE FOR YOUR ACTIONS THIS TIME.
I HAVE NO NEED FOR EXCUSES, MASTER YODA.
OH? THINK THIS WAS A SUCCESS, DO YOU?
WE WERE SENT TO A PLANET ON THE VERGE OF WAR. EVERY SIDE HAD THEIR OWN INTERESTS, THEIR OWN REASONS TO WANT US GONE. NO MATTER WHAT WE DID, WE WERE ONLY MAKING THINGS WORSE.
YES. UNCLEAR, A JEDI'S MISSION OFTEN IS. HARD TO SEE WHICH PATH LEADS TO VICTORY AND WHICH TO DEFEAT.
THIS WAS A VICTORY?
NO. NO ONE IS SAYING THAT.
THE FAILED REVOLUTION WOULD HAVE ENGULFED THE ENTIRE PLANET IN FLAMES.
THE COMPANY THAT HOPED TO ENRICH ITSELF AT THE COST OF OTHERS' LIVES WAS BROUGHT DOWN. AND THE CORRUPT PLANETARY GOVERNMENT IS BEING DEALT WITH IN REPUBLIC COURTS.
HOPEFULLY WE MAY FIND COMFORT IN THOSE THINGS.
SOME OF THE FYLARI HAVE AGREED TO HELP FORM A NEW JOINT GOVERNMENT OF ONTOTHO-FYLAR.
AND NERALLI?
THE DESTRUCTION OF THE TEMPLE RUPTURED A FAULT UNDER FYLARI LAND.
IT WILL MOST LIKELY REMAIN UNINHABITABLE FOR YEARS TO COME.
IF NERALLI AND HER LOYALISTS *DID* SURVIVE THE BATTLE, THEY'LL FIND NOTHING IN FYLAR BUT THE GHOSTS OF WHAT THEY LOST.

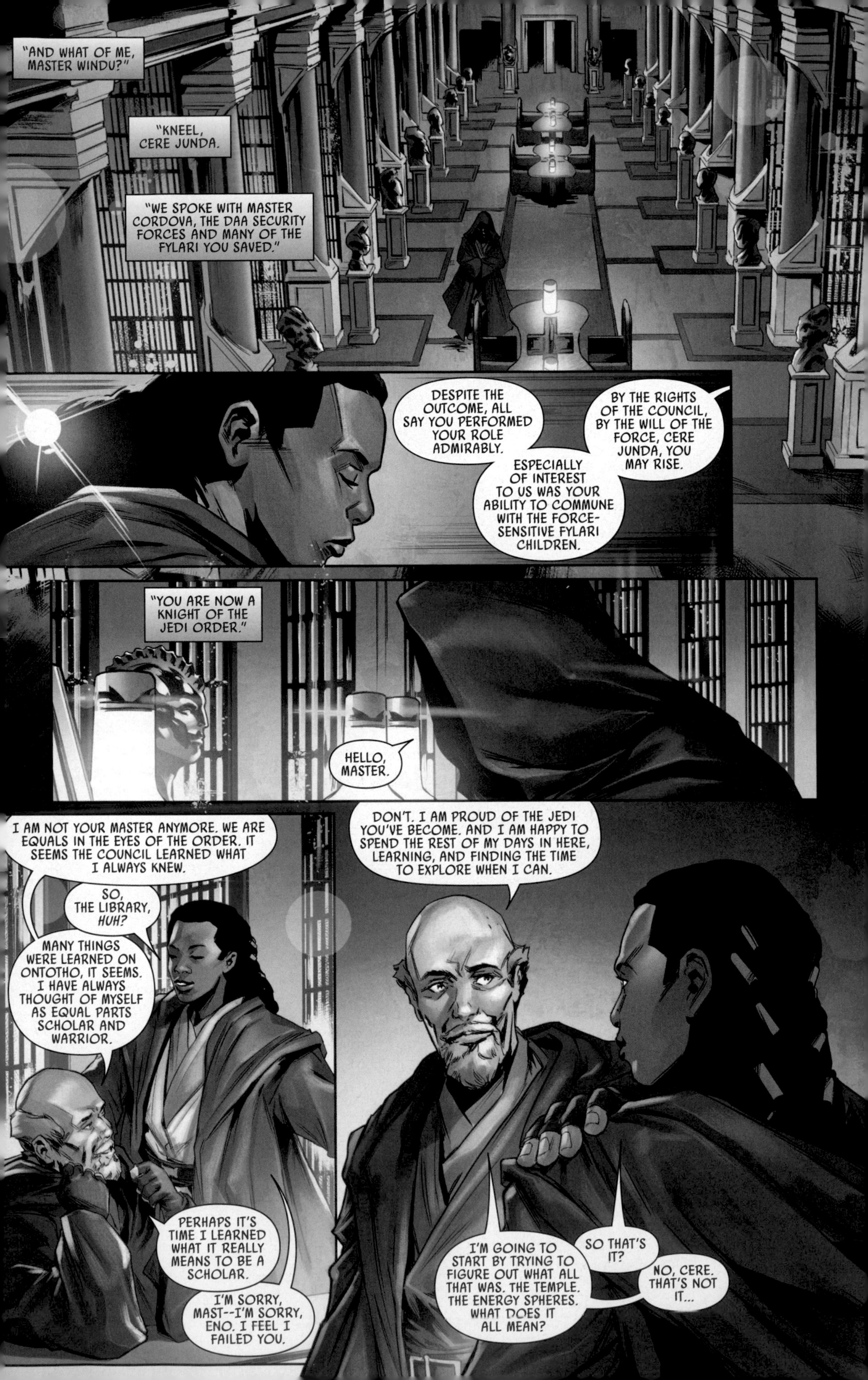
"AND WHAT OF ME, MASTER WINDU?"
"KNEEL, CERE JUNDA.
"WE SPOKE WITH MASTER CORDOVA, THE DAA SECURITY FORCES AND MANY OF THE FYLARI YOU SAVED."
DESPITE THE OUTCOME, ALL SAY YOU PERFORMED YOUR ROLE ADMIRABLY.
ESPECIALLY OF INTEREST TO US WAS YOUR ABILITY TO COMMUNE WITH THE FORCE-SENSITIVE FYLARI CHILDREN.
BY THE RIGHTS OF THE COUNCIL, BY THE WILL OF THE FORCE, CERE JUNDA, YOU MAY RISE.
"YOU ARE NOW A KNIGHT OF THE JEDI ORDER."
HELLO, MASTER.
I AM NOT YOUR MASTER ANYMORE. WE ARE EQUALS IN THE EYES OF THE ORDER. IT SEEMS THE COUNCIL LEARNED WHAT I ALWAYS KNEW.
SO, THE LIBRARY, HUH?
MANY THINGS WERE LEARNED ON ONTOTHO, IT SEEMS. I HAVE ALWAYS THOUGHT OF MYSELF AS EQUAL PARTS SCHOLAR AND WARRIOR.
PERHAPS IT'S TIME I LEARNED WHAT IT REALLY MEANS TO BE A SCHOLAR.
I'M SORRY, MAST--I'M SORRY, ENO. I FEEL I FAILED YOU.
DON'T. I AM PROUD OF THE JEDI YOU'VE BECOME. AND I AM HAPPY TO SPEND THE REST OF MY DAYS IN HERE, LEARNING, AND FINDING THE TIME TO EXPLORE WHEN I CAN.
I'M GOING TO START BY TRYING TO FIGURE OUT WHAT ALL THAT WAS. THE TEMPLE. THE ENERGY SPHERES. WHAT DOES IT ALL MEAN?
SO THAT'S IT?
NO, CERE. THAT'S NOT IT...

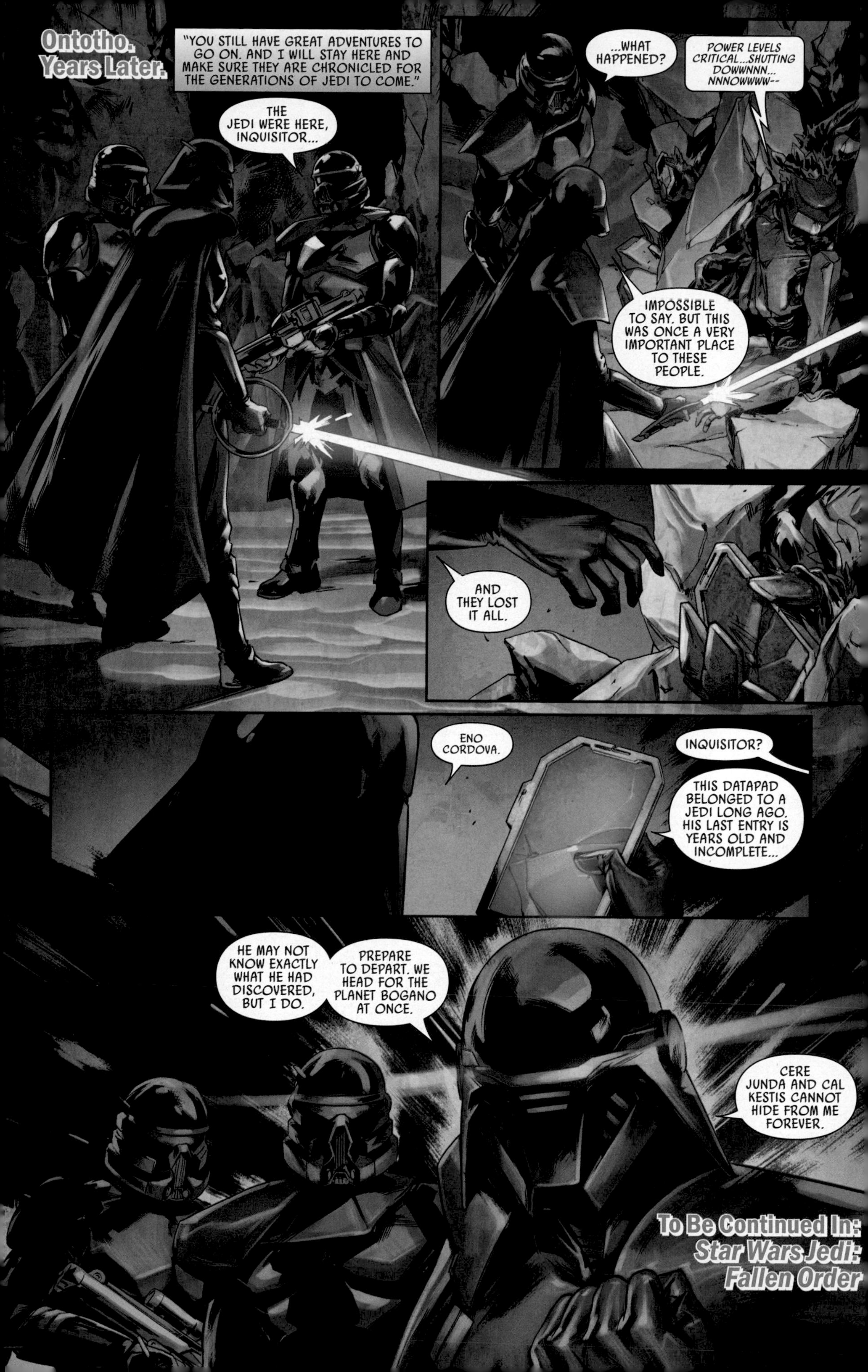
Ontotho. Years Later.
"YOU STILL HAVE GREAT ADVENTURES TO GO ON. AND I WILL STAY HERE AND MAKE SURE THEY ARE CHRONICLED FOR THE GENERATIONS OF JEDI TO COME."
THE JEDI WERE HERE, INQUISITOR...
...WHAT HAPPENED?
POWER LEVELS CRITICAL...SHUTTING DOWWNNN... NNNOWWWW--
IMPOSSIBLE TO SAY. BUT THIS WAS ONCE A VERY IMPORTANT PLACE TO THESE PEOPLE.
AND THEY LOST IT ALL.
ENO CORDOVA.
INQUISITOR?
THIS DATAPAD BELONGED TO A JEDI LONG AGO. HIS LAST ENTRY IS YEARS OLD AND INCOMPLETE...
HE MAY NOT KNOW EXACTLY WHAT HE HAD DISCOVERED, BUT I DO.
PREPARE TO DEPART. WE HEAD FOR THE PLANET BOGANO AT ONCE.
CERE JUNDA AND CAL KESTIS CANNOT HIDE FROM ME FOREVER.
To Be Continued In: Star Wars Jedi: Fallen Order

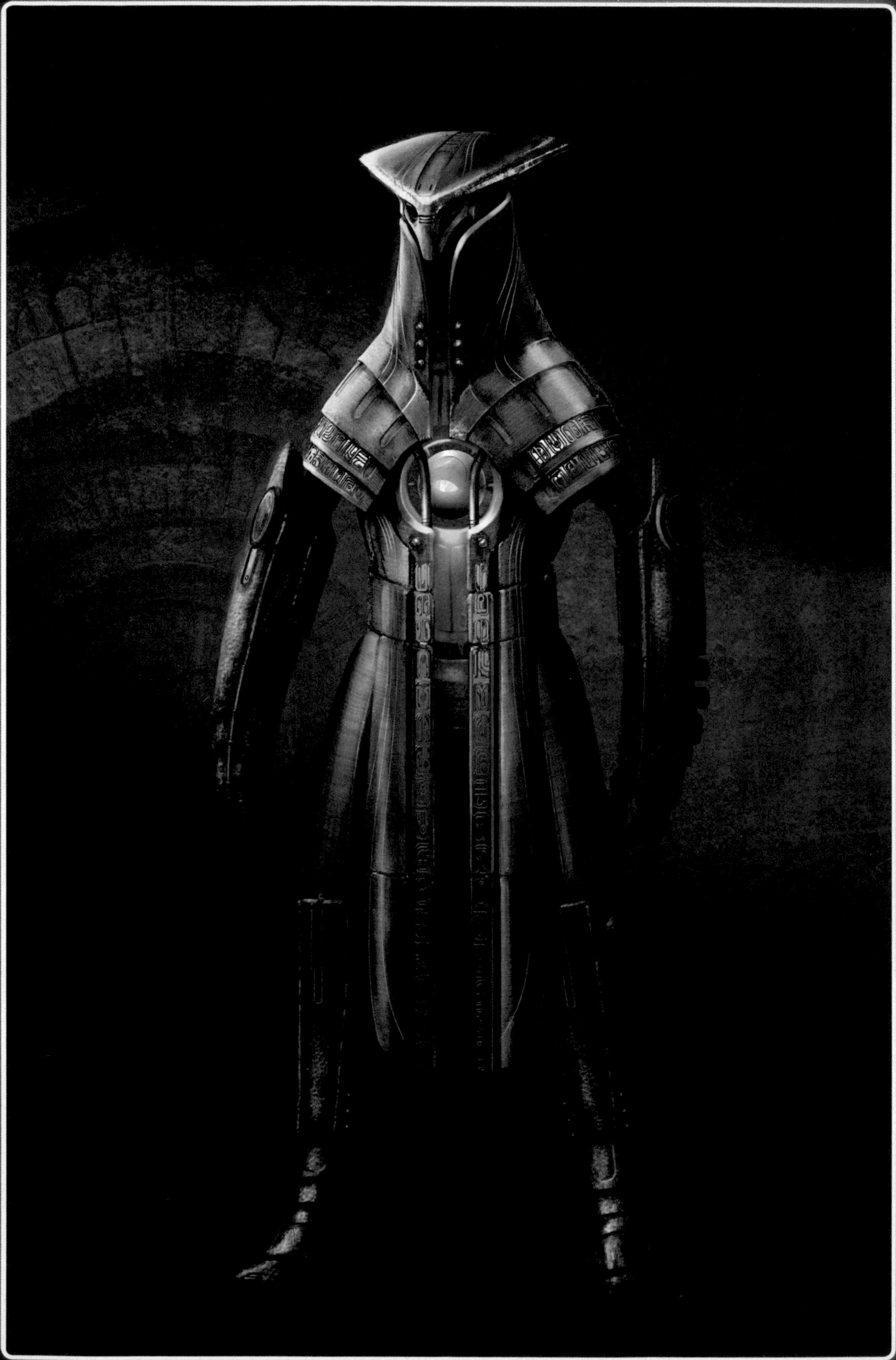

STAR WARS: JEDI FALLEN ORDER — DARK TEMPLE 1 **Game Variant**
Zeffo Temple Guardian by Jean-francois Rey, Respawn Entertainment

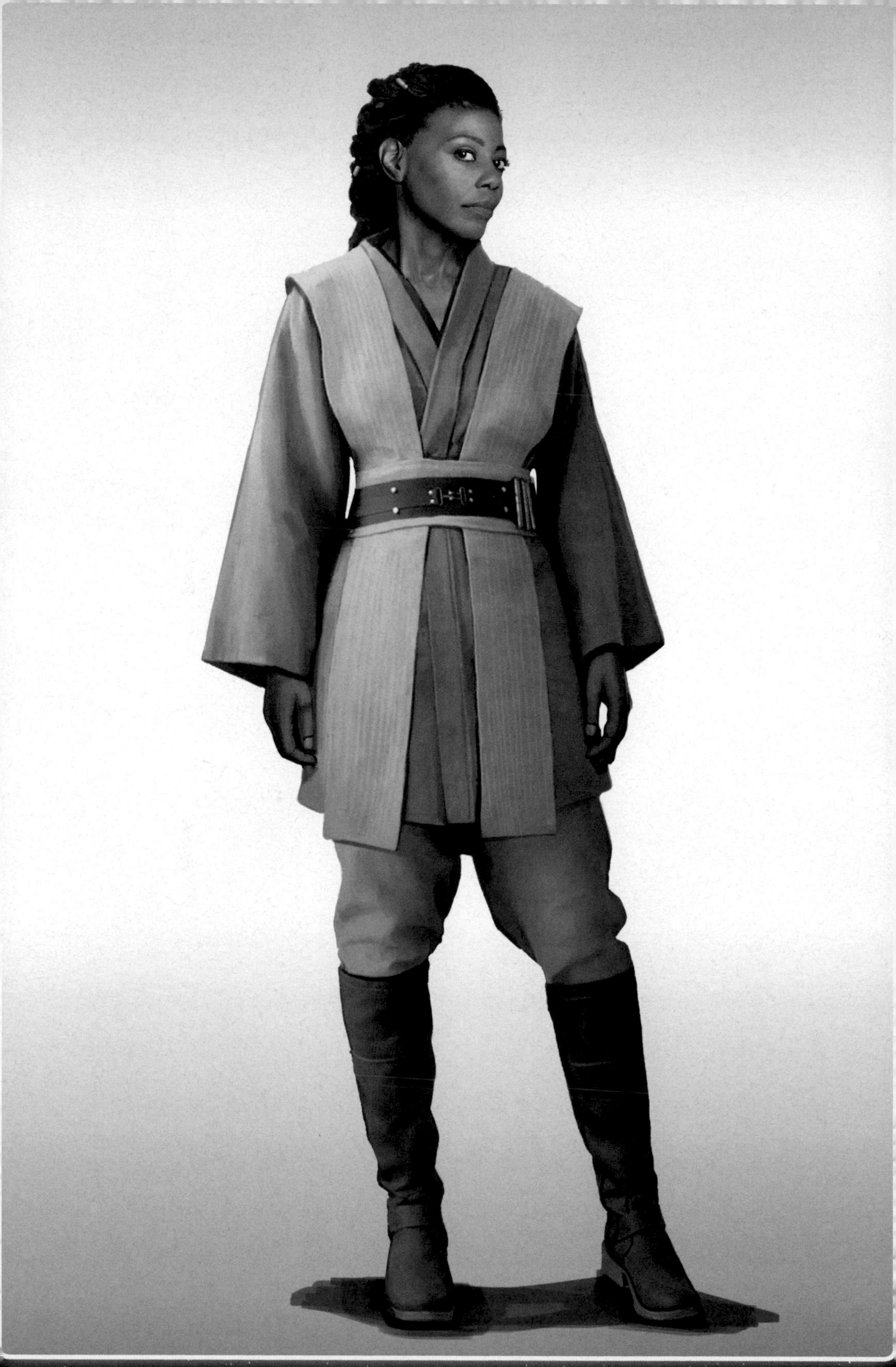

***STAR WARS: JEDI FALLEN ORDER — DARK TEMPLE* 2 Game Variant**
Cere Jedi Outfit by Jordan Lamarre-Wan and Theo Stylianides, Respawn Entertainment

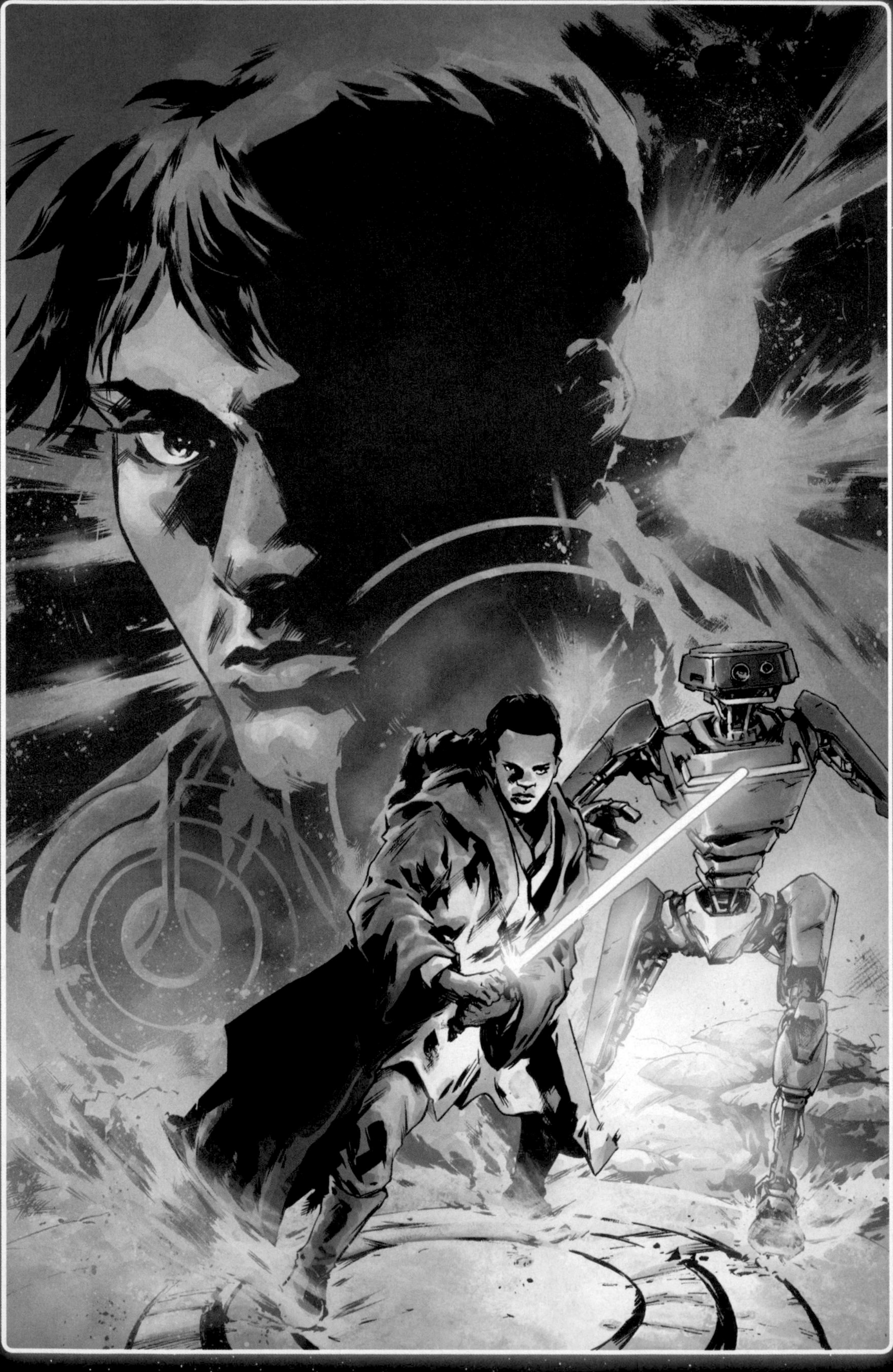

STAR WARS: JEDI FALLEN ORDER — DARK TEMPLE 3 Variant by
PAOLO VILLANELLI & NEERAJ MENON

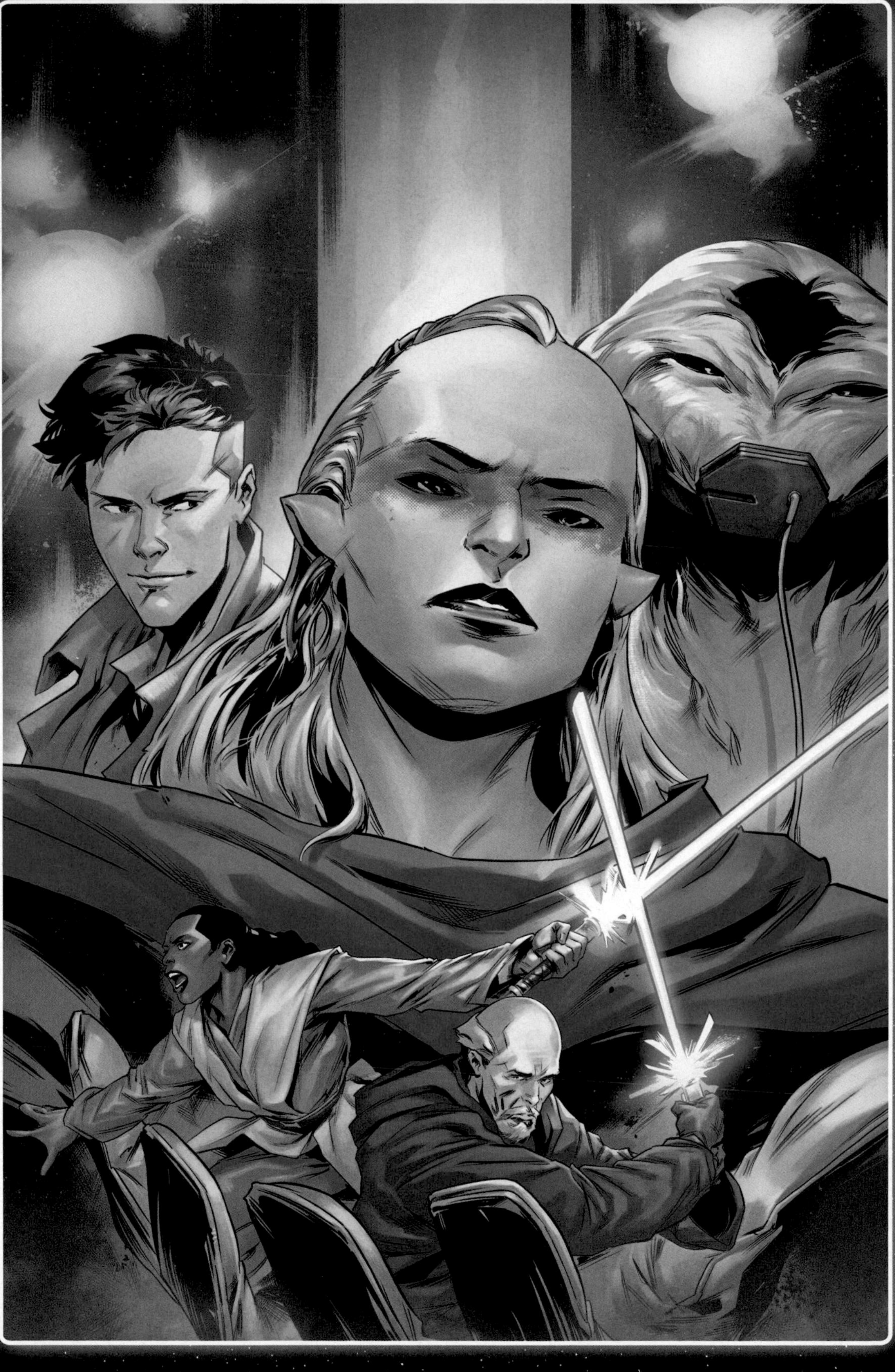

STAR WARS: JEDI FALLEN ORDER — DARK TEMPLE 4 **Variant by**

PAOLO VILLANELLI & ARIF PRIANTO

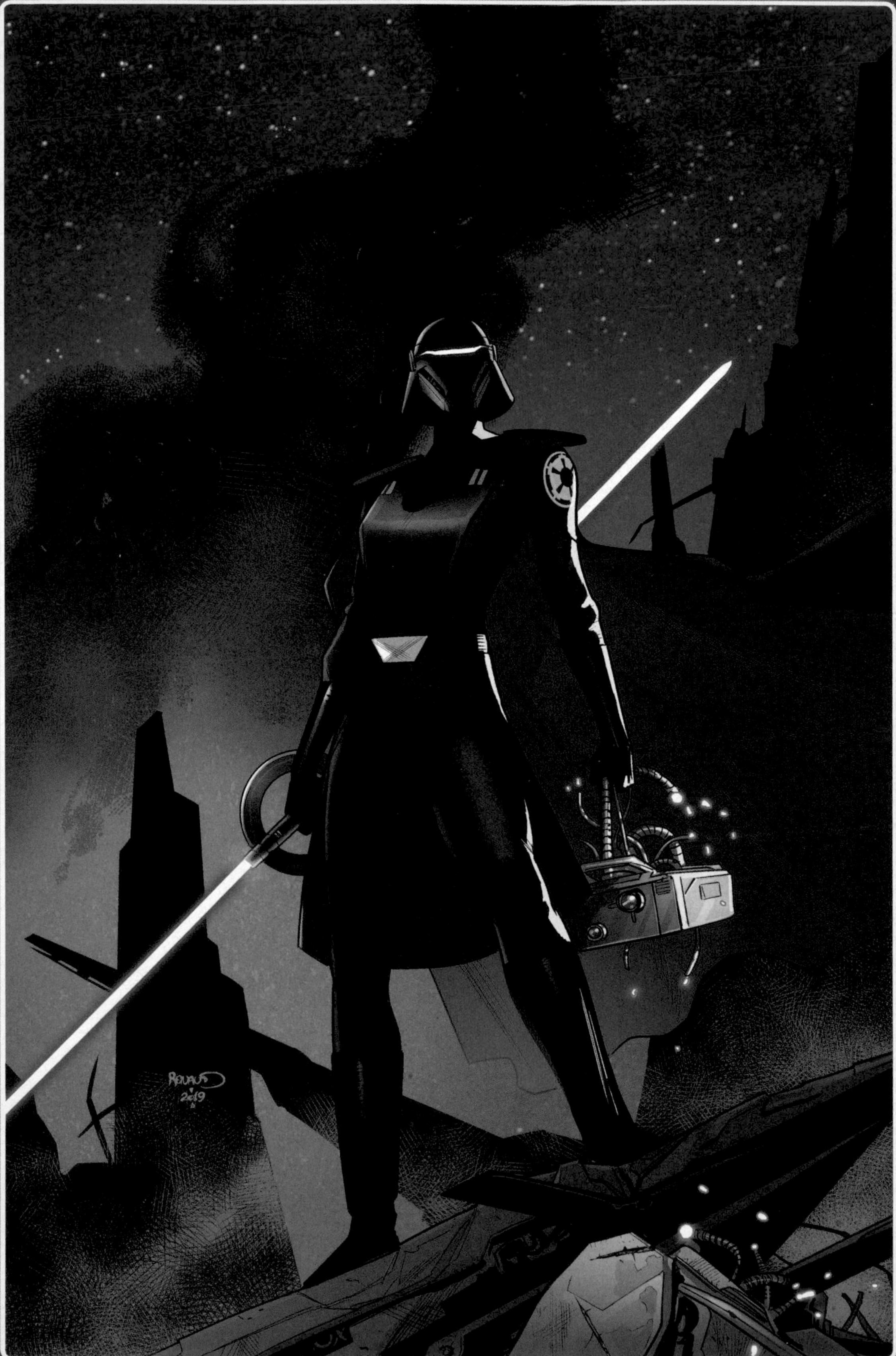
RENAUD
2019

STAR WARS: JEDI FALLEN ORDER — DARK TEMPLE 5 Variant by
PAUL RENAUD

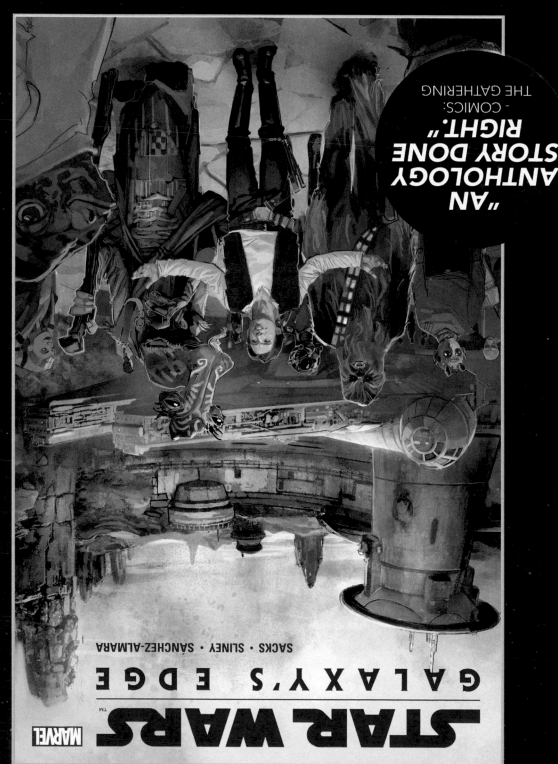

STAR WARS™

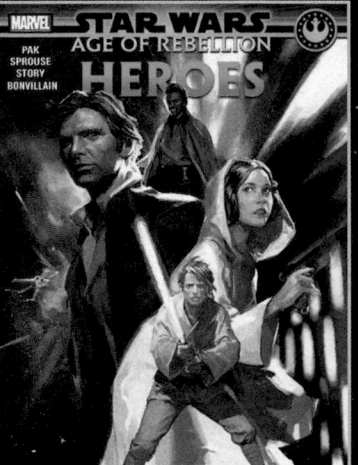
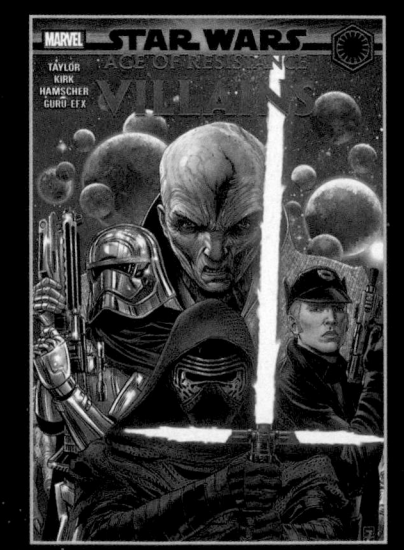

ROGUE ARCHAEOLOGIST DOCTOR APHRA THIEVES HER WAY ACROSS THE GALAXY!

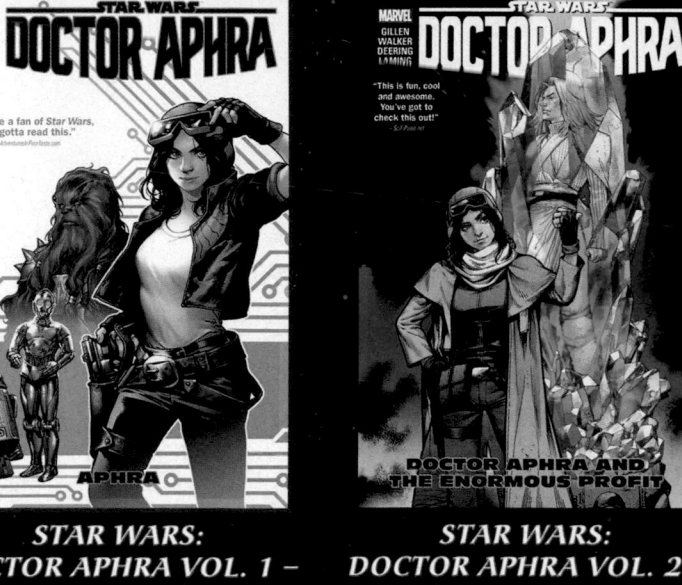

STAR WARS: DOCTOR APHRA VOL. 1 – APHRA TPB
ISBN: 978-1302913212

STAR WARS: DOCTOR APHRA VOL. 2 – DOCTOR APHRA AND THE ENORMOUS PROFIT TPB
ISBN: 978-1302907631

STAR WARS: DOCTOR APHRA VOL. 3 – REMASTERED TPB
ISBN: 978-1302911522

STAR WARS: DOCTOR APHRA VOL. 4 – THE CATASTROPHE CON TPB
ISBN: 978-1302911539

STAR WARS: DOCTOR APHRA VOL. 5 – WORST AMONG EQUALS TPB
ISBN: 978-1302914875

STAR WARS: DOCTOR APHRA VOL. 6 – UNSPEAKABLE REBEL SUPERWEAPON TPB
ISBN: 978-1302914882

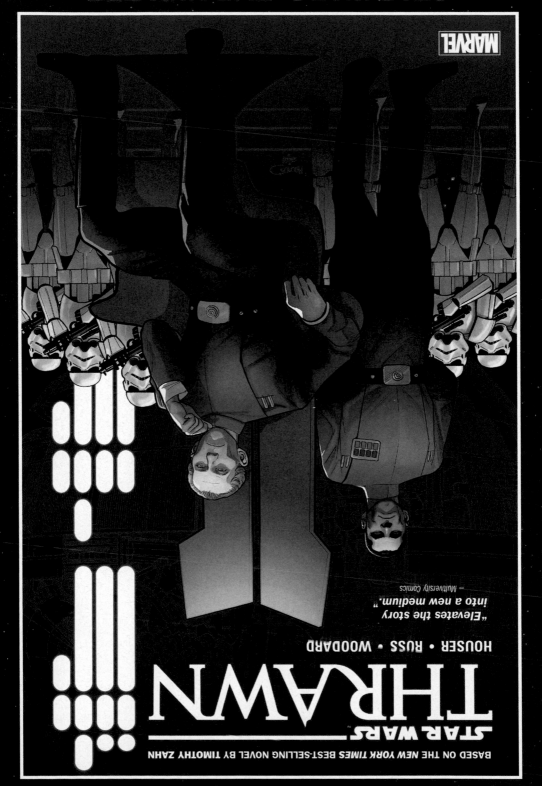

THE JEDI KNIGHTS ARE GONE AND FORGOTTEN.

DESTROYED BY THEIR ANCIENT ENEMIES — THE SITH — AFTER A LONG CIVIL WAR ENGINEERED TO BRING ABOUT THEIR DOWNFALL AND A NEW AGE: **THE AGE OF THE EMPIRE**.

BUT NOT LONG BEFORE, THE JEDI WERE THE GUARDIANS OF PEACE AND JUSTICE IN THE GALAXY. LOYAL TO THE REPUBLIC FOR MORE THAN 1,000 GENERATIONS AND WELL TRAINED IN THE MANY MYSTICAL POWERS OF THE FORCE, THE ORDER DISPERSED ITS WISE AND POWERFUL WARRIORS TO SETTLE DISPUTES, SEEK KNOWLEDGE AND KEEP THE PEOPLES OF COUNTLESS STAR SYSTEMS SAFE.

AND THE BOND OF ONE JEDI TEAM, A MASTER AND APPRENTICE, IS ABOUT TO BE TESTED LIKE NEVER BEFORE. THERE ARE SOME THREATS THAT ARE FAR TOO INSIDIOUS... AND FAR TOO ANCIENT TO BE OVERCOME WITH JUST THE SWING OF A LIGHTSABER. JEDI TRAINING CANNOT PREPARE A PADAWAN STUDENT FOR EVERYTHING....

Based on characters created for Respawn Entertainment's ***Star Wars Jedi: Fallen Order*** *video game.*

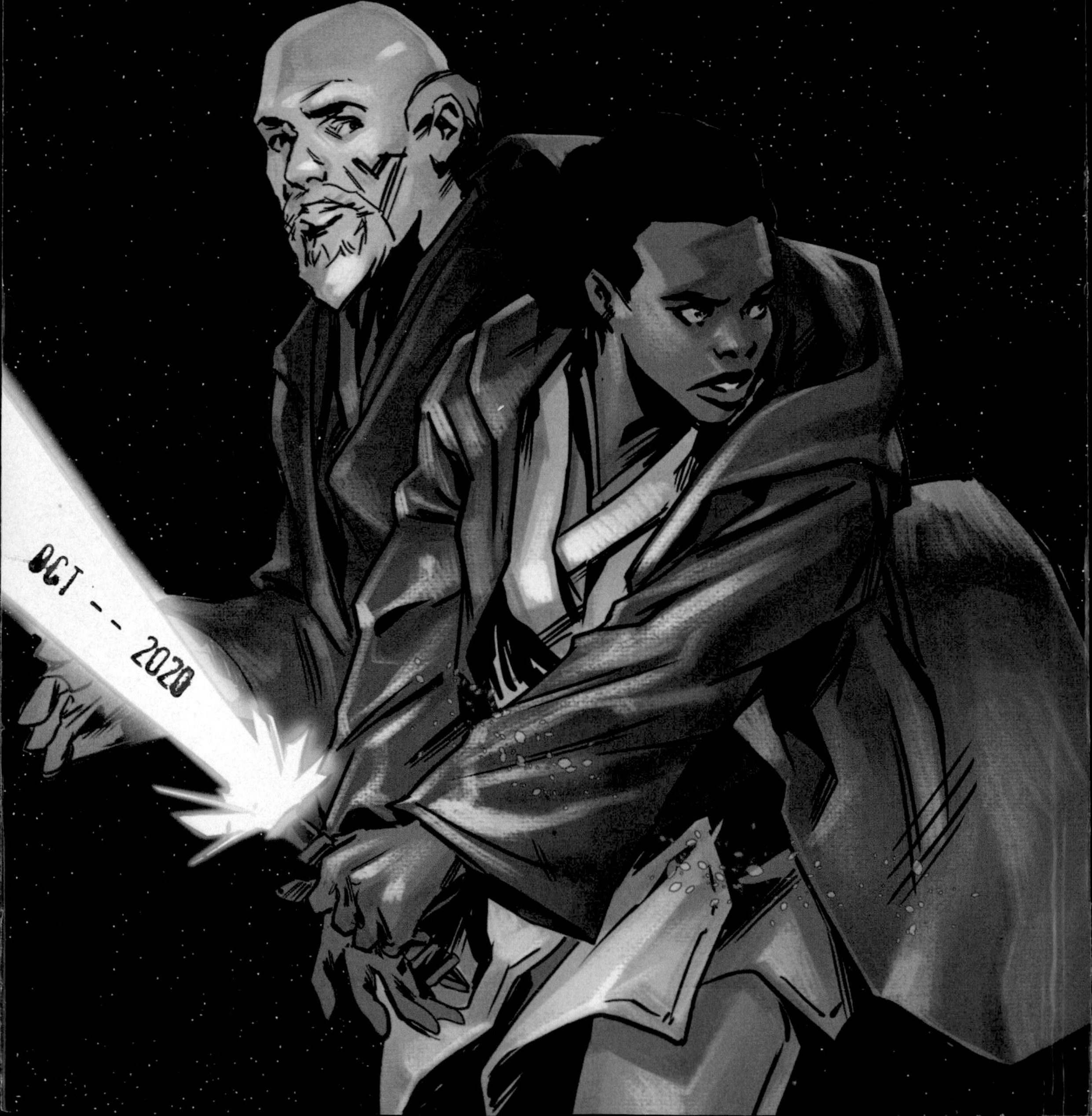

STAR WARS™

JEDI

FALLEN ORDER™

DARK TEMPLE